ELLIOTT WAVE PRINCIPLE
KEY TO MARKET BEHAVIOR

by

FROST and PRECHTER

With a Foreword by Charles J. Collins

PUBLISHED BY
NEW CLASSICS LIBRARY

www.elliottwave.com

ELLIOTT WAVE PRINCIPLE
KEY TO MARKET BEHAVIOR

Printed in the United States of America

First Edition: November 1978
Tenth Edition: 2005

For information, address the publishers:
New Classics Library
Post Office Box 1618
Gainesville, Georgia 30503 USA

www.elliottwave.com

ISBN: 978-0-932750-75-4
Library of Congress Control Number: 2004116120

PUBLISHER'S NOTE FOR THE
20ᵀᴴ ANNIVERSARY EDITION (1998)

Elliott Wave Principle came out in November 1978, with the Dow at 790. While reviewers immediately regarded it as the definitive textbook on the Wave Principle, it handily missed the best-seller list by several hundred thousand copies. Nevertheless, due to the spiraling interest in the book's content and the success of its long range forecast, it has sold more copies every year, achieving the status of a Wall Street classic. Like the Wave Principle itself, this book has stood the test of time.

What's more, *Elliott Wave Principle* has gotten better as it has evolved. The book fulfills its purpose as a comprehensive text more satisfactorily with each new edition, as Robert Prechter has meticulously refined, enhanced and expanded it through the years. This effort has borne fruit. In the 1970s, A.J. Frost had often recounted Hamilton Bolton's observation in the 1960s that "For every 100 people who know Dow Theory, only one has ever even *heard* of Elliott." In the summer of 1986, Frost called Prechter to say, "the tables are finally turning."

Until a few years ago, the idea that market movements are self-similarly patterned was highly controversial, but recent scientific discoveries have established that self-similar pattern formation is a fundamental characteristic of complex systems, which include financial markets. Some such systems undergo "punctuated growth," that is, periods of growth alternating with phases of non-growth or decline, building into similar patterns of increasing size. Nature is replete with such "fractals," and as we demonstrated in this book twenty years ago, and as R.N. Elliott revealed some sixty years ago, the stock market is no exception.

It is hard to believe that twenty years have gone by since we introduced the world to Frost and Prechter's vision of a great bull market in stocks. While its extent has been much more than they originally expected, the authors maintain their labeling of the advance as Cycle wave V. Today, the market's character is exactly as Prechter said it would be in his depiction of fifteen years ago: "At wave V's end, investor mass psychology should reach manic proportions, with elements of 1929, 1968 and 1973 all operating together and, at the end, to an even greater extreme." Here in 1998, every market statistic and every investor's racing heartbeat reflect exactly that condition.

This edition again keeps intact every word involving expectations for the future precisely as it originally appeared, allowing new readers to investigate both the successes and errors in the forecast presented by Frost and Prechter those many years ago. In referring to that forecast, investment analyst James W. Cowan says, *"Even allowing for minor stumbles, that 1978 prediction must go down as the most remarkable stock market prediction of all time."*

It remains to be seen whether this great bull market will be followed by the biggest bear market in U.S. history and thus fulfill the second half of the book's forecast. The authors, to be sure, stick by their scenario.

New Classics Library, Publisher

ACKNOWLEDGMENTS

The authors have tried to spell out everything that has been said of Elliott that is worthwhile saying. The book wouldn't be here, however, without the help of several people whom we will always remember with gratitude. Anthony Boeckh of Bank Credit Analyst fame generously opened his files. Jo-Anne Drew labored hours over the first draft and lent her artistic talents to its production. Mr. and Mrs. Robert R. Prechter, Sr. meticulously edited the final manuscript. Arthur Merrill of Merrill Analysis, Inc. gave us valuable advice and assistance in photography and production. Others too numerous to mention have sustained us in our efforts with advice and encouragement. To all, please accept our thanks.

Background charts for some of the illustrations were provided courtesy of the following sources: *Bank Credit Analyst*, Montreal, Canada (Figures 2-11, 5-5, 8-3); R.W. Mansfield, Jersey City, NJ (Figure 1-18); Merrill Lynch, Inc. (Figures 3-12; 6-8, 9, 10, 12; 7-5); Securities Research Co., Boston, MA (Figures 1-13, 6-1 through 6-7); Trendline, a division of Standard and Poor's Corp., New York (Figures 1-14, 17, 27, 37; 4-14). Figure 3-9 includes illustrations courtesy of *Fascinating Fibonaccis* by Trudi H. Garland (drawings), *Mathematics* by David Bergamini and the Editors of *Life* (spiral flower and Parthenon), *Omni* magazine, March 1988 (hurricane, whirlpool and shells), *Scientific American*, March 1969 (sunflower), *Science 86* magazine, May 1986 (pine cone), *Brain/Mind Bulletin*, June 1987 (DNA), *Fibonacci Quarterly*, December 1979 (human body), Nova-Adventures in Science (atomic particles), Daniel Schechtman, Technion, Haifa, Israel (quasi crystal), Hale Observatories, Pasadena, CA (galaxy). Some charts in the Appendix are provided by Ned Davis Research, Nokomis, FL; Foundation for the Study of Cycles, Wayne, PA; and *The Media General Financial Weekly*, Richmond, VA.

All illustrations not otherwise cited were done by Bob Prechter (original book) and Dave Allman (appendices). The formidable job of lettering and paste-up was patiently performed by Robin Machcinski. The jacket design was conceived by the authors and crafted by graphics artist Irene Goldberg of New Orleans, Louisiana. Production in later editions was handled by Jane Estes, Susan Willoughby, Paula Roberson, Karen Latvala, Debbie Iseler, Pete Kendall, Stephanie White, Leigh Tipton, Angie Barringer, Sally Webb, and Pam Greenwood.

The authors have tried to acknowledge all source material used in this book. Any omissions are accidental and will be corrected in future printings if brought to our attention.

CONTENTS

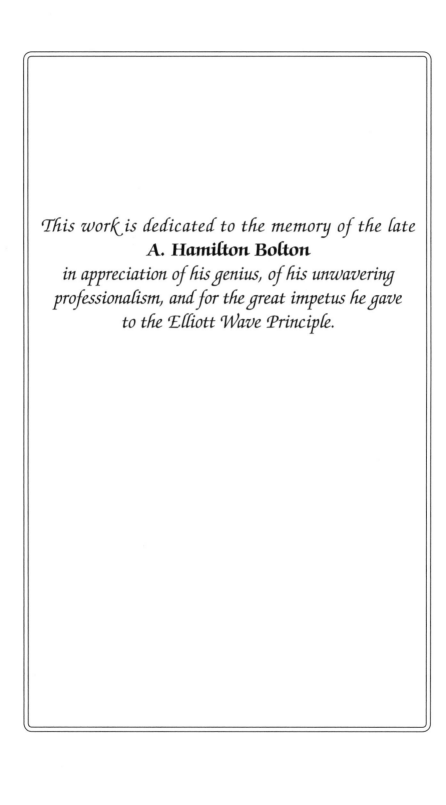

This work is dedicated to the memory of the late
A. Hamilton Bolton
in appreciation of his genius, of his unwavering professionalism, and for the great impetus he gave to the Elliott Wave Principle.

FOREWORD

Some two thousand years ago a man voiced a few words whose truth has rung down through the centuries:

> One generation passeth away, and another generation cometh, but the earth abideth forever. The sun also ariseth, and the sun goeth down, and hasteth to his place where he arose. The wind goeth toward the south, and turneth about unto the north; it whirleth about continually, and the wind returneth again according to his circuits. All the rivers run into the sea; yet the sea is not full; unto the flow from whence the rivers come, thither they return again.... *The thing that hath been, it is that which shall be; and that which is done is that which shall be done; and there is no new thing under the sun.*

A corollary of this profundity is that human nature does not change, nor does its pattern. Four men in our generation have built their reputations in the economic field on this truth: Arthur Pigou, Charles H. Dow, Bernard Baruch and Ralph Nelson Elliott.

Hundreds of theories have been advanced concerning the ups and downs of business, the so-called business cycle: variation in the money supply, inventory over-balance and under-balance, changes in world trade due to political edict, consumer attitude, capital expenditure, even sunspots and juxtapositions of the planets. Pigou, the English economist, reduced it to the human equation. The upward and downward swings of business, Pigou said, are caused by excesses of human optimism followed by excesses of pessimism. The pendulum swings too far one way and there is glut; it swings too far the other way and there is scarcity. An excess in one direction breeds an excess in the other, and so on and so on, diastole and systole in never-ending succession.

Charles H. Dow, one of America's most profound students of stock market movements, noted a certain repetition in the market's continuing gyrations. Out of this seeming confusion Dow observed that the market was not like a balloon plunging

aimlessly hither and thither in the wind but moved through orderly sequence. Dow enunciated two principles that have stood
the test of time. His first was that the market in its primary
uptrend was characterized by three upward swings. The first
swing he attributed to a rebound from the price over-pessimism
of the preceding primary downswing; the second upward swing
geared into the improving business and earnings picture; the
third and last swing was a price overdiscounting of value. Dow's
second principle was that at some point in every market swing,
whether up or down, there would be a reverse movement can-
celing three-eighths or more of such swing. While Dow may not
knowingly have tied these laws into the influence of the human
factor, the market is made by man and continuity or repetition,
noted by Dow, necessarily derives from that source.

Baruch, a multimillionaire through stock market operation
and adviser to American presidents, hit the nail on the head
in just a few words. "But what actually registers in the stock
market's fluctuations," he said, "are not the events themselves,
but the human reactions to these events. In short, how millions
of individual men and women feel these happenings may affect
their future." Baruch added, "Above all else, in other words, the
stock market is people. It is people trying to read the future. And
it is this intensely human quality that makes the stock market
so dramatic an arena, in which men and women pit their conflict-
ing judgments, their hopes and fears, strengths and weaknesses,
greeds and ideals."

Now we come to Ralph N. Elliott, who at the time he evolved
his theory had probably never heard of Pigou. Elliott had been
working down in Mexico but due to a physical malady — I think
he said it was anemia — had graduated to a rocking chair on a
front porch in California. With time on his hands, as he endea-
vored to throw off his difficulty, Elliott turned to a study of the
stock market as reflected by the history and movement of the Dow
Jones averages. Out of this protracted study Elliott dis-covered
the same repetitious phenomena so eloquently expressed, as
quoted in the opening paragraphs of this introduction, by the
Preacher of Ecclesiastes. Elliott, in developing his theory through
observation, study and thought, incorporated what Dow had
discovered but went well beyond Dow's theory in comprehensive-

ness and exactitude. Both men had sensed the involutions of the human equation that dominated market movements but Dow painted with broad strokes of the brush and Elliott in detail, with greater breadth.

I met Elliott through correspondence. I was publishing a national weekly stock market bulletin to which Elliott wished to join his efforts. Letters back and forth followed but the matter was triggered in the first quarter of 1935. On that occasion the stock market, after receding from a 1933 high to a 1934 low, had started up again but during 1935's first quarter the Dow Railroad Average broke to under its 1934 low point. Investors, economists, and stock market analysts had not recovered from the 1929-32 unpleasantness and this early 1935 breakdown was most discon-certing. Was the nation in for more trouble?

On the last day of the rail list decline I received a telegram from Elliott stating most emphatically that the decline was over, that it was only the first setback in a bull market that had much further to go. Ensuing months proved Elliott so right that I asked him to be my house guest in Michigan over a weekend. Elliott accepted and went over his theory in detail. I could not take him into my organization, however, since he insisted that all decisions be based on his theory. I did help him to locate in Wall Street and in appreciation of his disclosure to me of his work, wrote and put his theory into a booklet entitled *The Wave Principle* under his name.

Subsequently, I introduced Elliott to *Financial World* magazine for whom I had contributed and he, through a series of articles, covered the essentials of his theory therein. Later Elliott incorporated *The Wave Principle* into a larger work entitled *Nature's Law*. Therein he introduced the magic of Fibonacci and certain esoteric propositions that he believed confirmed his own views.

A.J. Frost and Robert R. Prechter, Jr., the authors of this book, are keen students of Elliott and those who wish to profit by Elliott's discoveries and their application to successful investing will find their work most rewarding.

Charles J. Collins
Grosse Pointe, Michigan, 1978

R. N. ELLIOTT
833 Beacon Avenue
Los Angeles, California
FEderal 2667

Nov. 28, 1934

Mr. C. J. Collins,   PERSONAL
Investment Counsel,   and
Detroit, Mich.   CONFIDENTIAL

Dear Mr. Collins:-,

      For some time I have been trying to formulate this letter, but unable to find expressions that would convey the desired impression and still doubt that I can do so. I am a stranger to you, but feel that I know you through the service letters which I admire very much. On my recommendation some friends have subscribed thereto. I was one of the first subscribers to Mr. Rhea's book and service.

      About six months ago I discovered 3 features in market action, and insofar as I know they are novel. I do not believe that it is egotistical to allege that they are a much needed complement to the Dow theory.

      Naturally I wish to benefit from these discoveries. You have a very extensive following and it has occurred to me that we might reach an arrangement mutually satis- factory. In your letters I have occasionally seen reference to "other sources of information" which prompted me to hope that you might become interested. Moreover from your service letters I judge that you are not familiar with my discoveries.

      Their adoption would in no wise necessitate any reference thereto in service letters. For example when the Dow-Jones Industrials made a top of 107 last April I could have forecasted the 85 bottom and the approximate date it would be reached but your letters could have used the Dow theory as a reason for abandoning long positions. I do not claim that this can always be done. Needless to say the prestige of your service would have materially benefited thereby. Incidently permit me to forecast that the present major bull swing will be followed by a major bear collapse. This is not an opinion but simply the application of a rule.

      These discoveries are much less mechanical than the Dow theory but add great forecasting value which it lacks. One gives reversal signals almost invariably at minor, intermediate and major terminals. Another classifies waves of all movements of which I find six. The other covers the time element which has been 83% correct since the 1932 bottom. When divergence occurs the time element slips out of gear temporarily.

      Unless you contemplate an early visit to the Coast, would you be willing to pay the expense of a trip to Detroit and back ? I know your agent here, Mr. Osbourn, and believe he would give me a "good character", but please note that neither he nor any one else knows anything about my discoveries.

                Yours very truly,

                  R. N. Elliott

DEC 2 1934

AUTHORS' NOTE

In coauthoring this book, we have not been unmindful of the little girl who, after reading a book about penguins, said, "This book has told me more about penguins than I really care to know." We have tried to explain the theory of the Wave Principle in simple, concise terms and avoid, for the most part, extensive elaboration and detailed examples of technical points.

When presented clearly, the basic tenets of the Wave Principle are easy to learn and apply. Unfortunately, the early works on the subject are now out of print, and the scattered nature of the writings since then has created problems since there has been no definitive reference text available for study. In this book, we have tried to produce a work that gives a complete treatment of the subject in a manner which we hope will succeed in introducing both experienced analysts and interested laymen to the fascinating field of Elliott.

We trust our readers will be encouraged to do their own research by keeping a chart of hourly fluctuations of the Dow until they can say with enthusiasm, "I see it!" Once you grasp the Wave Principle, you will have at your command a new and fascinating approach to market analysis, and even beyond that, a mathematical philosophy that can be applied in other spheres of life. It will not be the answer to all your problems, but it will give you perspective and at the same time enable you to appreciate the strange psychology of human behavior, especially market behavior. Elliott's concepts reflect a principle you can readily prove to yourself and evermore see the stock market in a new light.

— A.J. Frost and Robert R. Prechter, Jr., 1978

PART I
ELLIOTT THEORY

CHAPTER 1

THE BROAD CONCEPT

In *The Elliott Wave Principle — A Critical Appraisal*, Hamilton Bolton made this opening statement:

> As we have advanced through some of the most unpredictable economic climate imaginable, covering depression, major war, and postwar reconstruction and boom, I have noted how well Elliott's Wave Principle has fitted into the facts of life as they have developed, and have accordingly gained more confidence that this Principle has a good quotient of basic value.

In the 1930s, Ralph Nelson Elliott discovered that stock market prices trend and reverse in recognizable patterns. The patterns he discerned are repetitive in *form* but not necessarily in time or amplitude. Elliott isolated five such patterns, or "waves," that recur in market price data. He named, defined and illustrated these patterns and their variations. He then described how they link together to form larger versions of themselves, how they in turn link to form the same patterns of the next larger size, and so on, producing a structured progression. He called this phenomenon The Wave Principle.

Although it is the best forecasting tool in existence, the Wave Principle is not *primarily* a forecasting tool; it is a detailed description of how markets behave. Nevertheless, that description does impart an immense amount of knowledge about the market's position within the behavioral continuum and therefore about its probable ensuing path. The primary value of the Wave Principle is that it provides a *context* for market analysis. This context provides both a basis for disciplined thinking and a perspective on the market's general position and outlook. At times, its accuracy in identifying, and even anticipating, changes in direction is almost unbelievable. Many areas of mass human activity display the Wave Principle, but it is most popularly used in the stock market. Truly, however, the stock market is far more significant to the human condition than it appears to casual observers and even to those who make their living by it. The level of aggregate stock prices is a direct and immediate measure of the popular valuation of man's total productive capability. That this valuation has *form* is a fact of profound implications that will ultimately revolutionize the social sciences. That, however, is a discussion for another time.

R.N. Elliott's genius consisted of a wonderfully disciplined mental process, suited to studying charts of the Dow Jones Industrial Average and its predecessors with such thoroughness and precision that he could construct a network of principles that reflected all market action known to him up to the mid-1940s. At that time, with the Dow near 100, Elliott predicted a great bull market for the next several decades that would exceed all expectations at a time when most investors felt it impossible that the Dow could even better its 1929 peak. As we shall see, exceptional stock market forecasts, some of pinpoint accuracy years in advance, have accompanied the history of the application of the Elliott wave approach.

Elliott had theories regarding the origin and meaning of the patterns he discovered, which we will present and expand upon in Chapter 3. Until then, suffice it to say that the patterns described in Chapters 1 and 2 have stood the test of time.

Often one will hear several different interpretations of the market's Elliott wave status, especially when cursory, off-the-cuff studies of the averages are made by latter-day experts. However, most uncertainties can be avoided by keeping charts on both arithmetic and semilogarithmic scale and by taking care to follow the rules and guidelines as laid down in this book. Welcome to the world of Elliott.

BASIC TENETS

The Wave Principle is governed by man's social nature, and since he *has* such a nature, its expression generates forms. As the forms are repetitive, they have predictive value.

Sometimes the market appears to reflect outside conditions and events, but at other times it is entirely detached from what most people assume are causal conditions. The reason is that the market has a law of its own. It is not propelled by the external causality to which one becomes accustomed in the everyday experiences of life. The path of prices is *not* a product of news. Nor is the market the cyclically rhythmic machine that some declare it to be. Its movement reflects a repetition of forms that is independent both of presumed causal events and of periodicity.

The market's progression unfolds in *waves*. Waves are patterns of directional movement. More specifically, a wave is any one of the patterns that naturally occur, as described in the rest of this chapter.

The Five-Wave Pattern

In markets, progress ultimately takes the form of five waves of a specific structure. Three of these waves, which are labeled 1, 3 and 5, actually effect the directional movement. They are separated by two countertrend interruptions, which are labeled 2 and 4, as shown in Figure 1-1. The two interruptions are apparently a requisite for overall directional movement to occur.

Elliott noted three consistent aspects of the five-wave form. They are: Wave 2 never moves beyond the start of wave 1; wave 3 is never the shortest wave; wave 4 never enters the price territory of wave 1.

R.N. Elliott did not specifically say that there is only one overriding form, the "five-wave" pattern, but that is undeniably the case. At any time, the market may be identified as being somewhere in the basic five-wave pattern at the largest degree of trend. Because the five-wave pattern is the overriding form of market progress, all other patterns are subsumed by it.

Wave Mode

There are two modes of wave development: *motive* and *corrective*. Motive waves have a *five*-wave structure, while corrective waves have a *three*-wave structure or a variation thereof. Motive

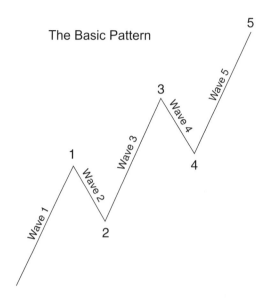

Figure 1-1

mode is employed by both the five-wave pattern of Figure 1-1 *and* its same-directional components, i.e., waves 1, 3 and 5. Their structures are called "motive" because they powerfully impel the market. Corrective mode is employed by all counter- trend interruptions, which include waves 2 and 4 in Figure 1-1. Their structures are called "corrective" because each one appears as a response to the preceding motive wave yet accomplishes only a partial retracement, or "correction," of the progress it achieved. Thus, the two modes are fundamentally different, both in their roles and in their construction, as will be detailed throughout this chapter.

The Complete Cycle

One complete cycle consisting of eight waves, then, is made up of two distinct phases, the five-wave motive phase (also called a "five"), whose subwaves are denoted by numbers, and the three-wave corrective phase (also called a "three"), whose subwaves are denoted by letters. Just as wave 2 corrects wave 1 in Figure 1-1, the sequence A, B, C corrects the sequence 1, 2, 3, 4, 5 in Figure 1-2.

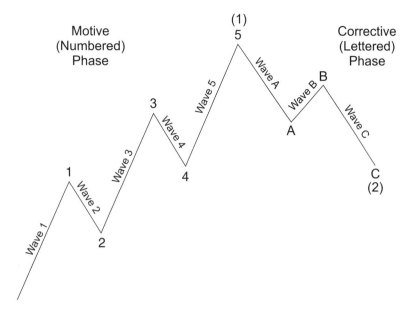

Figure 1-2

Compound Construction

When an initial eight-wave cycle such as shown in Figure 1-2 ends, a similar cycle ensues, which is then followed by another five-wave movement. This entire development produces a five-wave pattern of *one degree* (i.e., relative size) *larger* than the waves of which it is composed. The result is shown in Figure 1-3 up to the peak labeled (5). This five-wave pattern of larger degree is then corrected by a three-wave pattern of the same degree, completing a larger full cycle, depicted as Figure 1-3.

As Figure 1-3 illustrates, *each same-direction component of a motive wave* (i.e., wave 1, 3 and 5) *and each full-cycle component* (i.e., waves 1 + 2, or waves 3 + 4) *of a complete cycle, is a smaller version of itself.*

It is necessary to understand a crucial point: Figure 1-3 not only illustrates a *larger* version of Figure 1-2, it also illustrates *Figure 1-2 itself,* in greater detail. In Figure 1-2, each subwave 1, 3 and 5 is a motive wave that must subdivide into a "five," and each subwave 2 and 4 is a corrective wave that must subdivide into a "three." Waves (1) and (2) in Figure 1-3, if examined under a "microscope," would take the same form as waves ① and ②. Regardless of degree, the form is constant. We can use Figure

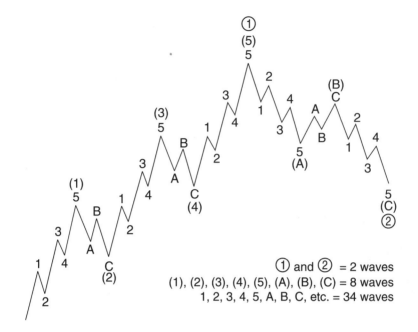

Figure 1-3

1-3 to illustrate two waves, eight waves or thirty-four waves, depending upon the degree to which we are referring.

The Essential Design

Now observe that within the corrective pattern illustrated as wave ② in Figure 1-3, waves (A) and (C), which point downward, are each composed of five waves: 1, 2, 3, 4 and 5. Similarly, wave (B), which points upward, is composed of three waves: A, B and C. This construction discloses a crucial point: Motive waves do not always point upward, and corrective waves do not always point downward. The mode of a wave is determined not by its absolute direction but primarily by its *relative* direction. Aside from five specific exceptions, which will be discussed later in this chapter, waves divide in *motive* mode (five waves) when trending in the same direction as the wave of one larger degree of which it is a part, and in *corrective* mode (three waves or a variation) when trending in the opposite direction. Waves (A) and (C) are motive, trending in the *same direction* as wave ②. Wave (B) is corrective because it corrects wave (A) and is *countertrend* to wave ②. In summary, the essential underlying tendency of the Wave Principle is that *action in the same direction as the one larger trend develops in five waves, while reaction against the one larger trend develops in three waves,* at all degrees of trend.

The phenomena of *form, degree* and *relative direction* are carried one step further in Figure 1-4. This illustration reflects the general principle that in any market cycle, waves will subdivide as shown in the table below.

Number of Waves at Each Degree

	Motive (Impulse)	+ Corrective (Zigzag)	= Cycle
Largest waves	1	1	2
Largest subdivisions	5	3	8
Next subdivisions	21	13	34
Next subdivisions	89	55	144

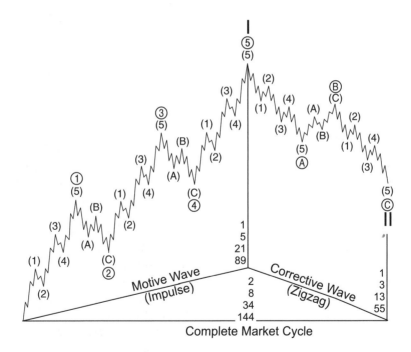

Figure 1-4

As with Figures 1-2 and 1-3, this larger cycle in Figure 1-4 automatically becomes two subdivisions of the wave of *next* higher degree. As long as progress continues, the process of building to greater degrees continues. The reverse process of subdividing into lesser degrees apparently continues indefinitely as well. As far as we can determine, then, all waves both *have* and *are* component waves.

Why 5-3?

Elliott himself never speculated on why the market's essential form is five waves to progress and three waves to regress. He simply noted that that was what was happening. Does the essential form have to be five waves and three waves? Think about it and you will realize that this is *the* minimum requirement for, and therefore the most efficient method of, achieving both *fluctuation* and *progress* in linear movement. *One* wave does not allow fluctuation. The fewest subdivisions to create fluctuation is three waves. Three waves (of unqualified size) in both directions would not allow progress. To progress in one direction despite periods of regress, movements in that direction must be at least five waves, simply to cover more ground than the intervening three waves. While there could be more waves than that, the most efficient form of punctuated progress is 5-3, and nature typically follows the most efficient path.

Wave Degree: Notation and Nomenclature

All waves may be categorized by relative size, or degree. The degree of a wave is determined by its size and position *relative to component, adjacent and encompassing waves*. Elliott named nine degrees of waves, from the smallest discernible on an hourly chart to the largest wave he could assume existed from the data then available. He chose the following terms for these degrees, from largest to smallest: Grand Supercycle, Supercycle, Cycle, Primary, Intermediate, Minor, Minute, Minuette, Subminuette. Cycle waves subdivide into Primary waves that subdivide into Intermediate waves that in turn subdivide into Minor waves, and so on. The specific terminology is not critical to the identification of degrees, although out of habit, today's practitioners have become comfortable with Elliott's nomenclature.

When labeling waves on a graph, some scheme is necessary to differentiate the degrees of waves in the market's progression. We have standardized a sequence of labels involving numbers and letters, as shown in the table below, which has several virtues heretofore lacking. The progression is infinite in both directions. It is based upon an easily memorized repetition. Motive waves are labeled with alternating sets of three Roman numerals followed by three Arabic numerals. The corrective-wave labels similarly alternate between three upper-case letters and three lower-case letters. Roman numerals always go with lower case letters, and Arabic numbers always go with upper case letters. Finally, all Roman numerals are lower case below Minor degree and upper case above Primary degree, so that a quick glance at a chart reveals some perspective on its time scale. (Several charts in this book deviate from this standard, as they were constructed prior to its adoption.)

(↑ continue progression: upper case Roman/Arabic numerals; upper/lower case letters)

Wave Degree	5's With the Trend					3's Against the Trend		
1 Supermillennium	①	②	③	④	⑤	Ⓐ	Ⓑ	Ⓒ
2 Millennium	(1)	(2)	(3)	(4)	(5)	(A)	(B)	(C)
3 Submillennium	1	2	3	4	5	A	B	C
4 Grand Supercycle	Ⓘ	Ⓘ Ⓘ	Ⓘ Ⓘ Ⓘ	Ⓘ Ⓥ	Ⓥ	ⓐ	ⓑ	ⓒ
5 Supercycle	(I)	(II)	(III)	(IV)	(V)	(a)	(b)	(c)
6 Cycle	I	II	III	IV	V	a	b	c
7 Primary	①	②	③	④	⑤	Ⓐ	Ⓑ	Ⓒ
8 Intermediate	(1)	(2)	(3)	(4)	(5)	(A)	(B)	(C)
9 Minor	1	2	3	4	5	A	B	C
10 Minute	①	ⓘⓘ	ⓘⓘⓘ	ⓘⓥ	ⓥ	ⓐ	ⓑ	ⓒ
11 Minuette	(i)	(ii)	(iii)	(iv)	(v)	(a)	(b)	(c)
12 Subminuette	i	ii	iii	iv	v	a	b	c
13 Micro	①	②	③	④	⑤	Ⓐ	Ⓑ	Ⓒ
14 Submicro	(1)	(2)	(3)	(4)	(5)	(A)	(B)	(C)
15 Miniscule	1	2	3	4	5	A	B	C

(↓ continue progression: lower case Roman/Arabic numerals; upper/lower case letters)

We may also refer to waves by their degree number. A wave of Cycle degree is a wave of degree six. The largest degree in progress, dating from the Stone Age, is degree zero (Epochal degree), so these numbers should serve all analytical endeavors. The most desirable form for scientific work would be 1_1, 1_2, 1_3, 1_4, 1_5, etc., with subscripts denoting degree, but it is difficult to read a large number of such notations on a graph. The above standard provides for rapid visual orientation.

It is important to understand that these names and labels refer to specifically identifiable degrees of waves. By using a nomenclature, an analyst can identify precisely the position of a wave in the overall progression of the stock market, much as longitude and latitude are used to identify a geographical location. To say, "The Dow Jones Industrial Average is in Minute wave ⓥ of Minor wave 1 of Intermediate wave (3) of Primary wave ⑤ of Cycle wave I of Supercycle wave (V) of the current Grand Supercycle" is to identify a specific point along the progression of market history.

All waves are of a specific degree. Yet it may be impossible to identify precisely the degree of developing waves, particularly subwaves at the start of a new wave. Degree is not based upon specific price or time lengths but upon *form*, which is a function of both price *and* time. Fortunately, the precise degree is usually irrelevant to successful forecasting since it is *relative* degree that matters most. To know a major advance is due is more important than its precise name. Later events always clarify degree.

Wave Function

Every wave serves one of two functions: *action* or *reaction*. Specifically, a wave may either advance the cause of the wave of one larger degree or interrupt it. The function of a wave is determined by its *relative direction*. An *actionary* or *trend* wave is any wave that trends in the *same* direction as the wave of one larger degree of which it is a part. A *reactionary* or *countertrend* wave is any wave that trends in the direction *opposite* to that of the wave of one larger degree of which it is part. Actionary waves are labeled with *odd* numbers and letters (for example, 1, 3, 5, a and c in Figure 1-2). Reactionary waves are labeled with even numbers and letters (for example, 2, 4 and b in Figure 1-2).

All reactionary waves develop in corrective mode. If all actionary waves developed in motive mode, then there would be no need for different terms. Indeed, most actionary waves do subdivide into five waves. However, as the following sections reveal, a few actionary waves develop in corrective mode, i.e., they subdivide into *three* waves or a variation thereof. A detailed knowledge of pattern construction is required in order to understand the distinction between *actionary* function and *motive* mode, which in the underlying model of Figures 1-1 through 1-4 are indistinct. A thorough understanding of the forms detailed later in this chapter will clarify why we have introduced these terms to the Elliott wave lexicon.

Variations on the Basic Theme

The Wave Principle would be simple to apply if the essential design described above were the complete description of market behavior. The real world, fortunately or unfortunately, is not so simple. While an idea such as cyclicality in markets or human experience implies precise repetition, the concept of waves allows for immense variability, which is in fact abundantly in evidence. The rest of this chapter fills out the description of how the market actually behaves. That is what Elliott set out to describe, and he succeeded in doing so.

There are a number of specific variations on the underlying theme, which Elliott meticulously described and illustrated. He also noted the important fact that each pattern has identifiable *requirements* as well as *tendencies*. From these observations, he was able to formulate numerous rules and guidelines for proper wave identification. A thorough knowledge of such details is necessary to understand what the market can do, and at least as important, what it does not do.

Chapters 2 and 4 present a number of guidelines to proper wave interpretation. If you do *not* wish to become a market analyst or are concerned that you will become bogged down in technical detail, skim the next paragraph and then skip to Chapter 3. A brief perusal of the highly condensed summary below should ensure that you will at least recognize the concepts and terms referenced in later chapters as necessary aspects of the Wave Principle.

Summary of Additional Technical Aspects

Additional technical aspects of waves, which are discussed in detail from here through Chapter 2, are herewith stated as briefly as possible: Most motive waves take the form of an impulse, i.e., a five-wave pattern like those shown in Figures 1-1 through 1-4, in which subwave 4 does not overlap subwave 1, and subwave 3 is not the shortest subwave. Impulses are typically bound by parallel lines. One motive wave in an impulse, i.e., 1, 3 *or* 5, is typically extended, i.e., much longer than the other two. There is a rare motive variation called a diagonal, which is a wedge-shaped pattern that appears at the start (wave 1 or A) or the end (wave 5 or C) of a larger wave. Corrective waves have numerous variations. The main ones are named *zigzag* (which is the one shown in Figures 1-2, 1-3 and 1-4), *flat* and *triangle* (whose labels include D and E). These three simple corrective patterns can string together to form more complex corrections (the components of which are labeled W, X, Y and Z). In impulses, waves 2 and 4 nearly always alternate in form, where one correction is typically of the zigzag family and the other is not. Each wave exhibits characteristic volume behavior and a "personality" in terms of attendant momentum and investor sentiment.

General readers may now skip to Chapter 3. For those who want to learn the details, we will turn our attention to the specifics of wave form.

DETAILED ANALYTICS

MOTIVE WAVES

Motive waves subdivide into *five* waves and always move in the same direction as the trend of one larger degree. They are straightforward and relatively easy to recognize and interpret.

Within motive waves, wave 2 always retraces less than 100% of wave 1, and wave 4 always retraces less than 100% of wave 3. Wave 3, moreover, always travels beyond the end of wave 1. The goal of a motive wave is to make progress, and these rules of formation assure that it will.

Elliott further discovered that in price terms, wave 3 is often the longest and never the shortest among the three actionary waves (1, 3 and 5) of a motive wave. As long as wave 3 undergoes a greater percentage movement than either wave 1 or 5, this rule is satisfied. It almost always holds on an arithmetic basis as well. There are two types of motive waves: *impulse* and *diagonal*.

Impulse

The most common motive wave is an *impulse,* per Figure 1-1. In an impulse, wave 4 does not enter the price territory of (i.e., "overlap") wave 1. This rule holds for all non-leveraged "cash" markets. Futures markets, with their extreme leverage, can induce short term price extremes that would not occur in cash markets. Even so, overlapping is usually confined to daily and intraday price fluctuations and even then is rare. In addition, the actionary subwaves (1, 3 and 5) of an impulse are themselves motive, and subwave 3 is always an impulse. Figures 1-2, 1-3 and 1-4 all depict impulses in the 1, 3, 5, A and C wave positions.

As detailed in the preceding three paragraphs, there are only a few simple rules for interpreting impulses properly. A *rule* is so called because it governs all waves to which it applies. Typical, yet not inevitable, characteristics of waves are called *guidelines*. Guidelines of impulse formation, including extension, truncation, alternation, equality, channeling, personality and ratio relationships are discussed below and throughout Chapters 2 and 4. A rule should never be disregarded. In many years of practice with countless patterns, the authors have found but one or two instances above Subminuette degree when all other rules and guidelines combined to suggest that a rule was broken. Analysts who routinely break any of the rules detailed in this section are practicing some form of analysis other than that guided by the Wave Principle. These rules have great practical utility in correct counting, which we will explore further in discussing extensions.

Extension

Most impulses contain what Elliott called an extension. An extension is an elongated impulse with exaggerated subdivisions. The vast majority of impulses contain an extension in one and only one of their three actionary subwaves. The rest either contain no extension or an extension in both subwaves three and five. At times, the subdivisions of an extended wave are nearly the same amplitude and duration as the other four waves of the larger impulse, giving a total count of nine waves of similar size rather than the normal count of "five" for the sequence. In a nine-wave sequence, it is occasionally difficult to say which wave extended. However, it is usually irrelevant anyway, since under the Elliott system, a count of nine and a count of five have the same technical significance. The diagrams in Figure 1-5, illustrating extensions, will clarify this point.

The fact that an extension typically occurs in only one actionary subwave provides a useful guide to the expected lengths of upcoming waves. For instance, if the first and third waves are of about equal length, the fifth wave will likely be a protracted surge. Conversely, if wave three extends, the fifth should be simply constructed and resemble wave one.

In the stock market, *the most commonly extended wave is wave 3*. This fact is of particular importance to real-time wave interpretation when considered in conjunction with two of the rules of impulse waves: Wave 3 is never the shortest actionary wave, and wave 4 may not overlap wave 1. To clarify, let us assume two situations involving an improper middle wave, as illustrated in Figures 1-6 and 1-7.

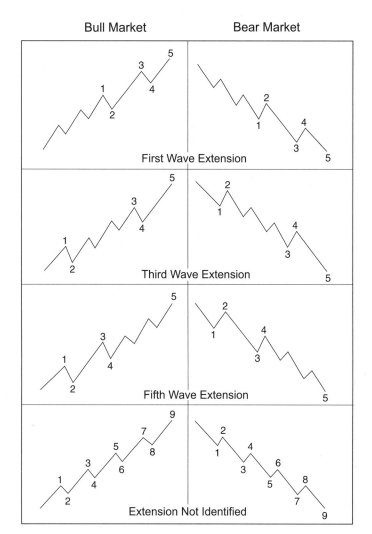

Bull Market   Bear Market

First Wave Extension

Third Wave Extension

Fifth Wave Extension

Extension Not Identified

Figure 1-5

Incorrect
Counting

Figure 1-6

Incorrect
Counting

Figure 1-7

Correct
Counting

Figure 1-8

In Figure 1-6, wave 4 overlaps the top of wave 1. In Figure 1-7, wave 3 is shorter than wave 1 and shorter than wave 5. According to the rules, neither is an acceptable labeling. Once the apparent wave 3 is proved unacceptable, it must be relabeled in some way that *is* acceptable. In fact, it is almost always to be labeled as shown in Figure 1-8, implying an extended wave (3) in the making. Do not hesitate to get into the habit of labeling the early stages of a third wave extension. The exercise will prove highly rewarding, as you will understand from the discussion under Wave Personality (see Chapter 2). Figure 1-8 is perhaps the single most useful guide to real time impulse wave counting in this book.

Extensions may also occur within extensions. In the stock market, the third wave of an extended third wave is typically an extension as well, producing a profile such as shown in Figure 1-9. A real-life example is shown in Figure 5-5. Figure 1-10 illustrates a fifth wave extension of a fifth wave extension. Extended fifths are quite common in major bull markets in commodities (see Chapter 6).

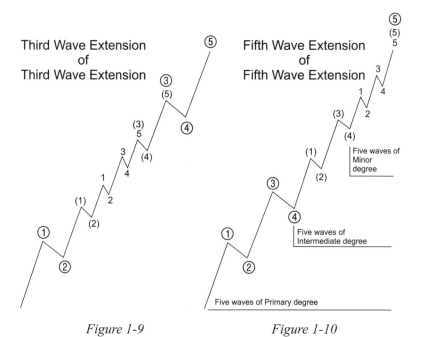

Figure 1-9   Figure 1-10

Truncation

Elliott used the word "failure" to describe a situation in which the fifth wave does not move beyond the end of the third. We prefer the less connotative term, "truncation," or "truncated fifth." A truncation can usually be verified by noting that the presumed fifth wave contains the necessary five subwaves, as illustrated in Figures 1-11 and 1-12. A truncation often occurs following a particularly strong third wave.

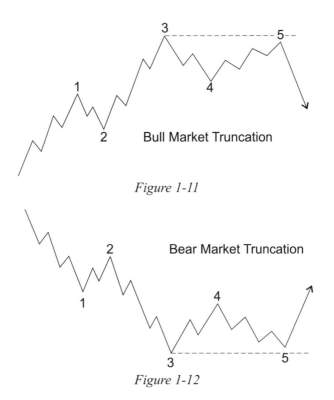

Bull Market Truncation

Figure 1-11

Bear Market Truncation

Figure 1-12

The U.S. stock market provides two examples of major-degree truncated fifths since 1932. The first occurred in October 1962 at the time of the Cuban crisis (see Figure 1-13). It followed the crash that occurred as wave 3. The second occurred at year-end in 1976 (see Figure 1-14). It followed the soaring and broad wave (3) that took place from October 1975 to March 1976.

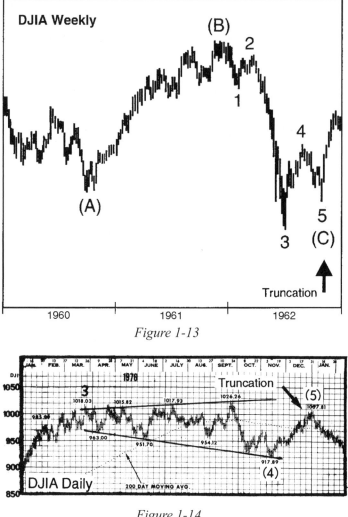

Figure 1-13

Figure 1-14

Diagonal

A diagonal is a motive pattern yet not an impulse, as it has two corrective characteristics. As with an impulse, no reactionary subwave fully retraces the preceding actionary subwave, and the third subwave is never the shortest. However, a diagonal is the only five-wave structure in the direction of the main trend within which wave four almost always moves into the price territory of (i.e., overlaps) wave one and within which all the waves are "threes," producing an overall count of 3-3-3-3-3. On rare occasions, a diagonal may end in a truncation, although in our experience such truncations occur only by the slimmest of margins. This pattern substitutes for an impulse at two specific locations in the wave structure.

Ending Diagonal

An ending diagonal occurs primarily in the fifth wave position at times when the preceding move has gone "too far too fast," as Elliott put it. A very small percentage of diagonals appear in the C-wave position of A-B-C formations. In double or triple threes (see next section), they appear only as the *final* C wave. In all cases, they are found at the *termination points of larger patterns*, indicating exhaustion of the larger movement.

A contracting diagonal takes a wedge shape within two converging lines. This most common form for an ending diagonal is illustrated in Figures 1-15 and 1-16 and shown in its typical position within a larger impulse wave.

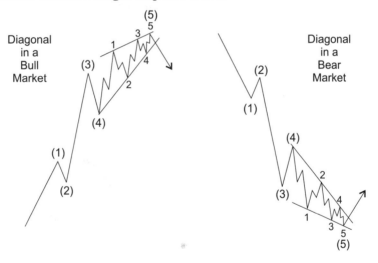

| *Figure 1-15* | *Figure 1-16* |

We have found one case in which an ending diagonal's boundary lines *diverged*, creating an expanding diagonal rather than a contracting one. However, it is unsatisfying analytically in that its third wave was the shortest actionary wave.

Ending diagonals have occurred recently in Minor degree as in early 1978, in Minute degree as in February-March 1976, and in Subminuette degree as in June 1976. Figures 1-17 and 1-18 show two of these periods, illustrating one upward and one downward "real life" formation. Figure 1-19 shows our real-life possible expanding diagonal. Notice that in each case, an important change of direction followed.

Although not so illustrated in Figures 1-15 and 1-16, the fifth wave of an ending diagonal often ends in a "throw-over," i.e., a brief break of the trendline connecting the end points of waves one and three. The real-life examples in Figures 1-17 and 1-19 show throw-overs. While volume tends to diminish as a diagonal of small degree progresses, the pattern always ends with a spike of relatively high volume when a throw-over occurs. On rare occasions, the fifth subwave falls short of its resistance trendline.

A rising ending diagonal is usually followed by a sharp decline retracing at least back to the level where it began and typically much further. A falling ending diagonal by the same token usually gives rise to an upward thrust.

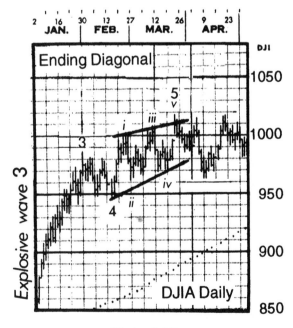

Figure 1-17

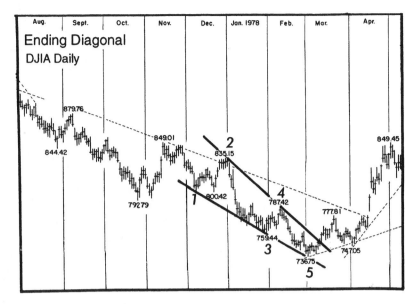

Figure 1-18

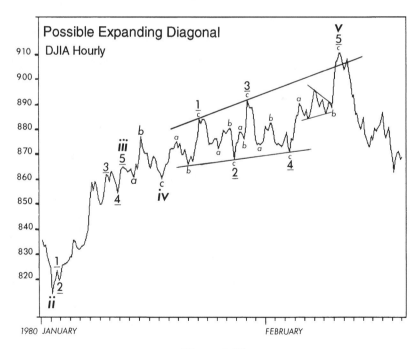

Figure 1-19

Fifth wave extensions, truncated fifths and ending diagonals all imply the same thing: *dramatic reversal ahead*. At some turning points, *two* of these phenomena have occurred together at different degrees, compounding the violence of the next move in the opposite direction.

Leading Diagonal

It has recently come to light that a diagonal occasionally appears in the wave 1 position of impulses and in the wave A position of zigzags. In the few examples we have, the subdivisions appear to be the same: 3-3-3-3-3, although in two cases, they can be labeled 5-3-5-3-5, so the jury is out on a strict definition. Analysts must be aware of this pattern to avoid mistaking it for a far more common development, a series of first and second waves, as illustrated in Figure 1-8. A leading diagonal in the wave one position is typically followed by a deep retracement (see Chapter 4).

Figure 1-20 shows a real-life leading diagonal. We have recently observed that a leading diagonal can also take an expanding shape. This form appears to occur primarily at the start of *declines* in the stock market (see Figure 21). These patterns were not originally discovered by R.N. Elliott but have appeared enough times and over a long enough period that the authors are convinced of their validity.

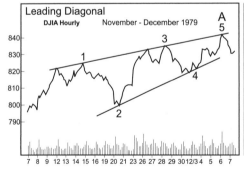

Figure 1-20   Figure 1-21

CORRECTIVE WAVES

Markets move *against* the trend of one greater degree only with a seeming struggle. Resistance from the larger trend appears to prevent a correction from developing a full motive structure. This struggle between the two oppositely-trending degrees generally makes corrective waves less clearly identifiable than motive waves, which always flow with comparative ease in the direction of the one larger trend. As another result of this conflict between trends, corrective waves are quite a bit more varied than motive waves. Further, they occasionally increase or decrease in complexity as they unfold so that what are technically subwaves of the same degree can by their complexity or time length appear to be of different degree (see Figures 2-4 and 2-5). For all these reasons, it can be difficult at times to fit corrective waves into recognizable patterns until they are completed and behind us. As the terminations of corrective waves are less predictable than those for motive waves, you must exercise more patience and flexibility in your analysis when the market is in a meandering corrective mood than when prices are in a persistent motive trend.

The single most important rule that can be gleaned from a study of the various corrective patterns is that *corrections are never fives*. Only motive waves are fives. For this reason, an initial five-wave movement against the larger trend is never the end of a correction, only part of it. The figures in this section should serve to illustrate this point.

Corrective processes come in two styles. *Sharp* corrections angle steeply against the larger trend. *Sideways* corrections, while always producing a net retracement of the preceding wave, typically contain a movement that carries back to or beyond its starting level, thus producing an overall sideways appearance. The discussion of the guideline of alternation in Chapter 2 explains the reason for noting these two styles.

Specific corrective patterns fall into three main categories:

Zigzag (5-3-5; includes three types: single, double and triple);

Flat (3-3-5; includes three types: regular, expanded and running);

Triangle (3-3-3-3-3; three types: contracting, barrier and expanding; and one variation: running.

A *combination* of the above forms comes in two types: double three and triple three.

Zigzag (5-3-5)

A *single zigzag* in a bull market is a simple three-wave declining pattern labeled A-B-C. The subwave sequence is 5-3-5, and the top of wave B is noticeably lower than the start of wave A, as illustrated in Figures 1-22 and 1-23.

In a bear market, a zigzag correction takes place in the opposite direction, as shown in Figures 1-24 and 1-25. For this reason, a zigzag in a bear market is often referred to as an inverted zigzag.

Occasionally zigzags will occur twice, or at most, three times in succession, particularly when the first zigzag falls short of a normal target. In these cases, each zigzag is separated by an intervening "three," producing what is called a *double zigzag* (see Figure 1-26) or *triple zigzag*. These formations are analogous to the extension of an impulse wave but are less common.

The correction in the Dow Jones Industrial Average from July to October 1975 (see Figure 1-27) can be labeled as a double zigzag, as can the correction in the Standard and Poor's 500 stock index from January 1977 to March 1978 (see Figure 1-28). Within impulses, second waves frequently sport zigzags, while fourth waves rarely do.

R.N. Elliott's original labeling of double and triple zigzags and double and triple threes (see later section) was a quick shorthand. He denoted the intervening movements as wave X, so that double corrections were labeled A-B-C-X-A-B-C. Unfortunately, this notation improperly indicated the degree of the actionary subwaves of each simple pattern. They were labeled as being only one degree less than the entire correction when in fact, they are two degrees smaller. We have eliminated this problem by introducing a useful notational device: labeling the successive actionary components of double and triple corrections as waves W, Y and Z, so that the entire pattern is counted "W-X-Y (-X-Z)." The letter W now denotes the first corrective pattern in a double or triple correction, Y the second, and Z the third of a triple. Each subwave thereof (A, B or C, as well as D or E of a triangle — see later section) is now properly seen as two degrees smaller than the entire correction. Each wave X is a reactionary wave and thus always a corrective wave, typically another zigzag.

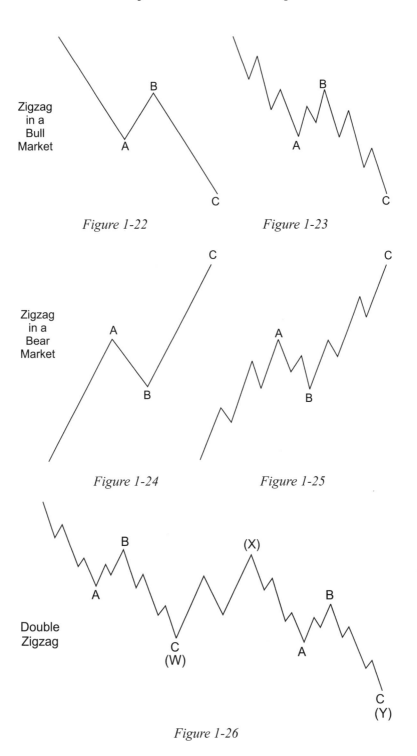

Zigzag
in a
Bull
Market

Figure 1-22

Figure 1-23

Zigzag
in a
Bear
Market

Figure 1-24

Figure 1-25

Double
Zigzag

Figure 1-26

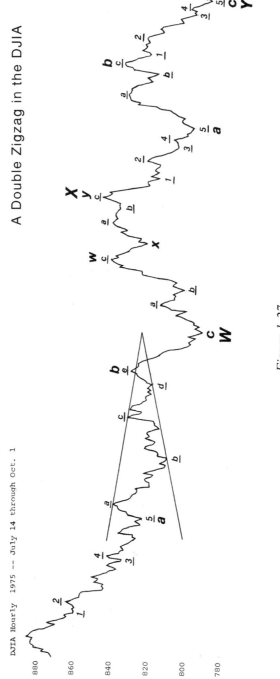

Figure 1-27

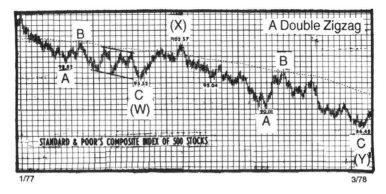

Figure 1-28

Flat (3-3-5)

A flat correction differs from a zigzag in that the subwave sequence is 3-3-5, as shown in Figures 1-29 and 1-30. Since the first actionary wave, wave A, lacks sufficient downward force to unfold into a full five waves as it does in a zigzag, the B wave reaction, not surprisingly, seems to inherit this lack of counter-trend pressure and terminates near the start of wave A. Wave C, in turn, generally terminates just slightly beyond the end of wave A rather than significantly beyond as in zigzags.

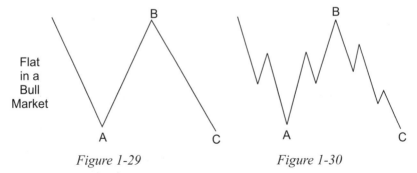

Flat
in a
Bull
Market

Figure 1-29   *Figure 1-30*

In a bear market, the pattern is the same but inverted, as shown in Figures 1-31 and 1-32.

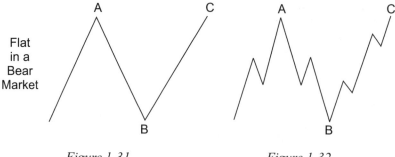

Flat
in a
Bear
Market

Figure 1-31   Figure 1-32

A flat correction usually retraces less of the preceding impulse wave than does a zigzag. It tends to occur when the larger trend is strong, so it virtually always precedes or follows an extension. The more powerful the underlying trend, the briefer the flat tends to be. Within an impulse, the fourth wave frequently sports a flat, while the second wave rarely does.

What might be called a "double flat" does occur. However, Elliott categorized such a formation as a "double three," a term we discuss later in this chapter.

The word "flat" is used as a catch-all name for any A-B-C correction that subdivides 3-3-5. In Elliott literature, however, three types of 3-3-5 corrections have been named by differences in their overall shape. In a *regular* flat correction, wave B terminates about at the level of the beginning of wave A, and wave C terminates a slight bit past the end of wave A, as we have shown in Figures 1-29 through 1-32. Far more common, however, is the variety we call an *expanded* flat, which contains a price extreme beyond that of the preceding impulse wave. Elliott called this variation an "irregular" flat, although the word is inappropriate as they are actually far more common than "regular" flats.

In expanded flats, wave B of the 3-3-5 pattern terminates beyond the starting level of wave A, and wave C ends more substantially beyond the ending level of wave A, as shown for bull markets in Figures 1-33 and 1-34 and bear markets in Figures 1-35 and 1-36. The formation in the DJIA from August to November 1973 was an expanded flat correction in a bear market, or an "inverted expanded flat" (see Figure 1-37).

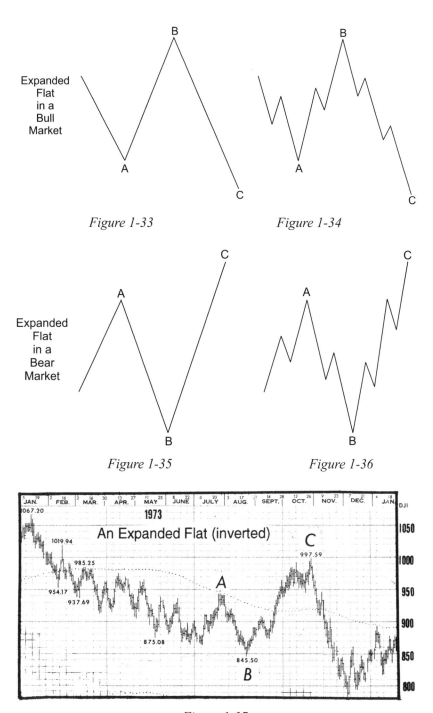

Expanded
Flat
in a
Bull
Market

Figure 1-33

Figure 1-34

Expanded
Flat
in a
Bear
Market

Figure 1-35

Figure 1-36

Figure 1-37

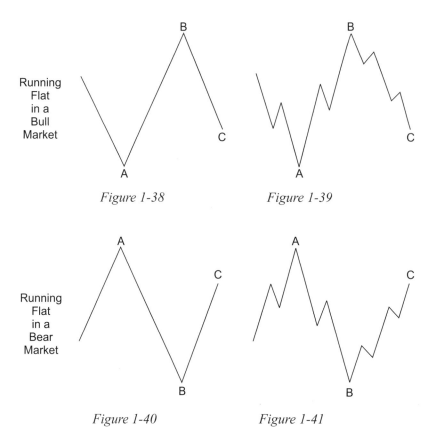

Running
Flat
in a
Bull
Market

Figure 1-38   *Figure 1-39*

Running
Flat
in a
Bear
Market

Figure 1-40   *Figure 1-41*

In a rare variation on the 3-3-5 pattern, which we call a *running* flat, wave B terminates well beyond the beginning of wave A as in an expanded flat, but wave C fails to travel its full distance, falling short of the level at which wave A ended, as in Figures 1-38 through 1-41. Apparently in this case, the forces in the direction of the larger trend are so powerful that the pattern is skewed in that direction. The result is akin to the truncation of an impulse.

It is always important, but particularly when concluding that a running flat has taken place, that the internal subdivisions adhere to Elliott's rules. If the supposed B wave, for instance, breaks down into five waves rather than three, it is more likely the first wave up of the impulse of next higher degree. The power of adjacent impulse waves is important in recognizing running corrections, which tend to occur only in strong and fast markets.

We must issue a warning, however. There are hardly any examples of this type of correction in the price record. Never label a correction prematurely this way, or you'll find yourself wrong nine times out of ten. A running *triangle*, in contrast, is much more common (see next section).

Triangle

A triangle appears to reflect a balance of forces, causing a sideways movement that is usually associated with decreasing volume and volatility. The triangle pattern contains five overlapping waves that subdivide 3-3-3-3-3 and are labeled A-B-C-D-E. A triangle is delineated by connecting the termination points of waves A and C, and B and D. Wave E can undershoot or overshoot the A-C line, and in fact, our experience tells us that it happens more often than not.

There are three varieties of triangles: contracting, barrier and expanding, as illustrated in Figure 1-42. Elliott contended that the horizontal line of a barrier triangle could occur on either side of the triangle, but such is not the case; it always occurs on the side that the next wave will exceed. Elliott's terms, "ascending" and "descending," are nevertheless useful shorthand in communicating whether the barrier triangle occurs in a bull or bear market, respectively.

Figure 1-42 depicts contracting and barrier triangles as taking place entirely within the area of preceding price action, which may be termed a *regular* triangle. Yet, it is extremely common for wave B of a contracting triangle to exceed the start of wave A in what may be termed a *running* triangle, as shown in Figure 1-43. Despite their sideways appearance, *all* triangles, including running triangles, effect a net retracement of the preceding wave at wave E's end.

There are several real life examples of triangles in the charts in this book (see Figures 1-28, 3-15, 5-5, 6-9, 6-10 and 6-12). As you will notice, most of the subwaves in a triangle are zigzags, but sometimes one of the subwaves (usually wave C) is more complex than the others and can take the shape of a multiple zigzag. In rare cases, one of the sub-waves (usually wave E) is itself a triangle, so that the entire pattern protracts into nine waves. Thus, triangles, like zigzags, occasionally display a development that is analogous to an extension. One example occurred in silver from 1973 through 1977 (see Figure 1-44).

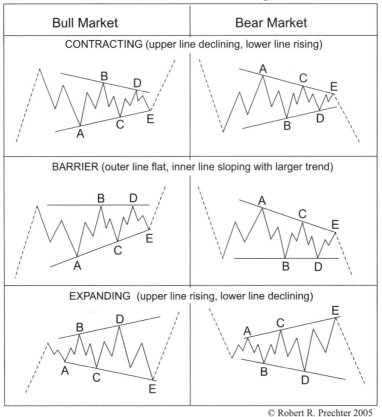

Figure 1-42

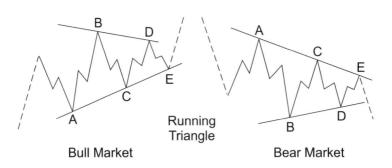

Figure 1-43

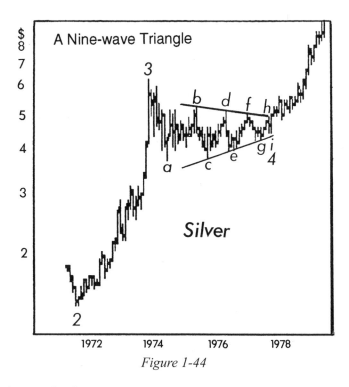

Figure 1-44

A triangle always occurs in a position *prior to* the final action-ary wave in the pattern of one larger degree, i.e., as wave four in an impulse, wave B in an A-B-C, or the final wave X in a double or triple zigzag or combination (see next section). A triangle may also occur as the final actionary pattern in a corrective combi-nation, as discussed in the next section, although even then it usually precedes the final actionary wave in the pattern of one larger degree than the corrective combination. Although upon extremely rare occasions a second wave in an impulse appears to take the form of a triangle, it is usually due to the fact that a triangle is *part* of the correction, which is in fact a double three (for example, see Figure 3-12).

In the stock market, when a triangle occurs in the fourth wave position, wave five is sometimes swift and travels approxi-mately the distance of the widest part of the triangle. Elliott used the word "thrust" in referring to this swift, short motive wave following a triangle. The thrust is usually an impulse but can be an ending diagonal. In powerful markets, there is no thrust, but instead a prolonged fifth wave. So if a fifth wave following a triangle pushes past a normal thrust movement, it is signaling a

likely protracted wave. Post-triangle advancing impulses in commodities at degrees above Intermediate are usually the longest
wave in the sequence, as explained in Chapter 6.

Many analysts are fooled into labeling a completed triangle
way too early. Triangles take time and go sideways. If you examine Figure 1-44 closely, you will see that one could have jumped
the gun in the middle of wave b, pronouncing the end of five
contracting waves. But the boundary lines of triangles almost
never collapse so quickly. Subwave C is typically a complex wave,
though wave B or D can fulfill that role. Give triangles time to
develop.

On the basis of our experience with triangles, as the examples in Figures 1-27 and later in 3-11 and 3-12 illustrate,
we propose that often the time at which the boundary lines of
a contracting triangle reach an apex coincides with a turning
point in the market. Perhaps the frequency of this occurrence
would justify its inclusion among the guidelines associated with
the Wave Principle.

Combination (Double and Triple Three)

Elliott called a sideways combination of two corrective patterns a "double three" and three patterns a "triple three." While
a single three is any zigzag or flat, a triangle is an allowable final
component of such combinations and in this context is called a
"three." A combination is composed of simpler types of corrections, including zigzags, flats and triangles. Their occurrence
appears to be the flat correction's way of extending sideways
action. As with double and triple zigzags, the simple corrective
pattern components are labeled W, Y and Z. Each reactionary
wave, labeled X, can take the shape of any corrective pattern but
is most commonly a zigzag. As with multiple zigzags, three patterns appear to be the limit, and even those are rare compared
to the more common double three.

Combinations of threes were labeled differently by Elliott
at different times, although the illustrative pattern always took
the shape of two or three juxtaposed flats, as shown in Figures
1-45 and 1-46. However, the component patterns more commonly
alternate in form. For example, a flat followed by a triangle is
a more typical type of double three (which we now know as of
1983; see Appendix), as illustrated in Figure 1-47.

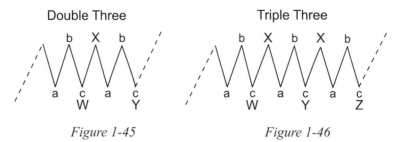

Double Three

Triple Three

Figure 1-45   *Figure 1-46*

A flat followed by a zigzag is another example, as shown in Figure 1-48. Naturally, since the figures in this section depict corrections in bull markets, they need only be inverted to observe them as upward corrections in bear markets.

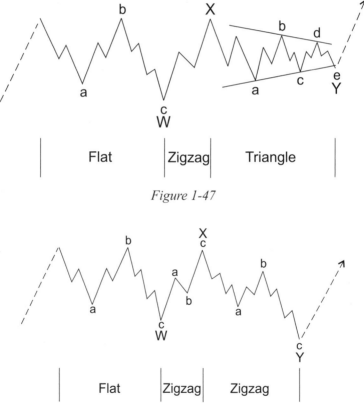

Flat   Zigzag   Triangle

Figure 1-47

Flat   Zigzag   Zigzag

Figure 1-48

For the most part, a combination is horizontal in character. Elliott indicated that the entire formation could slant against the larger trend, although we have never found this to be the case. One reason is that there never appears to be more than one zigzag in a combination. Neither is there more than one triangle. Recall that triangles occurring alone precede the final movement of a larger trend. Combinations appear to recognize this character and sport triangles only as the final wave in a double or triple three.

Although different in that their angle of trend is sharper than the sideways trend of combinations (see the guideline of alternation in Chapter 2), double and triple zigzags (see Figure 1-26) can be characterized as non-horizontal combinations, as Elliott seemed to suggest in *Nature's Law*. But double and triple threes are different from double and triple zigzags not only in their angle but in their goal. In a double or triple zigzag, the first zigzag is rarely large enough to constitute an adequate *price* correction of the preceding wave. The doubling or tripling of the initial form is usually necessary to create an adequately sized price retracement. In a combination, however, the first simple pattern often constitutes an adequate price correction. The doubling or tripling appears to occur mainly to extend the *duration* of the corrective process after price targets have been substantially met. Sometimes additional time is needed to reach a channel line or achieve a stronger kinship with the other correction in an impulse. As the consolidation continues, the attendant psychology and fundamentals extend their trends accordingly.

As this section makes clear, there is a qualitative difference between the series $3 + 4 + 4 + 4$, etc., and the series $5 + 4 + 4 + 4$, etc. Notice that while an impulse wave has a total count of 5, with extensions leading to 9 or 13 waves, and so on, a corrective wave has a count of 3, with combinations leading to 7 or 11 waves, and so on. The triangle appears to be an exception, although it can be counted as one would a triple three, totaling 11 waves. Thus, if an internal count is unclear, you can sometimes reach a reasonable conclusion merely by counting waves. A count of 9, 13 or 17 with few overlaps, for instance, is likely motive, while a count of 7, 11 or 15 with numerous overlaps is likely corrective. The main exceptions are diagonals of both types, which are hybrids of motive and corrective forces.

Orthodox Tops and Bottoms

Sometimes a pattern's end differs from the associated price extreme. In such cases, the end of the pattern is called the "orthodox" top or bottom in order to differentiate it from the actual price high or low that occurs intra-pattern or after the end of the pattern. For example, in Figure 1-14, the end of wave (5) is the orthodox top despite the fact that wave (3) registered a higher price. In Figure 1-13, the end of wave 5 is the orthodox bottom. In Figures 1-33 and 1-34, the starting point of wave A is the orthodox top of the preceding bull market despite the higher high of wave B. In Figures 1-35 and 1-36, the start of wave A is the orthodox bottom. In Figure 1-47, the end of wave Y is the orthodox bottom of the bear market even though the price low occurs at the end of wave W.

This concept is important primarily because a sucessful analysis always depends upon a proper labeling of the patterns. Assuming falsely that a particular price extreme is the correct starting point for wave labeling can throw analysis off for some time, while being aware of the requirements of wave form will keep you on track. Further, when applying the forecasting concepts that will be introduced in Chapter 4, the length and duration of a wave are typically determined by measuring from and projecting orthodox ending points.

Reconciling Function and Mode

Earlier in this chapter, we described the two functions waves may perform (action and reaction), as well as the two modes of structural development (motive and corrective) that they undergo. Now that we have reviewed all types of waves, we can summarize their labels as follows:

— The labels for actionary waves are 1, 3, 5, A, C, E, W, Y and Z.

— The labels for reactionary waves are 2, 4, B, D and X.

As stated earlier, *all* reactionary waves develop in corrective mode, and *most* actionary waves develop in motive mode. The preceding sections have described which actionary waves develop in corrective mode. They are:

— waves 1, 3 and 5 in an ending diagonal,

— wave A in a flat correction,

— waves A, C and E in a triangle,

— waves W and Y in a double zigzag and a double three,

— wave Z in a triple zigzag and a triple three.

Because the waves listed above are actionary in relative direction yet develop in corrective mode, we term them "actionary corrective" waves.

ADDITIONAL TERMINOLOGY (Optional)

Terms That Denote Purpose

Though action in five waves is followed by reaction in three waves at all degrees of trend *regardless of direction*, progress begins with an actionary impulse, which by convention is graphed in the upward direction. (Since all such graphs depict ratios, they could be depicted in the downward direction. Instead of dollars per share, for instance, one could plot shares per dollar.) Ultimately and most fundamentally, then, the long term trend of the stock market, which is a reflection of man's progress, is *upwardly directional*. Progress is carried out by the development of impulse waves of ever larger degree. Motive waves *downward* are merely parts of corrections and therefore are not synonymous with progress. Similarly, corrective waves *upward* are still corrective and thus ultimately do not achieve progress. Therefore, three additional terms are required to denote the *purpose* of a wave, to differentiate conveniently among waves that result in progress and those that do not.

Any motive wave upward that is not within a corrective wave of any larger degree will be termed a *progressive* wave. It must be labeled 1, 3 or 5. Any declining wave, regardless of mode, will be termed a *regressive* wave. Finally, an upward wave, regardless of mode, that occurs within a corrective wave of any larger degree will be termed a *proregressive* wave. Both regressive and proregressive waves are part or all of corrections. Only a progressive wave is independent of countertrend forces.

The reader may recognize that the commonly used term "bull market" would apply to a progressive wave, the term "bear market" would apply to a regressive wave, and the term "bear market rally" would apply to a proregressive wave. However, conventional definitions of terms such as "bull market," "bear market," "primary," "intermediate," "minor," "rally," "pullback" and "correction" attempt to include a quantitative element and are thus rendered useless because they are arbitrary. For instance, some people define a bear market as any decline of 20% or more. By this definition, a decline of 19.99% is not a bear market, just a "correction," while any decline of 20% *is* a bear market. Such terms are of questionable value. Although a whole list of quantitative terms could be developed (cub, mama bear, papa bear and grizzly, for instance), they cannot improve upon the simple use of a percentage. In contrast, Elliott wave terms are properly definitive because they are qualitative, i.e., they reflect concepts and pertain regardless of the size of the pattern. Thus, there are differing degrees of progressive, regressive and proregressive waves under the Wave Principle. A Supercycle B wave in a Grand Supercycle correction would be of sufficient amplitude and duration that it would be popularly identified as a "bull market." However, its proper label under the Wave Principle is a proregressive wave, or using the conventional term as it should be used, a bear market rally.

Terms That Denote Relative Importance

There are two classes of waves, which differ in fundamental importance. Waves denoted by numbers we term *cardinal* waves because they compose the essential wave form, the five-wave impulse, as shown in Figure 1-1. The market can *always* be identified as being in a cardinal wave at the largest degree. Waves denoted by letters we term *consonant* or *subcardinal* waves because they serve only as *components* of cardinal waves 2 and 4 and may not serve in any other capacity. A motive wave is composed, at one lesser degree, of cardinal waves, and a corrective wave is composed, at one lesser degree, of consonant waves. Our selection of these terms is due to their excellent double meanings. "Cardinal" means not only "of central or basic importance to any system, construction or framework of thought" but also denotes a primary number used in counting. "Consonant" means not only "harmonious with other parts [in] conforming to a pattern," but also is a type of letter in the alphabet. (Source: *The Merriam-Webster Unabridged Dictionary*.) There is little practical use for these terms, which is why this explanation has been relegated to the end of the chapter. However, they are useful in philosophical and theoretic discussions and so are presented to anchor the terminology.

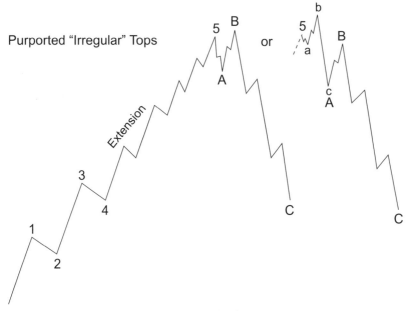

Purported "Irregular" Tops

Figure 1-49

ERRONEOUS CONCEPTS AND PATTERNS

In *The Wave Principle* and elsewhere, Elliott discussed what he called an "irregular top," an idea he developed with a great deal of specificity. He said that if an extended fifth wave terminates a fifth wave of one higher degree, the ensuing bear market will either *begin with* or *be* an expanded flat in which wave A is extremely (we would say impossibly) small relative to the size of wave C (see Figure 1-49). Wave B to a new high is the irregular top, "irregular" because it occurs after the end of the fifth wave. Elliott contended further that occurrences of irregular tops alternate with those of regular tops. His formulation is inaccurate, however, and complicates the description of phenomena that we describe accurately in the discussion of the behavior following fifth wave extensions and under "Depth of Corrective Waves" in Chapter 2.

The question is, how did Elliott end up with two extra waves that he had to explain away? The answer is that he was powerfully predisposed to marking a fifth wave extension when in fact the third wave had extended. Two impressive Primary degree fifth wave extensions occurred in the 1920s and 1930s, engendering that predisposition. In order to turn an extended third into an extended fifth, Elliott invented an A-B-C correction called an "irregular type 2." In this case, he said, wave B falls short of the level of the start of wave A, as in a zigzag, while wave C falls short of the level of the end of wave A, as in a running correction. He often asserted this labeling in the wave 2 position. These labels then left him with two extra waves at the peak. The "irregular type 2" idea got rid of an extension's first two waves, while the "irregular top" idea handled the two left over at the top. Thus, *these two erroneous concepts were born of the same tendency.* In fact, one *requires* the other. As you can see by the count illustrated in Figure 1-50, the a-b-c "irregular type 2" in the wave 2 position necessitates the "irregular top" labeling at the peak. In fact, there is nothing irregular about the wave structure except its false labeling!

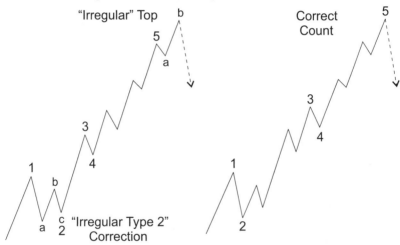

Figure 1-50

Elliott also contended that every fifth wave extension is "doubly retraced," i.e., followed by a "first retracement" to near the level of its beginning and a "second retracement" to above the level at which it began. Such movement happens naturally due to the guideline that corrections usually bottom in the area of the previous fourth wave (see Chapter 2); the "second retracement" is the next impulse wave. The term might apply reasonably well to waves A and B of an expanded flat following an extension, as per the discussion in Chapter 2 under "Behavior Following Fifth Wave Extensions." There is no point in giving this natural behavior a specific name.

In *Nature's Law*, Elliott referred to a shape called a "half moon." It was not a separate pattern but merely a descriptive phrase of how a decline within a bear market occasionally begins slowly, accelerates, and ends in a panic spike. This shape is found more often when declining prices are plotted on semilog scale and when advancing prices in a multi-year trend are plotted on arithmetic scale.

Also in *Nature's Law*, Elliott twice referred to a structure he called an "A-B base," in which after a decline ends on a satisfactory count, the market advances in three waves and then declines in three waves prior to the commencement of the true five-wave bull market. The fact is that Elliott invented this pattern during a period in which he was trying to force his Principle into the 13-year triangle concept, which no interpreter today accepts as valid under the rules of the Wave Principle. Indeed, it is clear that such a pattern, if it existed, would have the effect of invalidating the Wave Principle. The authors have never seen an "A-B base," and in fact it cannot exist. Its invention by Elliott merely goes to show that for all his meticulous study and profound discovery, he displayed a typical analyst's weakness in (at least once) allowing an opinion already formed to affect adversely his objectivity in analyzing the market.

As far as we know, this chapter lists all wave formations that can occur in the price movement of the broad stock market averages. Under the Wave Principle, no other formations than those listed here will occur. The authors can find no examples of waves above Minor degree that we cannot count satisfactorily by the Elliott method. The hourly readings are a nearly perfectly matched filter for detailing waves of Subminuette degree. Elliott waves of much smaller degree than Subminuette are revealed by computer generated charts of minute-by-minute transactions. Even the few data points (transactions) per unit of time at this low a degree are often enough to reflect the Wave Principle accurately by recording the rapid shifts in psychology occurring in the "pits" and on the exchange floor.

All rules and guidelines of the Wave Principle fundamentally apply to actual market mood, not its recording *per se* or lack thereof. Its clear manifestation requires free market pricing. When prices are fixed by government edict, such as those for gold and silver for half of the twentieth century, waves restricted by the edict are not allowed to register. When the available price record differs from what might have existed in a free market, rules and guidelines must be considered in that light. In the long run, of course, markets always win out over edicts, and edict enforcement is only possible if the mood of the market allows it. All rules and guidelines presented in this book presume that your price record is accurate.

Now that we have presented the rules and rudiments of wave formation, we can move on to some of the guidelines for successful analysis using the Wave Principle.

CHAPTER 2

GUIDELINES OF WAVE FORMATION

The guidelines presented throughout this chapter are discussed and illustrated in the context of a bull market. Except where specifically excluded, they apply equally in bear markets, in which context the illustrations and implications would be inverted.

Alternation

The guideline of alternation is very broad in its application and warns the analyst always to expect a difference in the next expression of a similar wave. Hamilton Bolton said,

> The writer is *not* convinced that alternation is *inevitable* in types of waves in larger formations, but there are frequent enough cases to suggest that one should look for it rather than the contrary.

Although alternation does not say precisely what is going to happen, it gives valuable notice of what *not* to expect and is therefore useful to keep in mind when analyzing wave formations and assessing future probabilities. It primarily instructs the analyst not to assume, as most people tend to do, that because the last market cycle behaved in a certain manner, this one is sure to be the same. As "contrarians" never cease to point out, the day that most investors "catch on" to an apparent habit of the market is the day it will change to one completely different. However, Elliott went further in stating that, in fact, alternation was virtually a law of markets.

Alternation Within An Impulse

If wave two of an impulse is a sharp correction, expect wave four to be a sideways correction, and vice versa. Figure 2-1 shows the most characteristic breakdowns of an impulse wave, either up or down, as suggested by the guideline of alternation. Sharp corrections never include a new price extreme, i.e., one that lies beyond the orthodox end of the preceding impulse wave. They are almost always zigzags (single, double or triple); occasionally they are double threes that *begin* with a zigzag. Sideways corrections include flats, triangles, and double and triple corrections. They usually include a new price extreme, i.e., one that lies beyond the orthodox end of the preceding impulse wave. In rare cases, a regular triangle (one that does not include a new price extreme) in the fourth wave position will take the place of a sharp correction and alternate with another type of sideways pattern in the second wave position. The idea of alternation within an impulse can be summarized by saying that one of the two corrective processes will contain a move back to or beyond the end of the preceding impulse, and the other will not.

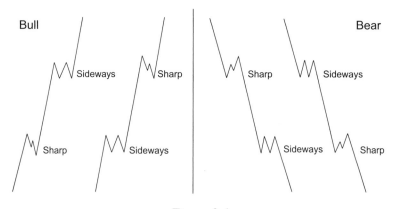

Figure 2-1

A diagonal does not display alternation between subwaves 2 and 4. Typically both corrections are zigzags. An extension is an expression of alternation, as the motive waves alternate their lengths. Typically the first is short, the third is extended, and the fifth is short again. An extension, which normally occurs as wave 3, sometimes occurs as wave 1 or 5, another manifestation of alternation.

Alternation Within Corrective Waves

If a correction begins with a flat a-b-c construction for wave A, expect a zigzag a-b-c formation for wave B, and vice versa (see Figures 2-2 and 2-3). With a moment's thought, it is obvious that this occurrence is sensible, since the first illustration reflects

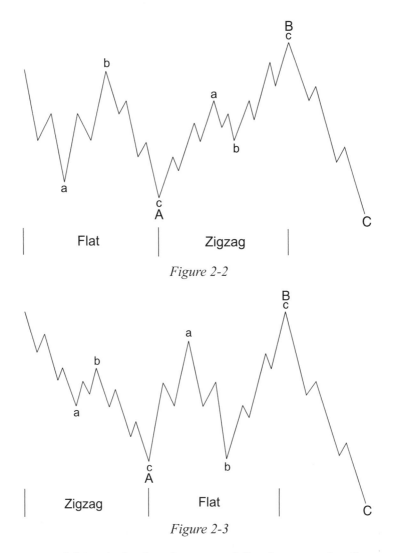

Figure 2-2

Figure 2-3

an upward bias in both subwaves while the second reflects a downward bias.

Quite often, when a large correction begins with a simple a-b-c zigzag for wave A, wave B will stretch out into a more intricately subdivided a-b-c zigzag to achieve a type of alternation, as in Figure 2-4. Sometimes wave C will be yet more complex, as in Figure 2-5. The reverse order of complexity is somewhat less common. An example of its occurrence can be found in wave 4 in Figure 2-16.

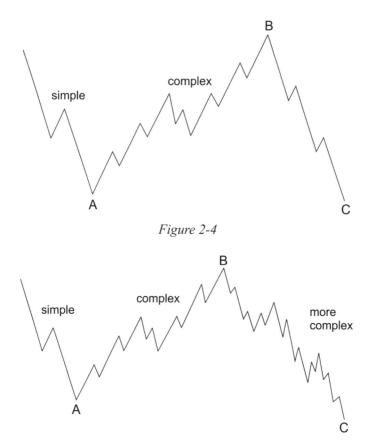

Figure 2-4

Figure 2-5

Depth of Corrective Waves

No market approach other than the Wave Principle gives a satisfactory answer to the question, "How far down can a bear market be expected to go?" The primary guideline is that corrections, especially when they themselves are fourth waves, tend to register their maximum retracement within the span of travel of the previous fourth wave of one lesser degree, most commonly near the level of its terminus.

Example #1: The 1929-1932 Bear Market

Our analysis of the period from 1789 to 1932 uses the chart of stock prices adjusted to constant dollars developed by Gertrude Shirk and presented in the January 1977 issue of *Cycles* magazine. Here we find that the 1932 Supercycle low bottomed within the area of the previous fourth wave of Cycle degree, an expanding triangle spanning the period between 1890 and 1921 (see Figure 5-4, page 161).

Example #2: The 1942 Bear Market Low

In this case, the Cycle degree bear market from 1937 to 1942 was a zigzag that terminated within the area of the fourth Primary wave of the bull market from 1932 to 1937 (see Figure 5-5, page 164).

Example #3: The 1962 Bear Market Low

The wave ④ plunge in 1962 brought the averages down to just above the 1956 high of the five-wave Primary sequence from 1949 to 1959. Ordinarily, the bear would have reached into the zone of wave (4), the fourth wave correction within wave ③. This narrow miss nevertheless illustrates why this guideline is not a rule. The preceding strong third wave extension and the shallow A wave and strong B wave within (4) indicated strength in the wave structure, which carried over into the moderate net depth of the correction (see Figure 5-5, page 164).

Example #4: The 1974 Bear Market Low

The final decline into 1974, ending the 1966-1974 Cycle degree wave IV correction of the entire wave III rise from 1942, brought the averages down to the area of the previous fourth wave of lesser degree (Primary wave ④). Again, Figure 5-5 on page 164 shows what happened.

Example #5: London Gold Bear Market, 1974-1976

Here we have an illustration from another market of the tendency for a correction to terminate in the area of travel of the preceding fourth wave of one lesser degree (see Figure 6-11, page 179).

Our analysis of small degree wave sequences over the last twenty years further validates the proposition that the usual limitation of any bear market is the travel area of the preceding fourth wave of one lesser degree, particularly when the bear market in question is itself a fourth wave. However, in a clearly reasonable modification of the guideline, it is often the case that if the *first* wave in a sequence extends, the correction following the fifth wave will have as a typical limit the bottom of the *second* wave of lesser degree. For example, the decline into March 1978 in the DJIA bottomed exactly at the low of the second wave in March 1975, which followed an extended first wave off the December 1974 low.

On occasion, a flat correction or triangle, particularly if it follows an extension, will fail, usually by a slim margin, to reach into the fourth wave area (see Example #3). A zigzag, on occasion, will cut deeply and move down into the area of the second wave of lesser degree, although this almost exclusively occurs when the zigzag is itself a second wave. "Double bottoms" are sometimes formed in this manner.

Behavior Following Fifth Wave Extensions

Having cumulatively observed the hourly changes in the DJIA for over twenty years, the authors are convinced that Elliott imprecisely stated some of his findings with respect to both the occurrence of extensions and the market action following an extension. The most important empirically derived rule that can be distilled from our observations of market behavior is that when the fifth wave of an advance is an extension, the ensuing correction will be sharp and find support at the level of the low of wave two of the extension. Sometimes the correction ends there, as illustrated in Figure 2-6, and sometimes only wave A ends there. Although a limited number of real life examples exist, the precision with which A waves have reversed at this level is remarkable. Figure 2-7 is an illustration showing both a zigzag and an expanded flat correction. An example involving a zigzag can be found in Figure 5-5 at the low of wave Ⓐ of II and an example involving an expanded flat can be found in Figure 2-16 at the low of wave a of A of 4. As you may be able to discern in Figure 5-5, wave a of (IV) bottoms near wave (2) of ⑤, which is an extension within the wave V from 1921 to 1929.

Since the low of the second wave of an extension is commonly in or near the price territory of the immediately preceding fourth wave of one larger degree, this guideline implies behavior similar to that of the preceding guideline. It is notable for its *precision*, however. Additional value is provided by the fact that fifth wave extensions are typically followed by *swift* retracements. Their occurrence, then, is an advance warning of a dramatic reversal

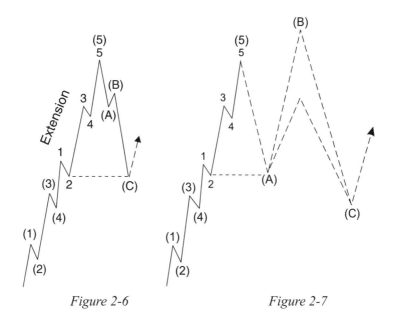

Figure 2-6   *Figure 2-7*

to a specific level, a powerful combination of knowledge. This guideline need not apply when the market is ending a fifth wave at more than one degree, yet the action in Figure 5-5 (see above reference) suggests that we should still view this level as at least potential or temporary support.

Wave Equality

One of the guidelines of the Wave Principle is that two of the motive waves in a five-wave sequence will tend toward equality in time and magnitude. This is generally true of the two non-extended waves when one wave is an extension, and it is especially true if the third wave is the extension. If perfect equality is lacking, a .618 multiple is the next likely relationship (see Chapters 3 and 4).

When waves are larger than Intermediate degree, the price relationships usually must be stated in percentage terms. Thus, within the entire extended Cycle wave advance from 1942 to 1966, we find that Primary wave ① traveled 120 points, a gain of 129%, in 49 months, while Primary wave ⑤ traveled 438 points, a gain of 80% (.618 times the 129% gain), in 40 months (see Figure 5-5, page 164), far different from the 324% gain of the third Primary wave, which lasted 126 months.

When waves are of Intermediate degree or below, the price equality can usually be stated in arithmetic terms, since the percentage lengths will also be nearly equivalent. Thus, in the year-end rally of 1976, we find that wave 1 traveled 35.24 points in 47 market hours while wave 5 traveled 34.40 points in 47 market hours. The guideline of equality is often extremely accurate.

Charting the Waves

A. Hamilton Bolton always kept an "hourly close" chart, i.e., one showing the end-of-hour prices, as do the authors. Elliott himself certainly followed the same practice, since in *The Wave Principle*, he presents an hourly chart of stock prices from February 23 to March 31, 1938. Every Elliott wave practitioner, or anyone interested in the Wave Principle, will find it instructive and useful to plot the hourly fluctuations of the DJIA, which are published by *The Wall Street Journal* and *Barron's*. It is a simple task that requires only a few minutes' work a week. Bar charts are fine but can be misleading by revealing fluctuations that occur near the time changes for each bar but not those that occur within the time for the bar. Actual print figures must be used on all plots. The so-called "opening" and "theoretical intraday" figures published for the Dow averages are statistical inventions that do not reflect the averages at any particular moment. Respectively, these figures represent a sum of the opening prices, which can occur at different times, and of the daily highs or lows of each individual stock in the average regardless of the time of day each extreme occurs.

The foremost aim of wave classification is to determine where prices are in the stock market's progression. This exercise is easy as long as the wave counts are clear, as in fast-moving, emotional markets, particularly in impulse waves, when minor movements generally unfold in an uncomplicated manner. In these cases, short term charting is necessary to view all subdivisions. However, in lethargic or choppy markets, particularly in corrections, wave structures are more likely to be complex and slow to develop. In these cases, a longer term chart often effectively condenses the action into a form that clarifies the pattern in progress. With a proper reading of the Wave Principle, there are times when a sideways trend can be forecasted (for instance, for a fourth wave when wave two is a zigzag). Even when anticipated, though, complexity and lethargy are two of the most frustrating occurrences for the analyst. Nevertheless, they are part of the reality of the market and must be taken into account. The authors highly recommend that during such periods you take some time off from the market to enjoy the profits made during the rapidly unfolding impulse waves. You can't "wish" the market into action; it isn't listening. When the market rests, do the same.

The correct method for tracking the stock market is to use semilogarithmic chart paper, since the market's history is sensibly related only on a percentage basis. The investor is concerned with percentage gain or loss, not the number of points traveled in a market average. For instance, ten points in the DJIA in 1980 meant a one percent move. In the early 1920s, ten points meant a ten percent move, quite a bit more important. For ease of charting, however, we suggest using semilog scale only for long term plots, where the difference is especially noticeable. Arithmetic scale is quite acceptable for tracking hourly waves since a 40 point rally with the DJIA at 800 is not much different in percentage terms from a 40 point rally with the DJIA at 900. Thus, channeling techniques work acceptably well on arithmetic scale with shorter term moves.

Channeling

Elliott noted that a parallel trend channel typically marks the upper and lower boundaries of an impulse wave, often with dramatic precision. You should draw one as early as possible to assist in determining wave targets and provide clues to the future development of trends.

The initial channeling technique for an impulse requires at least three reference points. When wave three ends, connect the points labeled 1 and 3, then draw a parallel line touching the point labeled 2, as shown in Figure 2-8. This construction provides an estimated boundary for wave four. (In most cases, third waves travel far enough that the starting point is excluded from the final channel's touch points.)

If the fourth wave ends at a point not touching the parallel, you must reconstruct the channel in order to estimate the boundary for wave five. First connect the ends of waves two and four. If waves one and three are normal, the upper parallel most

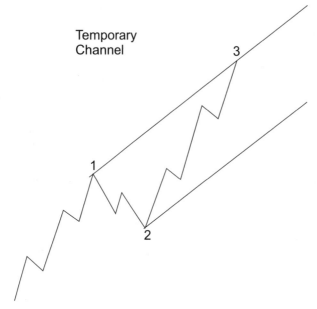

Figure 2-8

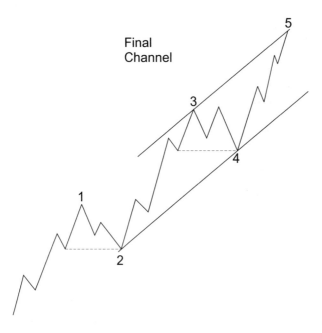

Figure 2-9

accurately forecasts the end of wave five when drawn touching the peak of wave three, as in Figure 2-9. If wave three is abnormally strong, almost vertical, then a parallel drawn from its top may be too high. Experience has shown that a parallel to the baseline that touches the top of wave one is then more useful, as in our depiction of gold bullion from August 1976 to March 1977 (see Figure 6-12, page 181). In some cases, it may be useful to draw both potential upper boundary lines to alert you to be especially attentive to the wave count and volume characteristics at those levels and then take appropriate action as the wave count warrants.

Always remember that all degrees of trend are operating at the same time. Sometimes, for instance, a fifth wave of Intermediate degree within a fifth wave of Primary degree will end when it reaches the upper channel lines at both degrees simultaneously. Or sometimes a throw-over at Supercycle degree will terminate precisely when prices reach the upper line of the channel at Cycle degree.

Zigzag corrections often form channels with four touch points. One line connects the starting point of wave A and then end of wave B; the other line touches the end of wave A and end end of wave C. Once the former line is established, a parallel line drawn from the end of wave A is an excellent tool for recognizing the exact end of the entire correction.

Throw-over

Within a parallel channel or the converging lines of a diagonal, if a fifth wave approaches its upper trendline on declining volume, it is an indication that the end of the wave will meet or fall short of it. If volume is heavy as the fifth wave approaches its upper trendline, it indicates a possible penetration of the upper line, which Elliott called a "throw-over." Near the point of throw-over, a fourth wave of small degree may trend sideways immediately below the parallel, allowing the fifth then to break it in a final burst of volume.

A throw-over is occasionally telegraphed by a preceding "throw-*under*," either by wave 4 or by wave two of 5, as suggested by the drawing shown as Figure 2-10, from Elliott's book, *The Wave Principle*. A throw-over is confirmed by an immediate reversal back below the line. A throw-over can also occur, with

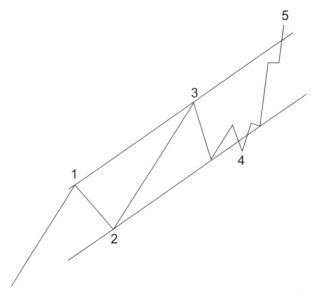

Figure 2-10

the same characteristics, in a declining market. Elliott correctly warned that a throw-over at large degree causes difficulty in identifying the waves of smaller degree during the throw-over, as smaller degree channels are sometimes penetrated on the upside during the final fifth wave. Figures 1-17, 1-19 and 2-11 show real-life examples of throw-overs.

Scale

Elliott contended that the necessity of channeling on semilog scale indicated the presence of inflation. To date, no student of the Wave Principle has questioned this assumption, which is demonstrably incorrect. Some of the differences apparent to Elliott may have been due to differences in the degree of waves that he was plotting, since the larger the degree, the more necessary a semilog scale usually becomes. On the other hand, the virtually perfect channels that were formed by the 1921-1929 market on semilog scale (see Figure 2-11) and the 1932-1937 market on arithmetic scale (see Figure 2-12) indicate that waves of the same degree will form the correct Elliott trend channel only when plotted selectively on the appropriate scale. On arithmetic scale, the 1920s bull market accelerates beyond the upper boundary,

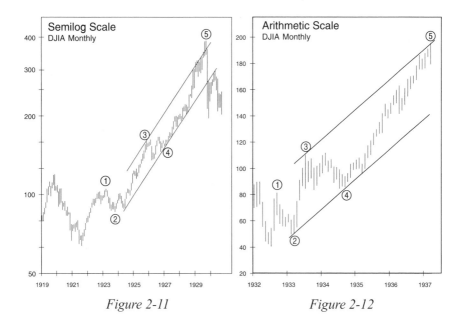

Figure 2-11   *Figure 2-12*

while on semilog scale the 1930s bull market falls far short of the upper boundary.

Regarding Elliott's contention concerning inflation, we note that the period of the 1920s actually accompanied mild deflation, as the Consumer Price Index declined an average of .5% per year, while the period from 1933 to 1937 was mildly inflationary, accompanying a rise in the CPI of 2.2% per year. This monetary background convinces us that inflation is not the reason behind the necessity for use of semilog scale. In fact, aside from this difference in channeling, these two waves of Cycle dimension are surprisingly similar: they create nearly the same multiples in price (six times and five times respectively), they both contain extended fifth waves, and the peak of the third wave is the same percentage gain above the bottom in each case. The essential difference between the two bull markets is the shape and time length of each individual subwave.

At most, we can state that the necessity for semilog scale indicates a wave that is in the process of acceleration, for whatever mass psychological reasons. Given a single price objective and a specific length of time allotted, anyone can draw a satisfactory hypothetical Elliott wave channel from the same point of origin on both arithmetic and semilog scale by adjusting the slope of the waves to fit. Thus, the question of whether to expect a parallel channel on arithmetic or semilog scale is still unresolved as far as developing a tenet on the subject. If the price development at any point does not fall neatly within two parallel lines on the scale you are using, switch to the other scale in order to observe the channel in correct perspective. To stay on top of all developments, you should always use both.

Volume

Elliott used volume as a tool for verifying wave counts and in projecting extensions. He recognized that in a bull market, volume has a natural tendency to expand and contract with the speed of price change. Late in a corrective phase, a decline in volume often indicates a decline in selling pressure. A low point in volume often coincides with a turning point in the market. In a normal fifth wave below Primary degree, volume tends to be less than in the third wave. If volume in an advancing fifth wave of less than Primary degree is equal to or greater than that in the third wave, an extension of the fifth is in force. While this outcome is often to be expected anyway if the first and third waves are about equal in length, it is an excellent warning of those rare times when both a third *and* a fifth wave are extended.

At Primary degree and greater, volume tends to be higher in an advancing fifth wave merely because of the natural long term growth in the number of participants in bull markets. Elliott noted, in fact, that volume at the terminal point of a bull market above Primary degree tends to run at an all-time high. Finally, as discussed earlier, volume often spikes briefly at the throw-over point of a parallel trend channel line or the resistance line of a diagonal. (Upon occasion, such a point can occur simultaneously, as when a diagonal fifth wave terminates right at the upper parallel of the channel containing the price action of one larger degree.)

In addition to these few valuable observations, we have expanded upon the importance of volume in various sections of this book. To the extent that volume guides wave counting or expectations, it is most significant. Elliott once said that volume independently follows the patterns of the Wave Principle, a claim for which the authors find no convincing evidence.

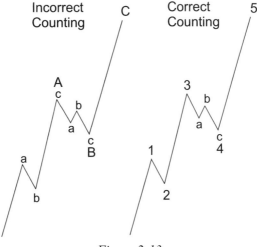

Figure 2-13

The "Right Look"

The overall appearance of a wave must conform to the appropriate illustration. Although any five-wave sequence can be forced into a three-wave count by labeling the first three subdivisions as a single wave A, as shown in Figure 2-13, it is incorrect to do so. Elliott analysis would lose its anchor if such contortions were allowed. If wave four terminates well above the top of wave one, a five-wave sequence must be classified as an impulse. Since wave A in this hypothetical case is composed of three waves, wave B would be expected to drop to about the start of wave A, as in a flat correction, which it clearly does not. While the internal count of a wave is a guide to its classification, the right overall shape is, in turn, often a guide to its correct internal count.

The "right look" of a wave is dictated by all the considerations we have outlined so far in the first two chapters. In our experience, we have found it extremely dangerous to allow our emotional involvement with the market to let us accept a wave count that reflects disproportionate wave relationships or a misshapen pattern merely on the basis that the Wave Principle's patterns are somewhat elastic.

Elliott cautioned that "the right look" may not be evident at all degrees of trend simultaneously. The solution is to focus on the degrees that are clearest. If the hourly chart is confusing, step back and look at the daily or weekly chart. Conversely, if the weekly chart offers too many possibilities, concentrate on the shorter term movements until the bigger picture clarifies. Generally speaking, you need short term charts to analyze subdivisions in fast moving markets and long term charts for slowly moving markets.

Wave Personality

The idea of wave personality is a substantial expansion of the Wave Principle. It has the advantage of bringing human behavior more personally into the equation.

The personality of each wave in the Elliott sequence is an integral part of the reflection of the mass psychology it embodies. The progression of mass emotions from pessimism to optimism and back again tends to follow a similar path each time around, producing similar circumstances at corresponding points in the wave structure. As the Wave Principle indicates, market history repeats but not exactly. Every wave has siblings (same-directional waves of the same degree within a larger wave) and cousins (same-degree and same-numbered waves within different larger waves) but no wave has a twin. Related waves — particularly cousins — have similar market and social characteristics. The personality of each wave type is manifest whether the wave is of Grand Supercycle degree or Subminuette. Waves' properties not only forewarn what to expect in the next sequence but at times can help determine the market's present location in the progression of waves, when for other reasons the count is unclear or open to differing interpretations. As waves are in the process of unfolding, there are times when several different wave counts are perfectly admissible under all known Elliott rules. It is at these junctures that a knowledge of wave personality can be invaluable. Recognizing the character of a single wave can often allow you to interpret correctly the complexities of the larger pattern. The following discussions relate to an underlying bull market picture, as illustrated in Figures 2-14 and 2-15. These observations apply in reverse when the actionary waves are downward and the reactionary waves are upward.

1) **First** waves — As a rough estimate, about half of first waves are part of the "basing" process and thus tend to be heavily corrected by wave two. In contrast to the bear market rallies within the previous decline, however, this first wave rise is technically more constructive, often displaying a subtle increase in

Idealized Elliott Wave Progression

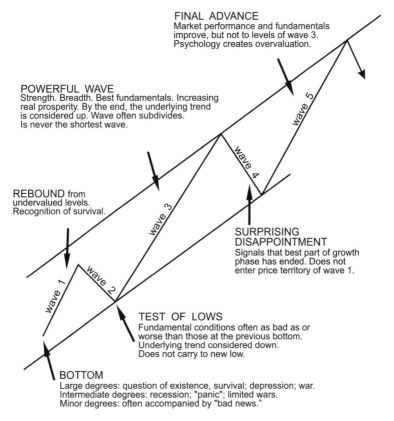

FINAL ADVANCE
Market performance and fundamentals improve, but not to levels of wave 3. Psychology creates overvaluation.

POWERFUL WAVE
Strength. Breadth. Best fundamentals. Increasing real prosperity. By the end, the underlying trend is considered up. Wave often subdivides. Is never the shortest wave.

REBOUND from undervalued levels. Recognition of survival.

SURPRISING DISAPPOINTMENT
Signals that best part of growth phase has ended. Does not enter price territory of wave 1.

TEST OF LOWS
Fundamental conditions often as bad as or worse than those at the previous bottom. Underlying trend considered down. Does not carry to new low.

BOTTOM
Large degrees: question of existence, survival; depression; war.
Intermediate degrees: recession; "panic"; limited wars.
Minor degrees: often accompanied by "bad news."

Figure 2-14

volume and breadth. Plenty of short selling is in evidence as the majority has finally become convinced that the overall trend is down. Investors have finally gotten "one more rally to sell on," and they take advantage of it. The other fifty percent of first waves rise from either large bases formed by the previous correction, as in 1949, from downside failures, as in 1962, or from extreme compression, as in both 1962 and 1974. From such beginnings, first waves are dynamic and only moderately retraced.

2) **Second** waves — Second waves often retrace so much of wave one that most of the profits gained up to that time are eroded away by the time it ends. This is especially true of call option purchases, as premiums sink drastically in the environ-

ment of fear during second waves. At this point, investors are thoroughly convinced that the bear market is back to stay. Second waves often end on very low volume and volatility, indicating a drying up of selling pressure.

3) **Third** waves — Third waves are wonders to behold. They are strong and broad, and the trend at this point is unmistakable. Increasingly favorable fundamentals enter the picture as confidence returns. Third waves usually generate the greatest volume and price movement and are most often the extended wave in a series. It follows, of course, that the third wave of a third wave, and so on, will be the most volatile point of strength in any wave sequence. Such points invariably produce breakouts, "continuation" gaps, volume expansions, exceptional breadth, major Dow Theory trend confirmations and runaway price movement, creating large hourly, daily, weekly, monthly or yearly gains in the market, depending on the degree of the wave. Virtually all stocks participate in third waves. Besides the personality of B waves, that of third waves produces the most valuable clues to the wave count as it unfolds.

4) **Fourth** waves — Fourth waves are predictable in both depth (see page 66) and form, because by alternation they should differ from the previous second wave of the same degree. More often than not they trend sideways, building the base for the final fifth wave move. Lagging stocks build their tops and begin declining during this wave, since only the strength of a third wave was able to generate any motion in them in the first place. This initial deterioration in the market sets the stage for non-confirmations and subtle signs of weakness during the fifth wave.

5) **Fifth** waves — Fifth waves in stocks are always less dynamic than third waves in terms of breadth. They usually display a slower maximum speed of price change as well, although if a fifth wave is an extension, speed of price change in the third *of* the fifth can exceed that of the third wave. Similarly, while it is common for volume to increase through successive impulse waves at Cycle degree or larger, it usually happens in a fifth wave below Primary degree only if the fifth wave extends. Otherwise, look for *lesser* volume as a rule in a fifth wave as opposed to the third. Market dabblers sometimes call for "blowoffs" at the end of long trends, but the stock market has no history of reaching maximum acceleration at a peak. Even if a fifth wave extends, the fifth of the fifth will lack the dynamism that preceded it. During advancing fifth waves, optimism runs extremely high despite a

narrowing of breadth. Nevertheless, market action does improve relative to prior corrective wave rallies. For example, the year-end rally in 1976 was unexciting in the Dow, but it was neverthe-less a motive wave as opposed to the preceding corrective wave advances in April, July and September, which, by contrast, had even less influence on the secondary indexes and the cumulative advance-decline line. As a monument to the optimism that fifth waves can produce, the advisory services polled two weeks after the conclusion of that rally turned in the lowest percentage of "bears," 4.5%, in the history of the recorded figures *despite* that fifth wave's failure to make a new high!

6) **A** waves — During the A wave of a bear market, the in-vestment world is generally convinced that this reaction is just a pullback pursuant to the next leg of advance. The public surges to the buy side despite the first really technically damaging cracks in individual stock patterns. The A wave sets the tone for the B wave to follow. A five-wave A indicates a zigzag for wave B, while a three-wave A indicates a flat or triangle.

7) **B** waves — B waves are phonies. They are sucker plays, bull traps, speculators' paradise, orgies of odd-lotter mental-ity or expressions of dumb institutional complacency (or both). They often involve a focus on a narrow list of stocks, are often "unconfirmed" (see Dow Theory discussion in Chapter 7) by other averages, are rarely technically strong, and are virtually always doomed to complete retracement by wave C. If the analyst can easily say to himself, "There is something wrong with this mar-ket," chances are it's a B wave. X waves and D waves in expanding triangles, both of which are corrective wave advances, have the same characteristics. Several examples will suffice to illustrate the point.

— The upward correction of 1930 was wave B within the 1929-1932 A-B-C zigzag decline. Robert Rhea describes the emotional climate well in his opus, *The Story of the Averages* (1934):

> ...many observers took it to be a bull market signal. I can remember having shorted stocks early in December, 1929, af-ter having completed a satisfactory short position in October. When the slow but steady advance of January and February carried above [the previous high], I became panicky and covered at considerable loss. ...I forgot that the rally might normally be expected to retrace possibly 66 percent or more of the 1929

Idealized Corrective Wave

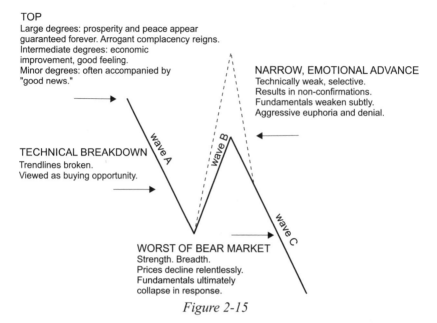

TOP
Large degrees: prosperity and peace appear
guaranteed forever. Arrogant complacency reigns.
Intermediate degrees: economic
improvement, good feeling.
Minor degrees: often accompanied by
"good news."

NARROW, EMOTIONAL ADVANCE
Technically weak, selective.
Results in non-confirmations.
Fundamentals weaken subtly.
Aggressive euphoria and denial.

TECHNICAL BREAKDOWN
Trendlines broken.
Viewed as buying opportunity.

wave A

wave B

wave C

WORST OF BEAR MARKET
Strength. Breadth.
Prices decline relentlessly.
Fundamentals ultimately
collapse in response.

Figure 2-15

downswing. Nearly everyone was proclaiming a new bull market. Services were extremely bullish, and the upside volume was running higher than at the peak in 1929.

— The 1961-1962 rise was wave (b) in an (a)-(b)-(c) expanded flat correction. At the top in early 1962, stocks were selling at unheard of price/earnings multiples that had not been seen up to that time and have not been seen since. Cumulative breadth had already peaked along with the top of the third wave in 1959.

— The rise from 1966 to 1968 was wave Ⓑ in a corrective pattern of Cycle degree. Emotionalism had gripped the public and "cheapies" were skyrocketing in the speculative fever, unlike the orderly and usually fundamentally justifiable participation of the secondaries within first and third waves. The Dow Industrials struggled unconvincingly upward throughout the advance and finally refused to confirm the phenomenal new highs in the secondary indexes.

— In 1977, the Dow Jones Transportation Average climbed to new highs in a B wave, miserably unconfirmed by the Industrials. Airlines and truckers were sluggish. Only the coal-carrying rails were participating as part of the energy play. Thus, breadth within the index was conspicuously lacking, confirming again that good breadth is generally a property of impulse waves, not corrections.

— For a discussion of the B wave in the gold market, see Chapter 6, page 180.

As a general observation, B waves of Intermediate degree and lower usually show a diminution of volume, while B waves of Primary degree and greater can display volume heavier than that which accompanied the preceding bull market, usually indicating wide public participation.

8) **C** waves — Declining C waves are usually devastating in their destruction. They are third waves and have most of the properties of third waves. It is during these declines that there is virtually no place to hide except cash. The illusions held throughout waves A and B tend to evaporate and fear takes over. C waves are persistent and broad. 1930-1932 was a C wave. 1962 was a C wave. 1969-1970 and 1973-1974 can be classified as C waves. Advancing C waves within upward corrections in larger bear markets are just as dynamic and can be mistaken for the start of a new upswing, especially since they unfold in five waves. The October 1973 rally (see Figure 1-37), for instance, was a C wave in an inverted expanded flat correction.

9) **D** waves — D waves in all but expanding triangles are often accompanied by increased volume. This is true probably because D waves in non-expanding triangles are hybrids, part corrective, yet having some characteristics of first waves since they follow C waves and are not fully retraced. D waves, being advances within corrective waves, are as phony as B waves. The rise from 1970 to 1973 was wave Ⓓ within the large wave IV of Cycle degree. The "one-decision" complacency that characterized the attitude of the average institutional fund manager at the time is well documented. The area of participation again was narrow, this time the "nifty fifty" growth and glamour issues. Breadth, as well as the Transportation Average, topped early, in 1972, and refused to confirm the extremely high multiples bestowed upon the favorite fifty. Washington was inflating at full steam to sustain the illusory prosperity during the entire advance in preparation for the presidential election. As with the preceding wave Ⓑ, "phony" was an apt description.

10) **E** waves — E waves in triangles appear to most market observers to be the dramatic kickoff of a new downtrend after a top has been built. They almost always are accompanied by

strongly supportive news. That, in conjunction with the tendency of E waves to stage a false breakdown through the triangle boundary line, intensifies the bearish conviction of market participants at precisely the time that they should be preparing for a substantial move in the opposite direction. Thus, E waves, being ending waves, are attended by a psychology as emotional as that of fifth waves.

****

Because the tendencies discussed here are not inevitable, they are stated not as rules, but as guidelines. Their lack of inevitability nevertheless detracts little from their utility. For example, take a look at Figure 2-16, an hourly chart of the most recent market action, the first four Minor waves in the DJIA rally off the March 1, 1978 low. The waves are textbook Elliott from beginning to end, from the length of waves to the volume pattern (not shown) to the trend channels to the guideline of equality to the retracement by the "a" wave following the extension to the expected low for the fourth wave to the perfect internal counts to alternation to the Fibonacci time sequences to the Fibonacci ratio relationships embodied within. Its only atypical aspect is the large size of wave 4. It might be worth noting that 914 would be a reasonable target in that it would mark a .618 retracement of the 1976-1978 decline.

There are exceptions to guidelines, but without those, market analysis would be a science of exactitude, not one of probability. Nevertheless, with a thorough knowledge of the guidelines of wave structure, you can be quite confident of your wave count. In effect, you can use the market action to confirm the wave count as well as use the wave count to predict market action.

Notice also that Elliott wave guidelines cover most aspects of traditional technical analysis, such as market momentum and investor sentiment. The result is that traditional technical analysis now has a greatly increased value in that it serves to aid the identification of the market's position in the Elliott wave structure. To that end, using such tools is by all means encouraged.

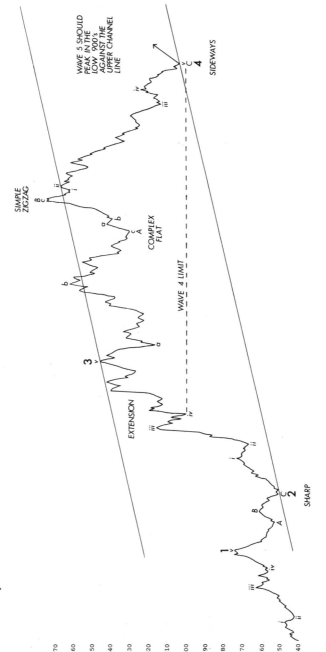

DJIA Hourly - 1978

WAVE 5 SHOULD
PEAK IN THE
LOW 900's
AGAINST THE
UPPER CHANNEL
LINE

SIMPLE
ZIGZAG

COMPLEX
FLAT

WAVE 4 LIMIT

EXTENSION

SHARP

SIDEWAYS

870 860 850 840 830 820 810 800 790 780 770 760 750 740

3/7   3/14   3/21   3/29   4/5   4/12   4/19   4/26   5/3   5/10   5/17   5/24   6/1   6/8   6/15   6/22   6/29

Figure 2-16

A Summary of Rules and Guidelines for Waves

From a theoretical standpoint, we must be careful not to confuse Elliott waves with their measures, which are as a thermometer is to heat. A thermometer is not designed to gauge rapid short-term fluctuations in air temperature and neither is an index of 30 stocks constructed so as to be able to record every short-term fluctuation in social mood. While we fully believe that the listed rules govern Elliott waves as a collective mental phenomenon, recordings of actions that Elliott waves induce — such as buying and selling certain lists of stocks — may not perfectly reflect those waves. Therefore recordings of such actions could deviate from a perfect expression of the rules simply because of the imperfection of the chosen gauge. That being said, we have found that the Dow Jones Industrial Average has followed Elliott's rules impeccably at Minor degree and above and almost always at lesser degrees as well. Below is a summary of the rules and known guidelines (excepting Fibonacci relationships) for the five main wave patterns, variations and combinations.

MOTIVE WAVES

Impulse
Rules
• An impulse always subdivides into five waves.
• Wave 1 always subdivides into an impulse or (rarely) a diagonal.
• Wave 3 always subdivides into an impulse.
• Wave 5 always subdivides into an impulse or a diagonal.
• Wave 2 always subdivides into a zigzag, flat or combination.
• Wave 4 always subdivides into a zigzag, flat, triangle or combination.
• Wave 2 never moves beyond the start of wave 1.
• Wave 3 always moves beyond the end of wave 1.
• Wave 3 is never the shortest wave.
• Wave 4 never moves beyond the end of wave 1.
• Never are waves 1, 3 and 5 all extended.

Guidelines
• Wave 4 will almost always be a different corrective pattern than wave 2.
• Wave 2 is usually a zigzag or zigzag combination.
• Wave 4 is usually a flat, triangle or flat combination.

• Sometimes wave 5 does not move beyond the end of wave 3 (in which case it is called a truncation).

• Wave 5 often ends when meeting or slightly exceeding a line drawn from the end of wave 3 that is parallel to the line connecting the ends of waves 2 and 4, on either arithmetic or semilog scale.

• The center of wave 3 almost always has the steepest slope of any equal period within the parent impulse except that sometimes an early portion of wave 1 (the "kickoff") will be steeper.

• Wave 1, 3 or 5 is usually extended. (An extension appears "stretched" because its corrective waves are small compared to its impulse waves. It is substantially longer, and contains larger subdivisions, than the non-extended waves).

• Often, the extended subwave is the same number (1, 3 or 5) as the parent wave.

• Rarely do two subwaves extend, although it is typical for waves 3 and 5 both to extend when they are of Cycle or Supercycle degree and within a fifth wave of one degree higher.

• Wave 1 is the least commonly extended wave.

• When wave 3 is extended, waves 1 and 5 tend to have gains related by equality or the Fibonacci ratio.

• When wave 5 is extended, it is often in Fibonacci proportion to the net travel of waves 1 through 3.

• When wave 1 is extended, it is often in Fibonacci proportion to the net travel of waves 3 thorough 5.

• Wave 4 typically ends when it is within the price range of subwave four of 3.

• Wave 4 often subdivides the entire impulse into Fibonacci proportion in time and/or price.

Diagonal
Rules

• A diagonal always subdivides into five waves.

• An ending diagonal always appears as wave 5 of an impulse or wave C of a zigzag or flat.

• A leading diagonal always appears as wave 1 of an impulse or wave A of a zigzag.

• Waves 1, 2, 3, 4 and 5 of an ending diagonal, and waves 2 and 4 of a leading diagonal, always subdivide into zigzags.

• Wave 2 never goes beyond the start of wave 1.

• Wave 3 always goes beyond the end of wave 1.

• Wave 4 never moves beyond the end of wave 2.

• Wave 4 always ends within the price territory of wave 1.*

• Going forward in time, a line connecting the ends of waves 2 and 4 converges towards (in the contracting variety) or diverges from (in the expanding variety) a line connecting the ends of waves 1 and 3.

• In a leading diagonal, wave 5 always ends beyond the end of wave 3.

• In the contracting variety, wave 3 is always shorter than wave 1, wave 4 is always shorter than wave 2, and wave 5 is always shorter than wave 3.

• In the expanding variety, wave 3 is always longer than wave 1, wave 4 is always longer than wave 2, and wave 5 is always longer than wave 3.

• In the expanding variety, wave 5 always ends beyond the end of wave 3.

Guidelines

• Waves 2 and 4 each usually retrace .66 to .81 of the preceding wave.

• Waves 1, 3 and 5 of a leading diagonal usually subdivide into zig-zags but sometimes appear to be impulses.

• Within an impulse, if wave 1 is a diagonal, wave 3 is likely to be extended.

• Within an impulse, wave 5 is unlikely to be a diagonal if wave 3 is not extended.

• In the contracting variety, wave 5 usually ends beyond the end of wave 3. (Failure to do so is called a truncation.)

• In the contracting variety, wave 5 usually ends at or slightly beyond a line that connects the ends of waves 1 and 3. (Ending beyond that line is called a throw-over.)

• In the expanding variety, wave 5 usually ends slightly before reaching a line that connects the ends of waves 1 and 3.

---

* We have found one diagonal in the Dow in which wave four did not reach the price territory of wave one. See Figure 1-18.

CORRECTIVE WAVES

Zigzag

Rules
• A zigzag always subdivides into three waves.
• Wave A always subdivides into an impulse or leading diagonal.
• Wave C always subdivides into an impulse or diagonal.
• Wave B always subdivides into a zigzag, flat, triangle or combination thereof.
• Wave B never moves beyond the start of wave A.

Guidelines
• Wave A almost always subdivides into an impulse.
• Wave C almost always subdivides into an impulse.
• Wave C is often about the same length as wave A.
• Wave C almost always ends beyond the end of wave A.
• Wave B typically retraces 38 to 79 percent of wave A.
• If wave B is a running triangle, it will typically retrace between 10 and 40 percent of wave A.
• If wave B is a zigzag, it will typically retrace 50 to 79 percent of wave A.
• If wave B is a triangle, it will typically retrace 38 to 50 percent of wave A.
• A line connecting the ends of waves A and C is often parallel to a line connecting the end of wave B and the start of wave A. (Forecasting guideline: Wave C often ends upon reaching a line drawn from the end of wave A that is parallel to a line connecting the start of wave A and the end of wave B.)

Flat

Rules
• A flat always subdivides into three waves.
• Wave A is never a triangle.
• Wave C is always an impulse or a diagonal.
• Wave B always retraces at least 90 percent of wave A.

Guidelines
• Wave B usually retraces between 100 and 138 percent of wave A.
• Wave C is usually between 100 and 165 percent as long as wave A.
• Wave C usually ends beyond the end of wave A.

Notes

• When wave B is more than 105 percent as long as wave A and wave C ends beyond the end of wave A, the entire formation is called an expanded flat.

• When wave B is more than 100 percent as long as wave A and wave C does not end beyond the end of wave A, the entire formation is called a running flat.

Contracting Triangle

Rules

• A triangle always subdivides into five waves.

• At least four waves among waves A, B, C, D and E each subdivide into a zigzag or zigzag combination.

• Wave C never moves beyond the end of wave A, wave D never moves beyond the end of wave B, and wave E never moves beyond the end of wave C. The result is that going forward in time, a line connecting the ends of waves B and D converges with a line connecting the ends of waves A and C.

• A triangle never has more than one complex subwave, in which case it is always a zigzag combination or a triangle.

Guidelines

• Usually, wave C subdivides into a zigzag combination that is longer lasting and contains deeper percentage retracements than each of the other subwaves.

• Sometimes, wave D subdivides into a zigzag combination that is longer lasting and contains deeper percentage retracements than each of the other subwaves.

• Sometimes one of the waves, usually wave C, D or E, subdivides into a contracting or barrier triangle. Often the effect is as if the entire triangle consisted of nine zigzags.

• About 60 percent of the time, wave B does not end beyond the start of wave A. When it does, the triangle is called a running triangle.

Barrier Triangle

• A barrier triangle has the same characteristics as a contracting triangle except that waves B and D end at essentially the same level. We have yet to observe a 9-wave barrier triangle, implying that this form may not extend.

• When wave 5 follows a triangle, it is typically either a brief, rapid movement or an exceptionally long extension.

Expanding Triangle

Rules

Most rules are the same as for contracting triangles, with these differences:

• Wave C, D and E each moves beyond the end of the preceding same-directional subwave. (The result is that going forward in time, a line connecting the ends of waves B and D diverges from a line connecting the ends of waves A and C.)

• Subwaves B, C and D each retrace at least 100 percent but no more than 150 percent of the preceding subwave.

Guidelines

• Most guidelines are the same, with these differences:

• Subwaves B, C and D usually retrace 105 to 125 percent of the preceding subwave.

• No subwave has yet been observed to subdivide into a triangle.

Combinations

Rules

• Combinations comprise two (or three) corrective patterns separated by one (or two) corrective pattern(s) in the opposite direction, labeled X. (The first corrective pattern is labeled W, the second Y, and the third, if there is one, Z.)

• A zigzag combination comprises two or three zigzags (in which case it is called a double or triple zigzag).

• A "double three" flat combination comprises (in order) a zigzag and a flat, a flat and a zigzag, a flat and a flat, a zigzag and a triangle or a flat and a triangle.

• A rare "triple three" flat combination comprises three flats.

• Double and triple zigzags take the place of zigzags, and double and triple threes take the place of flats and triangles.

• An expanding triangle has yet to be observed as a component of a combination.

Guidelines

• When a zigzag or flat appears too small to be the entire wave with respect to the preceding wave (or, if it is to be wave 4, the preceding wave 2), a combination is likely.

Learning the Basics

With a knowledge of the tools in Chapters 1 and 2, any dedicated student can perform expert Elliott wave analysis. Those who neglect to study the subject thoroughly or apply the tools rigorously give up before really trying. The best learning procedure is to keep an hourly chart and try to fit all the wiggles into Elliott wave patterns while keeping an open mind for all the possibilities. Slowly the scales should drop from your eyes, and you will be continually amazed at what you see.

It is important to remember that while investment tactics always must go with the most valid wave count, knowledge of alternative interpretations can be extremely helpful in adjusting to unexpected events, putting them immediately into perspective, and adapting to the changing market framework. The rigid rules of wave formation are of great value in narrowing the infinite possibilities to a relatively small list, while flexibility within the patterns eliminates cries that whatever the market is doing now is "impossible."

"When you have eliminated the impossible, whatever remains, *however improbable*, must be the truth." Thus eloquently spoke Sherlock Holmes to his constant companion, Dr. Watson, in Arthur Conan Doyle's *The Sign of Four*. This advice is a capsule summary of what you need to know to be successful with Elliott. The best approach is deductive reasoning. By knowing what Elliott rules will not allow, you can deduce that whatever remains is the proper perspective, no matter how improbable it may seem otherwise. By applying all the rules of extensions, alternation, overlapping, channeling, volume and the rest, you have a much more formidable arsenal than you might imagine at first glance. Unfortunately for many, the approach requires thought and work and rarely provides a mechanical signal. However, this kind of thinking, basically an elimination process, squeezes the best out of what Elliott has to offer and besides, it's fun! We sincerely urge you to give it a try.

As an example of such deductive reasoning, turn back to Figure 1-14 and cover up the price action from November 17, 1976 forward. Without the wave labels and boundary lines, the market would appear as formless. But with the Wave Principle as a guide, the meaning of the structures becomes clear. Now ask yourself, how would you go about predicting the next movement? Here is Robert Prechter's analysis from that date, from a letter to A.J. Frost summarizing a report he had issued for Merrill Lynch the previous day:

> Enclosed you will find my current opinion outlined on a recent Trendline chart, although I use only hourly point charts to arrive at these conclusions. My argument is that the third Primary wave, begun in October of 1975, *has not completed* its course as yet, and that the fifth Intermediate wave of that Primary is now underway. First and most important, I am convinced that October 1975 to March 1976 was so far a three-wave affair, not a five, and that only the possibility of a failure on May 11th could complete that wave as a five. However, the construction *following* that possible "failure" does not satisfy me as correct, since the first downleg to 956.45 would be of five waves, and the entire ensuing construction is obviously a flat. Therefore, I think that we have been in a fourth corrective wave since March 24th. This corrective wave satisfies *completely* the requirements for an expanding triangle formation, which of course can only be a fourth wave. The trendlines concerned are uncannily accurate, as is the downside objective, obtained by multiplying the first important length of decline (March 24th to June 7th, 55.51 points) by 1.618 to obtain 89.82 points. 89.82 points from the orthodox high of the third Intermediate wave at 1011.96 gives a downside target of 922, which was hit last week (actual hourly low 920.62) on November 11th. This would suggest now a fifth Intermediate back to new highs, completing the third Primary wave. The only problem I can see with this interpretation is that Elliott suggests that fourth wave declines usually hold above the previous fourth wave decline of lesser degree, in this case 950.57 on February 17th, which of course has been broken on the downside. I have found, however, that this rule is not steadfast. The reverse symmetrical triangle formation should be followed by a rally only approximating the width of the widest part of the triangle. Such a rally would suggest 1020-1030 and fall far short of the trendline target of 1090-1100. Also, *within* third waves, the first and fifth subwaves tend toward equality in time and magnitude. Since the first wave (Oct. 75-Dec.75) was a 10% move in two months, this fifth should cover about 100 points (1020-1030) and peak in January 1977, again short of the trendline mark.

Now uncover the rest of the chart to see how all these guidelines helped in assessing the market's likely path.

Christopher Morley once said, "Dancing is a wonderful training for girls. It is the first way they learn to guess what a man is going to do before he does it." In the same way, the Wave Principle trains the analyst to discern what the market is likely to do before it does it.

After you have acquired an Elliott "touch," it will be forever with you, just as a child who learns to ride a bicycle never forgets. Thereafter, catching a turn becomes a fairly common experience and not really too difficult. Furthermore, by giving you a feeling of confidence as to where you are in the progress of the market, a knowledge of Elliott can prepare you psychologically for the fluctuating nature of price movement and free you from sharing the widely practiced analytical error of forever projecting today's trends linearly into the future. Most important, the Wave Principle often indicates in advance the relative *magnitude* of the next period of market progress or regress. Living in harmony with those trends can make the difference between success and failure in financial affairs.

Practical Application

The practical goal of any analytical method is to identify market lows suitable for buying (or covering shorts) and market highs suitable for selling (or selling short). When developing a system of trading or investing, you should adopt certain patterns of thought that will help you remain both flexible and decisive, both defensive and aggressive, depending upon the demands of the situation. The Elliott Wave Principle is not such a system, but is unparalleled as a basis for creating one.

Despite the fact that many analysts do not treat it as such, the Wave Principle is by all means an objective study, or as Collins put it, "a disciplined form of technical analysis." Bolton used to say that one of the hardest things he had to learn was to believe what he saw. If you do not believe what you see, you are likely to read into your analysis what you think should be there for some other reason. At this point, your count becomes subjective and worthless.

How can you remain objective in a world of uncertainty? It is not difficult once you understand the proper goal of your analysis.

Without Elliott, there appear to be an infinite number of possibilities for market action. What the Wave Principle provides is a means of first *limiting the possibilities* and then *ordering the relative probabilities* of possible future market paths. Elliott's highly specific rules reduce the number of valid alternatives to a minimum. Among those, the best interpretation, sometimes called the "preferred count," is the one that satisfies the largest number of guidelines. Other interpretations are ordered accordingly. As a result, competent analysts applying the rules and guidelines of the Wave Principle objectively should usually agree on both the list of possibilities and the order of probabilities for various possible outcomes at any particular time. That order can usually be stated with certainty. Do not assume, however, that certainty about the order of probabilities is the same as certainty about one specific outcome. Under only the rarest of circumstances do you ever *know exactly* what the market is going to do. You must understand and accept that even an approach that can identify high odds for a fairly specific event must be wrong some of the time.

You can prepare yourself psychologically for such outcomes through the continual updating of the *second best interpretation*, sometimes called the "alternate count." Because applying the Wave Principle is an exercise in probability, the ongoing maintenance of alternative wave counts is an essential part of using it correctly. In the event that the market violates the expected scenario, the alternate count puts the unexpected market action into perspective and immediately becomes your new preferred count. If you're thrown by your horse, it's useful to land right atop another.

Always invest with the preferred wave count. Not infrequently, the two or even three best counts comfortably dictate the same investment stance. Sometimes being continuously sensitive to alternatives can allow you to make money even when your preferred count is in error. For instance, after a minor low that you erroneously consider of major importance, you may recognize *at a higher level* that the market is vulnerable again to new lows. This recognition occurs after a clear-cut *three*-wave rally follows the minor low rather than the necessary five, since a three-wave rally is the sign of an upward correction. Thus, what happens *after* the turning point often helps confirm or refute the assumed status of the low or high, well in advance of danger.

Even if the market allows no such graceful change of opinion, the Wave Principle still offers exceptional value. Most other approaches to market analysis, whether fundamental, technical or cyclical, have no good way of forcing a reversal of opinion or position if you are wrong. The Wave Principle, in contrast, provides a built-in objective method for placing a stop. Since wave analysis is based upon price patterns, a pattern identified as having been completed *is either over or it isn't*. If the market changes direction, the analyst has caught the turn. If the market moves beyond what the apparently completed pattern allows, the conclusion is wrong, and any funds at risk can be reclaimed immediately.

Of course, there are often times when, despite a rigorous analysis, there is no clearly preferred interpretation. At such times, you must wait until the count resolves itself. When after a while the apparent jumble gels into a clear picture, the probability that a turning point is at hand can suddenly and excitingly rise to nearly 100%. It is a thrilling experience to pinpoint a turn, and the Wave Principle is the only approach that can occasionally provide the opportunity to do so.

The ability to *identify* such junctures is remarkable enough, but the Wave Principle is the only method of analysis that also provides guidelines for *forecasting*. Many of these guidelines are specific and can occasionally yield stunningly precise results. If indeed markets are patterned, and if those patterns have a recognizable geometry, then regardless of the variations allowed, certain price and time relationships are likely to recur. In fact, experience shows that they do.

It is our practice to try to determine in advance where the next move will likely take the market. One advantage of setting a target is that it gives a sort of backdrop against which to monitor the market's actual path. This way, you are alerted quickly when something is wrong and can shift your inter-pretation to a more appropriate one if the market does not do what you expect. The second advantage of choosing a target well in advance is that it prepares you psychologically for buying when others are selling out in despair, and selling when others are buying confidently in a euphoric environment.

No matter what your convictions, it pays never to take your eyes off what is happening in the wave structure in real time. Ultimately, the market is the message, and a change in behavior can dictate a change in outlook. All one really needs to know *at the time* is whether to be long, short or out, a decision that can sometimes be made with a swift glance at a chart and other times only after painstaking work.

Despite all your knowledge and skill, however, absolutely nothing can prepare you fully for the ordeal of risking your own money in the market. Paper trading won't do it. Watching others won't do it. Simulation games won't do it. Once you have con-quered the essential task of applying a method expertly, you have done little more than gather the tools for the job. When you *act* on that method, you encounter the real work: battling your own emotions. This is why anaylsis and making money are two different skills. There is no way to understand that battle off the field. Only financial speculation prepares you for financial speculation.

If you decide to attempt to do what only one person in a thousand can do — trade or invest in markets successfully — set aside a specific amount of money that is significantly less than your total net worth. That way, when you inevitably lose it all at the end of stage one, you will have funds to live on while you investigate the reasons for your losses. When those reasons begin to sink in, you will finally be on your way to stage two: the long process of conquering your emotions so that your reason will prevail. This is a task for which *no one* can prepare you; you must do it yourself. However, what we *can* provide is a good basis for your analysis. Countless potential trading and investment careers have been doomed from the start from choosing a worthless analytical approach. We say: choose the Wave Principle. It will start you *thinking properly*, and that is the first step on the path to investment success.

No approach guarantees market omniscience, and that includes the Wave Principle. However, viewed in the proper light, it delivers everything it promises.

Statue of Leonardo Fibonacci, Pisa, Italy.
The inscription reads, "A. Leonardo Fibonacci, Insigne
Matematico Piisano del Secolo XII."

Photo by Robert R. Prechter, Sr.

CHAPTER 3

HISTORICAL AND MATHEMATICAL BACKGROUND OF THE WAVE PRINCIPLE

The Fibonacci (pronounced fib-eh-nah´-chee) sequence of numbers was discovered (actually rediscovered) by Leonardo Fibonacci da Pisa, a thirteenth century mathematician. We will outline the historical background of this amazing man and then discuss more fully the sequence (technically it is a sequence and not a series) of numbers that bears his name. When Elliott wrote *Nature's Law*, he explained that the Fibonacci sequence provides the mathematical basis of the Wave Principle. (For a further discussion of the mathematics behind the Wave Principle, see "Mathematical Basis of Wave Theory," by Walter E. White, in a forthcoming book from New Classics Library.)

Leonardo Fibonacci da Pisa

The Dark Ages were a period of almost total cultural eclipse in Europe. They lasted from the fall of Rome in 476 A.D. until around 1000 A.D. During this period, mathematics and philosophy waned in Europe but flowered in India and Arabia since the Dark Ages did not extend to the East. As Europe gradually began to emerge from its stagnant state, the Mediterranean Sea developed into a river of culture that directed the flow of commerce, mathematics and new ideas from India and Arabia.

During the Middle Ages, Pisa became a strongly walled city-state and a flourishing commercial center whose waterfront reflected the Commercial Revolution of that day. Leather, furs, cotton, wool, iron, copper, tin and spices were traded within the walls of Pisa, with gold serving as an important currency. The port was filled with ships ranging up to four hundred tons and eighty feet in length. The Pisan economy supported leather and shipbuilding industries and an iron works. Pisan politics were well constructed even according to today's standards. The

Chief Magistrate of the Republic, for instance, was not paid for his services until after his term of office had expired, at which time his administration could be investigated to determine if he had earned his salary. In fact, our man Fibonacci was one of the examiners.

Born between 1170 and 1180, Leonardo Fibonacci, the son of a prominent merchant and city official, probably lived in one of Pisa's many towers. A tower served as a workshop, fortress and family residence and was constructed so that arrows could be shot from the narrow windows and boiling tar poured on strangers who approached with aggressive intent. During Fibonacci's lifetime, the bell tower known as the Leaning Tower of Pisa was under construction. It was the last of the three great edifices to be built in Pisa, as the cathedral and the baptistery had been completed some years earlier.

As a schoolboy, Leonardo became familiar with customs houses and commercial practices of the day, including the operation of the abacus, which was widely used in Europe as a calculator for business purposes. Although his native tongue was Italian, he learned several other languages, including French, Greek and even Latin, in which he was fluent.

Soon after Leonardo's father was appointed a customs official at Bogia in North Africa, he instructed Leonardo to join him in order to complete his education. Leonardo began making many business trips around the Mediterranean. After one of his trips to Egypt, he published his famous *Liber Abacci* (Book of Calculation) which introduced to Europe one of the greatest mathematical discoveries of all time, namely the decimal system, including the positioning of zero as the first digit in the notation of the number scale. This system, which included the familiar symbols 0, 1, 2, 3, 4, 5, 6, 7, 8 and 9, became known as the Hindu-Arabic system, which is now universally used.

Under a true digital or place-value system, the actual value represented by any symbol placed in a row along with other symbols depends not only on its basic numerical value but also on its position in the row, i.e., 58 has a different value from 85. Though thousands of years earlier the Babylonians and Mayas of Central America separately had developed digital or place-value systems of numeration, their methods were awkward in other respects. For this reason, the Babylonian system, which was the first to use zero and place values, was never carried forward into the mathematical systems of Greece, or even Rome, whose numeration comprised the seven symbols I, V, X, L, C, D, and M, with non-digital values assigned to those symbols. Addition, subtraction, multiplication and division in a system using these non-digital symbols is not an easy task, especially when large numbers are involved. Paradoxically, to overcome this problem, the Romans used the very ancient digital device known as the abacus. Because this instrument is digitally based and contains the zero principle, it functioned as a necessary supplement to the Roman computational system. Throughout the ages, bookkeepers and merchants depended on it to assist them in the mechanics of their tasks. Fibonacci, after expressing the basic principle of the abacus in *Liber Abacci*, started to use his new system during his travels. Through his efforts, the new system, with its easy method of calculation, was eventually transmitted to Europe. Gradually Roman numerals were replaced by the Arabic numeral system. The introduction of the new system to Europe was the first important achievement in the field of mathematics since the fall of Rome over seven hundred years before. Fibonacci not only kept mathematics alive during the Middle Ages, but laid the foundation for great developments in the field of higher mathematics and the related fields of physics, astronomy and engineering.

Although the world later almost lost sight of Fibonacci, he was unquestionably a man of his time. His fame was such that Frederick II, a scientist and scholar in his own right, sought him out by arranging a visit to Pisa. Frederick II was Emperor of the Holy Roman Empire, the King of Sicily and Jerusalem, scion of two of the noblest families in Europe and Sicily, and the most powerful prince of his day. His ideas were those of an absolute monarch, and he surrounded himself with all the pomp of a Roman emperor.

The meeting between Fibonacci and Frederick II took place in 1225 A.D. and was an event of great importance to the town of Pisa. The Emperor rode at the head of a long procession of trumpeters, courtiers, knights, officials and a menagerie of animals. Some of the problems the Emperor placed before the famous mathematician are detailed in *Liber Abacci*. Fibonacci apparently solved the problems posed by the Emperor and forever more was welcome at the king's court. When Fibonacci revised

Liber Abacci in 1228 A.D., he dedicated the revised edition to Frederick II.

It is almost an understatement to say that Leonardo Fibonacci was the greatest mathematician of the Middle Ages. In all, he wrote three major mathematical works: the *Liber Abacci,* published in 1202 and revised in 1228, *Practica Geometriae*, published in 1220, and *Liber Quadratorum.* The admiring citizens of Pisa documented in 1240 A.D. that he was "a discreet and learned man," and very recently Joseph Gies, a senior editor of the Encyclopedia Britannica, stated that future scholars will in time "give Leonard of Pisa his due as one of the world's great intellectual pioneers." His works, after all these years, are only now being translated from Latin into English. For those interested, the book entitled *Leonard of Pisa and the New Mathematics of the Middle Ages*, by Joseph and Frances Gies, is an excellent treatise on the age of Fibonacci and his works.

Although he was the greatest mathematician of medieval times, Fibonacci's only monuments are a statue across the Arno River from the Leaning Tower and two streets that bear his name, one in Pisa and the other in Florence. It seems strange that so few visitors to the 179-foot marble Tower of Pisa have ever heard of Fibonacci or seen his statue. Fibonacci was a contemporary of Bonanna, the architect of the Tower, who started building in 1174 A.D. Both men made contributions to the world, but the one whose influence far exceeds the other's is almost unknown.

The Fibonacci Sequence

In *Liber Abacci*, a problem is posed that gives rise to the sequence of numbers 1, 1, 2, 3, 5, 8, 13, 21, 34, 55, 89, 144, and so on to infinity, known today as the Fibonacci sequence. The problem is this:

> How many pairs of rabbits placed in an enclosed area can be produced in a single year from one pair of rabbits if each pair gives birth to a new pair each month starting with the second month?

In arriving at the solution, we find that each pair, including the first pair, needs a month's time to mature, but once in production, begets a new pair each month. The number of pairs is

The Rabbit Family Tree

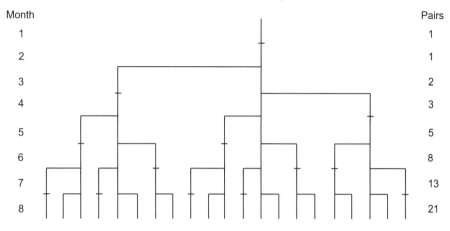

In twelve months, Mr. and Mrs. Rabbit would have a family of 144 pairs.

12   144

Figure 3-1

the same at the beginning of each of the first two months, so the sequence is 1, 1. This first pair finally doubles its number during the second month, so that there are two pairs at the beginning of the third month. Of these, the older pair begets a third pair the following month so that at the beginning of the fourth month, the sequence expands 1, 1, 2, 3. Of these three, the two older pairs reproduce, but not the youngest pair, so the number of rabbit pairs expands to five. The next month, three pairs reproduce so the sequence expands to 1, 1, 2, 3, 5, 8 and so forth. Figure 3-1 shows the Rabbit Family Tree with the family growing with exponential acceleration. Continue the sequence for a few years and the numbers become astronomical. In 100 months, for instance, we would have to contend with 354,224,848,179,261,915,075 pairs of rabbits. The Fibonacci sequence resulting from the rabbit problem has many interesting properties and reflects an almost constant relationship among its components.

The sum of any two adjacent numbers in the sequence forms the next higher number in the sequence, viz., 1 plus 1 equals 2, 1 plus 2 equals 3, 2 plus 3 equals 5, 3 plus 5 equals 8, and so on to infinity.

The Golden Ratio

After the first several numbers in the sequence, the ratio of any number to the next higher is approximately .618 to 1 and to the next lower number approximately 1.618 to 1. The further along the sequence, the closer the ratio approaches *phi* (denoted ϕ) which is an irrational number, .618034.... Between alternate numbers in the sequence, the ratio is approximately .382, whose inverse is 2.618. Refer to Figure 3-2 for a ratio table interlocking all Fibonacci numbers from 1 to 144.

Phi is the only number that when added to 1 yields its inverse: $1 + .618 = 1 \div .618$. This alliance of the additive and the multiplicative produces the following sequence of equations:

$$.618^2 = 1 - .618,$$
$$.618^3 = .618 - .618^2,$$
$$.618^4 = .618^2 - .618^3,$$
$$.618^5 = .618^3 - .618^4, \text{ etc.}$$

or alternatively,

$$1.618^2 = 1 + 1.618,$$
$$1.618^3 = 1.618 + 1.618^2,$$
$$1.618^4 = 1.618^2 + 1.618^3,$$
$$1.618^5 = 1.618^3 + 1.618^4, \text{ etc.}$$

Some statements of the interrelated properties of these four main ratios can be listed as follows:

$$1.618 - .618 = 1,$$
$$1.618 \times .618 = 1,$$
$$1 - .618 = .382,$$
$$.618 \times .618 = .382,$$
$$2.618 - 1.618 = 1,$$
$$2.618 \times .382 = 1,$$
$$2.618 \times .618 = 1.618,$$
$$1.618 \times 1.618 = 2.618.$$

Besides 1 and 2, any Fibonacci number multiplied by four, when added to a selected Fibonacci number, gives another Fibonacci number, so that:

Fibonacci Ratio Table

NUMERATOR → DENOMINATOR ↓	1	2	3	5	8	13	21	34	55	89	144
1	1.00	2.00	3.00	5.00	8.00	13.00	21.00	34.00	55.00	89.00	144.00
2	.50	1.00	1.50	2.50	4.00	6.50	10.50	17.00	27.50	44.50	72.00
3	.333	.667	1.00	1.667	2.667	4.33	7.00	11.33	18.33	29.67	48.00
5	.20	.40	.60	1.00	1.60	2.60	4.20	6.80	11.00	17.80	28.80
8	.125	.25	.375	.625	1.00	1.625	2.625	4.25	6.875	11.125	18.00
13	.077	.154	.231	.385	.615	1.00	1.615	2.615	4.23	6.846	11.077
21	.0476	.0952	.1429	.238	.381	.619	1.00	1.619	2.619	4.238	6.857
34	.0294	.0588	.0882	.147	.235	.3824	.6176	1.00	1.618	2.618	4.235
55	.01818	.03636	.0545	.0909	.1455	.236	.3818	.618	1.00	1.618	2.618
89	.011236	.02247	.0337	.05618	.08989	.146	.236	.382	.618	1.00	1.618
144	.006944	.013889	.0208	.0347	.05556	.0903	.1458	.236	.382	.618	1.00

Toward perfect ratios

Figure 3-2

$$3 \times 4 = 12; + 1 = 13,$$
$$5 \times 4 = 20; + 1 = 21,$$
$$8 \times 4 = 32; + 2 = 34,$$
$$13 \times 4 = 52; + 3 = 55,$$
$$21 \times 4 = 84; + 5 = 89, \text{ and so on.}$$

As the new sequence progresses, a third sequence begins in those numbers that are added to the 4x multiple. This relationship is possible because the ratio between *second* alternate Fibonacci numbers is 4.236, where .236 is both its inverse *and* its difference from the number 4. Other multiples produce different sequences, all based on Fibonacci multiples.

We offer a partial list of additional phenomena relating to the Fibonacci sequence as follows:

1) No two consecutive Fibonacci numbers have any common factors.

2) If the terms of the Fibonacci sequence are numbered 1, 2, 3, 4, 5, 6, 7, etc., we find that, except for the fourth Fibonacci number (3), each time a prime Fibonacci number (one divisible only by itself and 1) is reached, the sequence number is prime as well. Similarly, except for the fourth Fibonacci number (3), all composite sequence numbers (those divisible by at least two numbers besides themselves and 1) denote composite Fibonacci numbers, as in the table below. The converses of these phenomena are not always true.

Fibonacci: Prime vs. Composite

P	P	P	X	P		P				P		P			
1	1	2	3	5	8	13	21	34	55	89	144	233	377	610	987
1	2	3	4	5	6	7	8	9	10	11	12	13	14	15	16
			X	C			C	C	C		C		C	C	C

3) The sum of any ten numbers in the sequence is divisible by 11.

4) The sum of all Fibonacci numbers in the sequence up to any point, plus 1, equals the Fibonacci number two steps ahead of the last one added.

5) The sum of the squares of any consecutive sequence of Fibonacci numbers beginning at the first 1 will always equal the last number of the sequence chosen times the next higher number.

6) The square of a Fibonacci number minus the square of the second number below it in the sequence is always a Fibonacci number.

7) The square of any Fibonacci number is equal to the number before it in the sequence multiplied by the number after it in the sequence plus or minus 1. The plus 1 and minus 1 alternate along the sequence.

8) The square of one Fibonacci number F_n plus the square of the next Fibonacci number F_{n+1} equals the Fibonacci number of F_{2n+1}. The formula $F_n^2 + F_{n+1}^2 = F_{2n+1}$ is applicable to right-angle triangles, for which the sum of the squares of the two shorter sides equals the square of the longest side. At right is an example, using F_5, F_6 and $\sqrt{F}_{11}$.

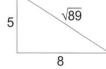

9) One formula illustrating a relationship between the two most ubiquitous irrational numbers in mathematics, *pi* and *phi*, is as follows:

$F_n \approx 100 \times \pi^2 \times \phi^{(15-n)}$, where $\phi = .618...$, n represents the numerical position of the term in the sequence and F_n represents the term itself. In this case, the number "1" is represented only once, so that $F_1 \approx 1$, $F_2 \approx 2$, $F_3 \approx 3$, $F_4 \approx 5$, etc.

For example, let n = 7. Then,

$$F_7 \approx 100 \times 3.1416^2 \times .6180339^{(15-7)}$$
$$\approx 986.97 \times .6180339^8$$
$$\approx 986.97 \times .02129 \approx 21.01 \approx 21$$

10) One mind stretching phenomenon, which to our knowledge has not previously been mentioned, is that the ratios between Fibonacci numbers yield numbers which very nearly are thousandths of other Fibonacci numbers, the difference being a thousandth of a third Fibonacci number, all in sequence (see ratio table, Figure 3-2). Thus, in ascending direction, identical Fibonacci numbers are related by 1.00, or .987 plus .013; adjacent Fibonacci numbers are related by 1.618, or 1.597 plus .021; alternate Fibonacci numbers are related by 2.618, or 2.584 plus .034; and so on. In the descending direction, adjacent Fibonacci numbers are related by .618, or .610 plus .008; alternate Fibonacci numbers are related by .382, or .377 plus .005; second alternates are related by .236, or .233 plus .003; third alternates are related by .146, or .144 plus .002; fourth alternates are related by .090, or .089 plus .001; fifth alternates are related by .056, or .055 plus .001; sixth through twelfth alternates are related by ratios which

are themselves thousandths of Fibonacci numbers beginning with .034. It is interesting that by this analysis, the ratio then between thirteenth alternate Fibonacci numbers begins the series back at .001, one thousandth of where it began! On all counts, we truly have a creation of "like from like," of "reproduction in an endless series," revealing the properties of "the most binding of all mathematical relations," as its admirers have characterized it.

Finally, we note that $(\sqrt{5} + 1)/2 = 1.618$ and $(\sqrt{5} - 1)/2 = .618$, where $\sqrt{5} = 2.236$. 5 is the most important number in the Wave Principle, and its square root is a mathematical key to *phi*.

1.618 (or .618) is known as the Golden Ratio or Golden Mean. Its proportions are pleasing to the eye and ear. It appears throughout biology, music, art and architecture. William Hoffer, writing for the December 1975 *Smithsonian Magazine*, said:

> ...the proportion of .618034 to 1 is the mathematical basis for the shape of playing cards and the Parthenon, sunflowers and snail shells, Greek vases and the spiral galaxies of outer space. The Greeks based much of their art and architecture upon this proportion. They called it "the golden mean."
>
> Fibonacci's abracadabric rabbits pop up in the most unexpected places. The numbers are unquestionably part of a mystical natural harmony that feels good, looks good and even sounds good. Music, for example, is based on the 8-note octave. On the piano this is represented by 8 white keys, 5 black ones — 13 in all. It is no accident that the musical harmony that seems to give the ear its greatest satisfaction is the major sixth. The note E vibrates at a ratio of .62500 to the note C.* A mere .006966 away from the exact golden mean, the proportions of the major sixth set off good vibrations in the cochlea of the inner ear — an organ that just happens to be shaped in a logarithmic spiral.
>
> The continual occurrence of Fibonacci numbers and the golden spiral in nature explains precisely why the proportion of .618034 to 1 is so pleasing in art. Man can see the image of life in art that is based on the golden mean.

---

* Note: The author means a major sixth to C# or a minor sixth to C. — Ed.

Nature uses the Golden Ratio in its most intimate building blocks and in its most advanced patterns, in forms as minuscule as microtubules in the brain and the DNA molecule (see Figure 3-9) to those as large as planetary distances and periods. It is involved in such diverse phenomena as quasi crystal arrangements, reflections of light beams on glass, the brain and nervous system, musical arrangement, and the structures of plants and animals. Science is rapidly demonstrating that there is indeed a basic proportional principle of nature. By the way, you are holding this book with two of your *five* appendages, which have *three* jointed parts, *five* digits at the end, and *three* jointed sections to each digit, a 5-3-5-3 progression that mightily suggests the Wave Principle.

The Golden Section

Any length can be divided in such a way that the ratio between the smaller part and the larger part is equivalent to the ratio between the larger part and the whole (see Figure 3-3). That ratio is always .618.

Figure 3-3

The Golden Section occurs throughout nature. In fact, the human body is a tapestry of Golden Sections (see Figure 3-9) in everything from outer dimensions to facial arrangement. "Plato, in his *Timaeus*," says Peter Tompkins, "went so far as to consider *phi*, and the resulting Golden Section proportion, the most binding of all mathematical relations, and considers it the key to the physics of the cosmos." In the sixteenth century, Johannes Kepler, in writing about the Golden, or "Divine Section," said that it described virtually all of creation and specifically symbolized God's creation of "like from like." Man is divided at the navel into a Golden Section. The statistical average is approximately .618. The ratio holds true separately for men, and separately for women, a fine symbol of the creation of "like from like." Is mankind's progress also a creation of "like from like?"

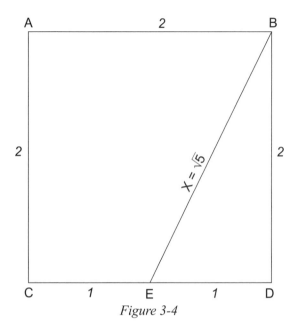

Figure 3-4

The Golden Rectangle

The sides of a Golden Rectangle are in the proportion of 1.618 to 1. To construct a Golden Rectangle, start with a square of 2 units by 2 units and draw a line from the midpoint of one side of the square to one of the corners formed by the opposite side as shown in Figure 3-4.

Triangle EDB is a right-angled triangle. Pythagoras, around 550 B.C., proved that the square of the hypotenuse (X) of a right-angled triangle equals the sum of the squares of the other two sides. In this case, therefore, $X^2 = 2^2 + 1^2$, or $X^2 = 5$. The length of the line EB, then, must be the square root of 5. The next step in the construction of a Golden Rectangle is to extend the line CD, making EG equal to the square root of 5, or 2.236, units in length, as shown in Figure 3-5. When completed, the sides of the rectangles are in the proportion of the Golden Ratio, so both the rectangle AFGC and BFGD are Golden Rectangles. The proofs are as follows:

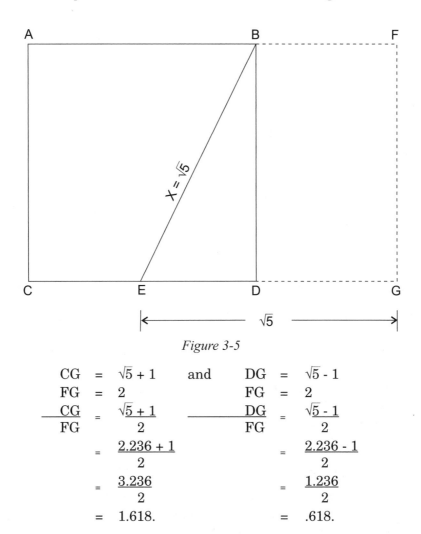

Figure 3-5

CG = √5 + 1   and   DG = √5 - 1
FG = 2   FG = 2

$$\frac{CG}{FG} = \frac{\sqrt5 + 1}{2}$$ $$\frac{DG}{FG} = \frac{\sqrt5 - 1}{2}$$

$$= \frac{2.236 + 1}{2}$$ $$= \frac{2.236 - 1}{2}$$

$$= \frac{3.236}{2}$$ $$= \frac{1.236}{2}$$

$$= 1.618.$$ $$= .618.$$

Since the sides of the rectangles are in Golden Ratio proportion, then the rectangles are, by definition, Golden Rectangles.

Works of art have been greatly enhanced with knowledge of the Golden Rectangle. Fascination with its value and use was particularly strong in ancient Egypt and Greece and during the Renaissance, all high points of civilization. Leonardo da Vinci attributed great meaning to the Golden Ratio. He also found it pleasing in its proportions and said, "If a thing does not have the right look, it does not work." Many of his paintings had the right look because he consciously used the Golden Rectangle to enhance their appeal. Ancient and modern architechts, most famously those who designed the Parthenon in Athens, have applied the Golden Rectangle deliberately in their designs.

Apparently, the *phi* proportion does have an effect upon the viewer of forms. Experimenters have determined that people find it aesthetically pleasing. For instance, subjects have been asked to choose one rectangle from a group of different types of rectangles. The average choice is generally found to be close to the Golden Rectangle shape. When asked to cross one bar with another in a way they liked best, subjects generally used one to divide the other into the *phi* proportion. Windows, picture frames, buildings, books and cemetery crosses often approximate Golden Rectangles.

As with the Golden Section, the value of the Golden Rectangle is hardly limited to beauty, but apparently serves function as well. Among numerous examples, the most striking is that the double helix of DNA itself creates precise Golden Rectangles at regular intervals of its twists (see Figure 3-9).

While the Golden Section and the Golden Rectangle represent static forms of natural and man-made aesthetic beauty and function, the representation of an aesthetically pleasing dynamism, an orderly progression of growth or progress, is more effectively made by one of the most remarkable forms in the universe, the Golden Spiral.

The Golden Spiral

A Golden Rectangle can be used to construct a Golden Spiral. Any Golden Rectangle, as in Figure 3-5, can be divided into a square and a smaller Golden Rectangle, as shown in Figure 3-6. This process theoretically can be continued to infinity. The resulting squares we have drawn, which appear to be whirling inward, are marked A, B, C, D, E, F and G.

The dotted lines, which are themselves in golden proportion to each other, diagonally bisect the rectangles and pinpoint the theoretical center of the whirling squares. From near this central point, we can draw the spiral shown in Figure 3-7 by connecting with a curve the points of intersection for each whirling square, in order of increasing size. As the squares whirl inward and outward, their connecting points trace out a Golden Spiral.

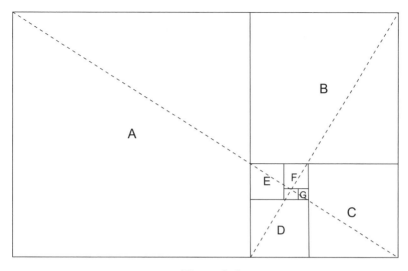

Figure 3-6

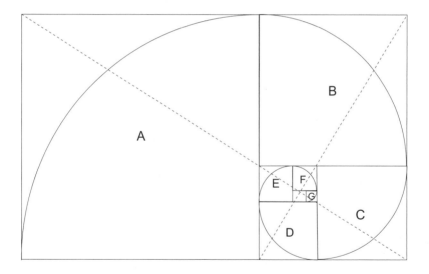

Figure 3-7

At any point in the evolution of the Golden Spiral, the ratio of the length of the arc to its diameter is 1.618. The diameter and radius, in turn, are related by 1.618 to the diameter and radius 90° away, as illustrated in Figure 3-8.

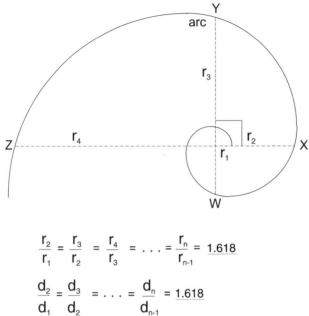

$$\frac{r_2}{r_1} = \frac{r_3}{r_2} = \frac{r_4}{r_3} = \ldots = \frac{r_n}{r_{n-1}} = 1.618$$

$$\frac{d_2}{d_1} = \frac{d_3}{d_2} = \ldots = \frac{d_n}{d_{n-1}} = 1.618$$

(where $d_1 = r_1 + r_3$, $d_2 = r_2 + r_4$, etc.)

$$\frac{\text{arcXY}}{\text{arcWX}} = \frac{\text{arcYZ}}{\text{arcXY}} \text{, etc.} = \frac{\text{arcXZ}}{\text{arcWY}} = 1.618$$

$$\frac{\text{arcWY}}{\text{diam. (WY)}} = \frac{\text{arcXZ}}{\text{diam. (XZ)}} \text{, etc.} = 1.618$$

Figure 3-8

The Golden Spiral, which is a type of logarithmic, or equian-gular, spiral, has no boundaries and is a constant shape. From any point along it, the spiral proceeds infinitely in both the outward and inward directions. The center is never met, and the outward reach is unlimited. The core of the logarithmic spiral in Figure 3-8, if viewed through a microscope, would have the same look as its expansion would from light years away.

While Euclidean geometric forms (except perhaps for the ellipse) typically imply stasis, a spiral implies motion: growth and decay, expansion and contraction, progress and regress. The logarithmic spiral is the quintessential expression of natural growth phenomena found throughout the universe. It covers scales as small as the motion of atomic particles and as large as galaxies. As David Bergamini, writing for *Mathematics* (in Time-Life Books' Science Library series) points out, the tail of a comet curves away from the sun in a logarithmic spiral. The epeira spider spins its web into a logarithmic spiral. Bacteria grow at an accelerating rate that can be plotted along a logarithmic spiral. Meteorites, when they rupture the surface of the Earth, cause depressions that correspond to a logarithmic spiral. An electron microscope trained upon a quasi crystal reveals logarithmic spirals. Pine cones, sea horses, snail shells, mollusk shells, ocean waves, ferns, animal horns and the arrangement of seed curves on sunflowers and daisies all form logarithmic spirals. Hurricane clouds, whirlpools and the galaxies of outer space swirl in logarithmic spirals. Even the human finger, which is composed of three bones in Golden Section to one another, takes the spiral shape of the dying poinsettia leaf (see Figure 3-9) when curled. In Figure 3-9, we see a reflection of this cosmic influence in numerous forms. Eons of time and light years of space separate the pine cone and the galaxy, but the design is the same: a logarithmic spiral, a primary shape governing natural dynamic structures. Most of the illustrated forms involve the Fibonacci ratio, whether precisely or roughly. For example, the pine cone and sunflower have a Fibonacci number of units in their whorls; a quasi crystal displays the five-pointed star; and the radii of a Nautilus shell expand at a rate of a 1.6-1.7 multiple per half cycle. The logarithmic spiral spreads before us in symbolic form as one of nature's grand designs, a force of endless expansion and contraction, a static law governing a dynamic process, sustained by the 1.618 ratio, the Golden Mean.

The Meaning of *Phi*

The greatest intellects of the ages profoundly appreciated the value of this ubiquitous phenomenon. History abounds with examples of exceptionally learned men who held a special fascination for this mathematical formulation. Pythagoras chose the five-pointed star, in which every segment is in golden ratio to the next smaller segment, as the symbol of his Order; celebrated 17th century mathematician Jacob Bernoulli directed that the Golden Spiral be etched into his headstone; Isaac Newton had the same spiral carved on the headboard of his bed (owned today by the Gravity Foundation, New Boston, NH). The earliest known aficionados were the architects of the Gizeh pyramid in Egypt, who recorded the knowledge of *phi* in its construction nearly 5000 years ago. Egyptian engineers consciously incorporated

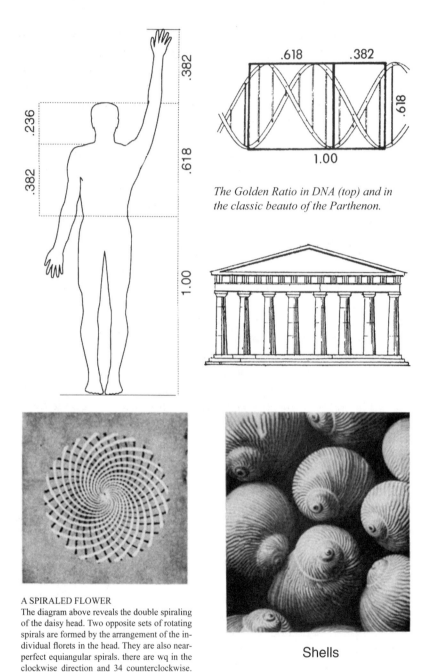

The Golden Ratio in DNA (top) and in the classic beauto of the Parthenon.

A SPIRALED FLOWER
The diagram above reveals the double spiraling of the daisy head. Two opposite sets of rotating spirals are formed by the arrangement of the individual florets in the head. They are also near-perfect equiangular spirals. there are wq in the clockwise direction and 34 counterclockwise. This 21:34 ratio is composed of two adjacent terms in the mysterious Fibonacci sequence.

Shells

Figure 3-9 (four pages)

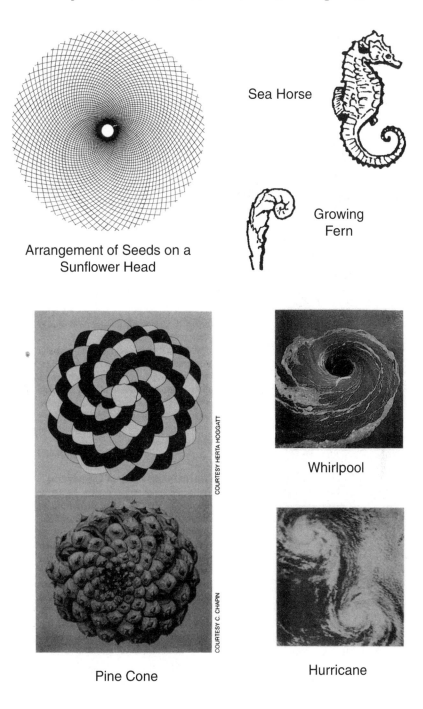

Sea Horse

Growing
Fern

Arrangement of Seeds on a
Sunflower Head

COURTESY HERTA HOGGATT

COURTESY C. CHAPIN

Whirlpool

Pine Cone

Hurricane

Figure 3-9

D. Schechtman, Technion, Israel

Quasi crystal under
an electron microscope

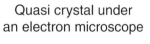

Dying
Poinsettia
Leaf

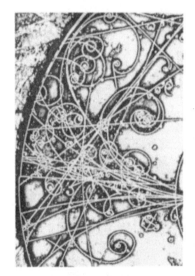

Atomic Particles in
Bubble Chamber

Horn

Ocean Waves

Nautilus

Figure 3-9

Spiraling Galaxy

Figure 3-9

the Golden Ratio in the Great Pyramid by giving its faces a slope height equal to 1.618 times half its base, so that the vertical height of the pyramid is at the same time the square root of 1.618 times half its base. According to Peter Tompkins, author of *Secrets of the Great Pyramid* (Harper & Row, 1971), "This relation shows Herodotus' report to be indeed correct, in that the square of the height of the pyramid is $\sqrt{\phi}$ x $\sqrt{\phi}$ = ϕ, and the areas of the face 1 x ϕ = ϕ." Furthermore, using these proportions, the Egyptian designers (apparently in order to build a scale model of the Northern Hemisphere) used *pi* and *phi* in an approach so mathematically sophisticated that it accomplished the feat of squaring the circle and cubing the sphere (i.e., making them of equal area and volume respectively), a feat that was not duplicated for well over four thousand years.

While the mere mention of the Great Pyramid may serve as an engraved invitation to skepticism (perhaps for good reason), keep in mind that its form reflects the same fascination held by pillars of scientific, mathematical, artistic and philosophic thought, including Plato, Pythagoras, Bernoulli, Kepler, DaVinci and Newton. Those who designed and built the pyramid were likewise demonstrably brilliant scientists, astronomers, mathematicians and engineers. Clearly they wanted to enshrine for millennia the Golden Ratio as something of transcendent importance. That such a caliber of intellects, who were later joined by some of the greatest minds of Ancient Greece and the Enlightenment in their fascination for this ratio, undertook this task is itself important. As for *why*, all we have is conjecture from a few authors. Yet that conjecture, however obtuse, curiously pertains to our own observations. It has been surmised that the Great Pyramid, for centuries after it was built, was used as a temple of initiation for those who proved themselves worthy of understanding the great universal secrets. Only those who could rise above the crude acceptance of things as they *seemed* in order to discover what, in actuality, they *were*, could be instructed in "the mysteries," i.e., the complex truths of eternal order and growth. Did such "mysteries" include *phi*? Tompkins explains, "The pharaonic Egyptians, says Schwaller de Lubicz, considered *phi* not as a number, but as a symbol of the creative function, or of reproduction in an endless series. To them it represented 'the fire of life, the male action of sperm, the *logos* [referenced in] the gospel of St. John.'" *Logos*, a Greek word, was defined variously by

Heraclitus and subsequent pagan, Jewish and Christian philosophers as meaning the rational order of the universe, an immanent natural law, a life-giving force hidden within things, the universal structural force governing and permeating the world.

Consider when reading such grand yet vague descriptions that these people could not clearly *see* what they sensed. They did not have graphs and the Wave Principle to make nature's growth pattern manifest and were doing the best they could to describe an organizational principle that they discerned as shaping the natural world. If these ancient philosophers were right that a universal structural force governs and permeates the world, should it not govern and permeate the world of man? If forms throughout the universe, including man's body, brain and DNA, reflect the form of *phi*, might man's activities reflect it as well? If *phi* is the growth-force in the universe, might it be the impulse behind the progress in man's productive capacity? If *phi* is a symbol of the creative function, might it govern the creative activity of man? If man's progress is based upon production and reproduction "in an endless series," is it not possible, even reasonable, that such progress has a spiraling form based on *phi*, and that this form is discernible in the movement of the valuation of his productive capacity, i.e., the stock market? Intelligent Egyptians apparently learned that there are hidden truths of order and growth in the universe behind the apparent randomness. Similarly, the stock market, in our opinion, can be understood properly only if it is taken for what it *is* rather than for what it crudely appears to be upon cursory consideration. The stock market is not a random, formless mess reacting to current news events but a remarkably precise recording of the formal structure of the progress of man.

Compare this concept with astronomer William Kingsland's words in *The Great Pyramid in Fact and in Theory* that Egyptian astronomy/astrology was a "profoundly esoteric science connected with the great cycles of man's evolution." The Wave Principle explains the great cycles of man's evolution and reveals how and why they unfold as they do. Moreover, it encompasses micro as well as macro scales, all of which are based upon a paradoxical principle of dynamism and variation within an unaltered form.

It is this form that gives structure and unity to the universe. Nothing in nature suggests that life is disorderly or formless.

The word "universe" means "one order." If life has form, then we must not reject the probability that human progress, which is part of the reality of life, also has order and form. By extension, the stock market, which values man's productive enterprise, will have order and form as well. All technical approaches to understanding the stock market depend on the basic principle of order and form. Elliott's theory, however, goes beyond all others. It postulates that no matter how minute or how large the form, *the basic design remains constant.*

Elliott, in his second monograph, used the title *Nature's Law — The Secret of the Universe* in preference to "The Wave Principle" and applied it to all sorts of human activity. Elliott may have gone too far in saying that the Wave Principle was *the* secret of the universe, as nature appears to have created numerous forms and processes, not just one simple design. Nevertheless, some of history's greatest scientists, mentioned earlier, would probably have agreed with Elliott's formulation. At minimum, it is credible to say that the Wave Principle is one of the most important secrets of the universe.

Fibonacci in the Spiraling Stock Market

Can we both theorize and observe that the stock market operates on the same mathematical basis as so many natural phenomena? The answer is yes. As Elliott explained in his final unifying conclusion, the progress of waves has the same mathematical base. The Fibonacci sequence governs the numbers of waves that form in the movement of aggregate stock prices, in an expansion upon the underlying 5:3 relationship described at the beginning of Chapter 1.

As we first showed in Figure 1-4, the essential structure of the market generates the complete Fibonacci sequence. The simplest expression of a correction is a straight-line decline. The simplest expression of an impulse is a straight-line advance. A complete cycle is two lines. In the next degree of complexity, the corresponding numbers are 3, 5 and 8. As illustrated in Figure 3-10, this sequence can be taken to infinity. The fact that waves produce the Fibonacci sequence of numbers reveals that *man's collectively expressed emotions are keyed to this mathematical law of nature.*

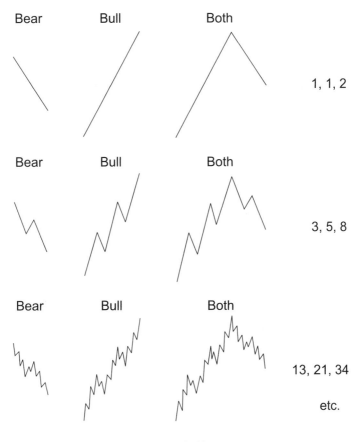

Figure 3-10

Now compare the formations shown in Figures 3-11 and 3-12. Each illustrates the natural law of the inwardly directed Golden Spiral and is governed by the Fibonacci ratio. Each wave relates to the previous wave by .618. In fact, the distances in terms of the Dow points themselves reflect Fibonacci mathematics. In Figure 3-11, showing the 1930-1942 sequence, the market swings cover approximately 260, 160, 100, 60, and 38 points respectively, closely resembling the declining list of Fibonacci ratios: 2.618, 1.618, 1.00, .618 and .382.

Starting with wave X in the 1977 upward correction shown in Figure 3-12, the swings are almost exactly 55 points (wave X), 34 points (waves a through c), 21 points (wave d), 13 points

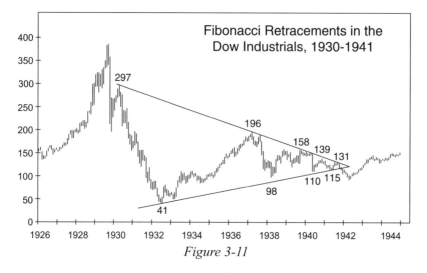

Figure 3-11

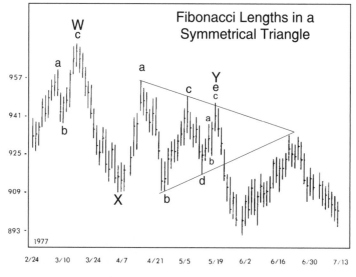

Figure 3-12

(wave a of e) and 8 points (wave b of e), the Fibonacci sequence itself. The total net gain from beginning to end is 13 points, and the apex of the triangle lies on the level of the correction's beginning at 930, which is also the level of the peak of the subsequent reflex rally in June. Whether one takes the actual number of points in the waves as coincidence or part of the design, one can be certain that the precision manifest in the constant .618 ratio between each successive wave is not coincidence. Chapters 4 and 7 will elaborate substantially on the appearance of the Fibonacci ratio in market patterns.

Does the Fibonacci-based behavior of the stock market reflect spiral growth? Once again, the answer is yes. The idealized Elliott concept of the progression of the stock market, as presented in Figure 1-3, is an excellent base from which to construct a logarithmic spiral, as Figure 3-13 illustrates with a rough approximation. In this construction, the top of each successive wave of higher degree is the touch point of the exponential expansion.

In these two crucial ways (Fibonacci and spiraling), the sociological valuation of man's productive enterprise reflects other growth forms found throughout nature. We conclude, therefore, *they all follow the same law.*

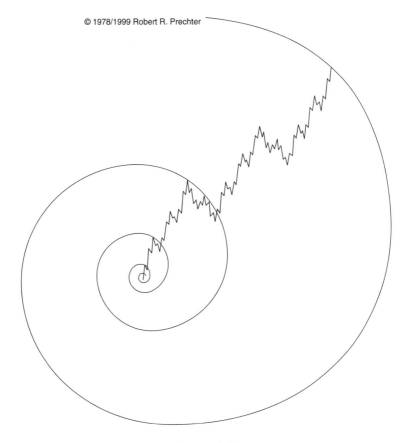

Figure 3-13

The Fibonacci Construction of Wave Pattern Complexity

© 1994-2006 Robert R. Prechter, Jr.

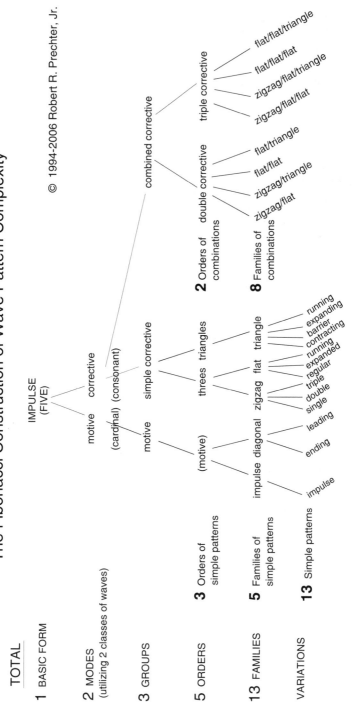

Figure 3-14

Fibonacci Mathematics in the Structure of the Wave Principle

Even the ordered structural complexity of Elliott wave *forms* reflects the Fibonacci sequence. There is 1 basic form: the five wave sequence. There are 2 modes of waves: motive (which subdivide into the cardinal class of waves, numbered) and corrective (which subdivide into the consonant class of waves, lettered). There are 3 orders of simple patterns of waves: fives, threes and triangles (which have characteristics of both fives and threes). There are 5 families of simple patterns: impulse, diagonal, zigzag, flat and triangle. There are 13 variations of simple patterns: impulse, ending diagonal, leading diagonal, zigzag, double zigzag, triple zigzag, regular flat, expanded flat, running flat, contracting triangle, barrier triangle, expanding triangle and running triangle.

The corrective mode has two groups, simple and combined, bringing the total number of groups to 3. There are 2 orders of corrective combinations (double correction and triple correction), bringing the total number of orders to 5. Allowing only one triangle per combination and one zigzag per combination (as required), there are 8 families of corrective combinations in all: zig/flat, zig/tri, flat/flat, flat/tri, zig/flat/flat, zig/flat/tri, flat/flat/flat and flat/flat/tri, which brings the total number of families to 13. The total number of simple patterns and combination families is 21.

Figure 3-14 is a depiction of this developing tree of complexity. Listing permutations of those combinations, or further variations of lesser importance within waves, such as which wave, if any, is extended, which ways alternation is satisfied, whether an impulse does or does not contain a diagonal, which types of triangles are in each of the combinations, etc., may serve to keep this progression going.

There may be an element of contrivance in this ordering process, as one can conceive of some possible variations in acceptable categorization. Still, that a principle about Fibonacci appears to reflect Fibonacci is itself worth some reflection.

Phi and Additive Growth

As we will show in subsequent chapters, market action is governed by the Golden Ratio. Even Fibonacci numbers appear

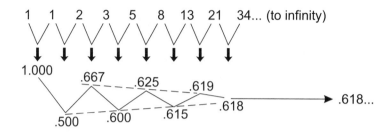

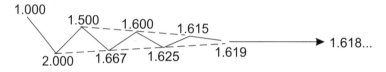

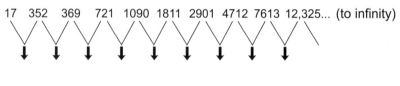

Figure 3-15

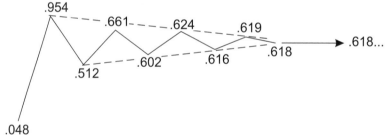

Figure 3-16

in market statistics more often than mere chance would allow. However, it is crucial to understand that while the numbers themselves do have theoretic weight in the grand concept of the Wave Principle, it is the *ratio* that is the fundamental key to growth patterns of this type. Although it is rarely pointed out in the literature, the Fibonacci ratio results from this type of additive sequence no matter what two numbers start the sequence. The Fibonacci sequence is the basic additive sequence of its type since it begins with the number 1 (see Figure 3-15), which is the starting point of mathematical growth. However, we may also take any two *randomly selected numbers*, such as 17 and 352, and add them to produce a third, continuing in that manner to produce additional numbers. As this sequence progresses, the ratio between adjacent terms always approaches the limit *phi* very quickly. This relationship becomes obvious by the time the eighth term is produced (see Figure 3-16). Thus, while the specific numbers making up the Fibonacci sequence reflect the ideal progression of waves in markets, the Fibonacci *ratio* is a fundamental law of geometric progression in which two preceding units are summed to create the next. That is why this ratio governs so many relationships in data series relating to natural phenomena of growth and decay, expansion and contraction, and advancement and retreat.

In its broadest sense, the Wave Principle suggests the idea that the same law that shapes living creatures and galaxies is inherent in the spirit and activities of men *en masse*. Because the stock market is the most meticulously tabulated reflector of mass psychology in the world, its data produce an excellent recording of man's social psychological states and trends. This record of the fluctuating self-evaluation of social man's own productive enterprise makes manifest specific patterns of progress and regress. What the Wave Principle says is that mankind's progress (of which the stock market is a popularly determined valuation) does not occur in a straight line, does not occur randomly, and does not occur cyclically. Rather, progress takes place in a "three steps forward, two steps back" fashion, a form that nature prefers. More grandly, as the activity of social man is linked to the Fibonacci sequence and the spiral pattern of progression, it is apparently no exception to the general law of ordered growth in the universe. In our opinion, the parallels between the Wave Principle and other natural phenomena are too great to be dismissed as just so much nonsense. On the balance of probabilities, we have come to the conclusion that there is a principle, everywhere present, giving shape to social affairs, and that Einstein knew what he was talking about when he said, "God does not play dice with the universe." The stock market is no exception, as mass behavior is undeniably linked to a law that can be studied and defined. The briefest way to express this principle is a simple mathematical statement: the 1.618 ratio.

The *Desiderata,* by poet Max Ehrmann, reads, "You are a child of the Universe, no less than the trees and the stars; you have a right to be here. And whether or not it is clear to you, no doubt the Universe is unfolding as it should." Order in life? Yes. Order in the stock market? Apparently.

PART II

ELLIOTT APPLIED

In 1939, *Financial World* magazine published twelve articles by R.N. Elliott entitled "The Wave Principle." The original publisher's note, in the introduction to the articles, stated the following:

> During the past seven or eight years, publishers of financial magazines and organizations in the investment advisory field have been virtually flooded with "systems" for which their proponents have claimed great accuracy in forecasting stock market movements. Some of them appeared to work for a while. It was immediately obvious that others had no value whatever. All have been looked upon by *The Financial World* with great skepticism. But after investigation of Mr. R.N. Elliott's Wave Principle, *The Financial World* became convinced that a series of articles on this subject would be interesting and instructive to its readers. To the individual reader is left the determination of the value of the Wave Principle as a working tool in market forecasting, but it is believed that it should prove at least a useful check upon conclusions based on economic considerations.
>
> — The Editors of *The Financial World*

In Part II of this book, we reverse the editors' suggested procedure and argue that economic considerations at best may be thought of as an ancillary tool in checking market forecasts based entirely upon the Elliott Wave Principle.

CHAPTER 4

RATIO ANALYSIS
AND FIBONACCI TIME SEQUENCES

Ratio Analysis

Ratio analysis is the assessment of the proportionate relationship, in time and amplitude, of one wave to another. In discerning the working of the Golden Ratio in the five up and three down movement of the stock market cycle, one might anticipate that on completion of any bull phase, the ensuing correction would be three-fifths of the previous rise in both time and amplitude. Such simplicity is seldom seen. However, the underlying tendency of the market to conform to relationships suggested by the Golden Ratio is always present and helps generate the right look for each wave.

The study of wave amplitude relationships in the stock market can often lead to such startling discoveries that some Elliott wave practitioners have become almost obsessive about its importance. Although Fibonacci time ratios are far less common, years of plotting the averages have convinced the authors that the amplitude (measured either arithmetically or in percentage terms) of virtually every wave is related to the amplitude of an adjacent, alternate and/or component wave by one of the ratios between Fibonacci numbers. However, we shall endeavor to present some evidence and let it stand or fall on its own merit.

The first data reflecting time and amplitude ratios in the stock market come from, of all suitable sources, the works of the great Dow Theorist, Robert Rhea. In 1934, Rhea, in his book *The Story of the Averages*, compiled a consolidated summary of market data covering nine Dow Theory bull markets and nine bear markets spanning a thirty-six year time period from 1896 to 1932. He had this to say about why he felt it was necessary to present the data despite the fact that no use for it was immediately apparent:

Whether or not [this review of the averages] has contributed anything to the sum total of financial history, I feel certain that the statistical data presented will save other students many months of work.... Consequently, it seemed best to record all the statistical data we had collected rather than merely that portion which appeared to be useful.... The figures presented under this heading probably have little value as a factor in estimating the probable extent of future movements; nevertheless, as a part of a general study of the averages, the treatment is worthy of consideration.

One of the observations was this one:

The footings of the tabulation shown above (considering only the industrial average) show that the nine bull and bear markets covered in this review extended over 13,115 calendar days. Bull markets were in progress 8,143 days, while the remaining 4,972 days were in bear markets. The relationship between these figures tends to show that bear markets run *61.1* percent of the time required for bull periods.

And finally,

Column 1 shows the sum of all primary movements in each bull (or bear) market. It is obvious that such a figure is considerably greater than the net difference between the highest and lowest figures of any bull market. For example, the bull market discussed in Chapter II started (for Industrials) at 29.64 and ended at 76.04, and the difference, or net advance, was 46.40 points. Now this advance was staged in four primary swings of 14.44, 17.33, 18.97, and 24.48 points respectively. The sum of these advances is 75.22, which is the figure shown in Column 1. If the net advance, 46.40, is divided into the sum of advances, 75.22, the result is *1.621*, which gives the percent shown in Column 1. Assume that two traders were infallible in their market operations, and that one bought stocks at the low point of the bull market and retained them until the high day of that market before selling. Call his gain 100 percent. Now assume that the other trader bought at the bottom, sold out at the top of each primary swing, and repurchased the same stocks at the bottom of each secondary reaction — his profit would be *162.1*, compared with 100 realized by the first trader. Thus the total of secondary reactions retraced *62.1* percent of the net advance. [Emphasis added.]

So in 1934 Robert Rhea discovered, without knowing it, the Fibonacci ratio and its function relating bull phases to bear in both time and amplitude. Fortunately, he felt that there was value in presenting data that had no immediate practical utility, but that might be useful at some future date. Similarly, we feel that there is much to learn on the ratio front, and our introduction, which merely scratches the surface, could be valuable in leading some future analyst to answer questions we have not even thought to ask.

Ratio analysis has revealed a number of precise price relationships that occur often among waves. There are two categories of relationships: retracements and multiples.

Retracements

Occasionally, a correction retraces a Fibonacci percentage of the preceding wave. As illustrated in Figure 4-1, sharp corrections tend more often to retrace 61.8% or 50% of the previous wave, particularly when they occur as wave 2 of an impulse, wave B of a larger zigzag, or wave X in a multiple zigzag. A leading diagonal in the wave one position is typically followed by a zigzag retracement of 78.6% ($\sqrt{\phi}$). Sideways corrections tend more often to retrace 38.2% of the previous impulse wave, particularly when they occur as wave 4, as shown in Figure 4-2.

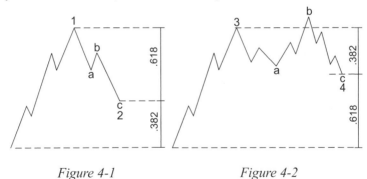

Figure 4-1   *Figure 4-2*

Retracements come in all sizes. The ratios shown in Figures 4-1 and 4-2 are merely tendencies. Unfortunately, that is where most analysts place an inordinate focus because measuring retracements is easy. Far more precise and reliable, however, are relationships between *alternate* waves, or lengths unfolding in the same direction, as explained in the next section.

Motive Wave Multiples

Chapter 2 mentioned that when wave 3 is extended, waves
1 and 5 tend towards equality or a .618 relationship, as illustrated in Figure 4-3. Actually, all three motive waves tend to be
related by Fibonacci mathematics, whether by equality, 1.618 or
2.618 (whose inverses are .618 and .382). These impulse wave
relationships usually occur in *percentage* terms. For instance,
wave I from 1932 to 1937 gained 371.6%, while wave III from
1942 to 1966 gained 971.7%, or 2.618 times as much. Semilog
scale is required to reveal these relationships. Of course, at small
degrees, arithmetic and percentage scales produce essentially the
same result, so that the number of *points* in each impulse wave
reveals the same multiples.

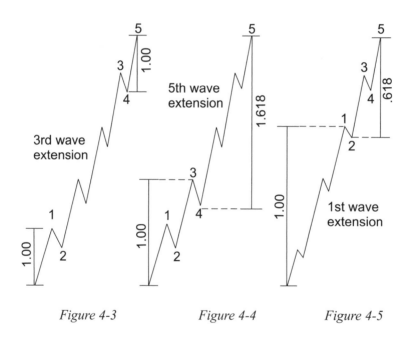

Figure 4-3   Figure 4-4   Figure 4-5

Another typical development is that wave 5's length is
sometimes related by the Fibonacci ratio to the length of wave 1
through wave 3, as illustrated in Figure 4-4, showing an extended
fifth wave. .382 and .618 relationships occur when wave five is
not extended. In those rare cases when wave 1 is extended, it is
wave 2, quite reasonably, that often subdivides the entire impulse
wave into the Golden Section, as shown in Figure 4-5.

Here is a generalization that subsumes some of the observations we have already made: Unless wave 1 is extended, wave 4 often divides the price range of an impulse wave into the Golden Section. In such cases, the latter portion is .382 of the total distance when wave 5 is not extended, as shown in Figure 4-6, and .618 when it is, as shown in Figure 4-7. Real life examples are shown in Figures 6-8 and 6-9. This guideline is somewhat loose in that the exact point within wave 4 that effects the subdivision varies. It can be its start, end or extreme countertrend point. Thus, it provides, depending on the circumstances, two or three closely clustered targets for the end of wave 5. This guideline explains why the target for a retracement following a fifth wave often is doubly indicated both by the end of the preceding fourth wave and the .382 retracement point.

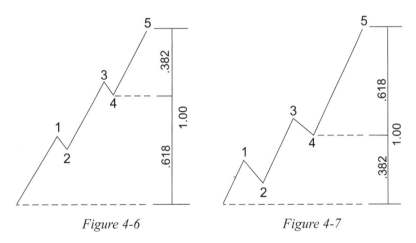

Figure 4-6   Figure 4-7

Corrective Wave Multiples

In a zigzag, the length of wave C is usually equal to that of wave A, as shown in Figure 4-8, although it is not uncommonly 1.618 or .618 times the length of wave A. This same relationship applies to a second zigzag relative to the first in a double zigzag pattern, as shown in Figure 4-9.

In a regular flat correction, waves A, B and C are, of course, approximately equal, as shown in Figure 4-10. In an expanded flat correction, wave C is often 1.618 times the length of wave A. Sometimes wave C will terminate beyond the end of wave A by .618 times the length of wave A. Each of these tendencies is illustrated in Figure 4-11. In rare cases, wave C is 2.618 times

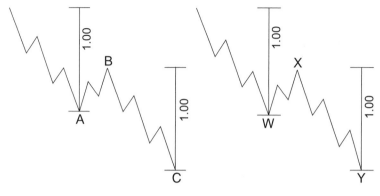

Figure 4-8   Figure 4-9

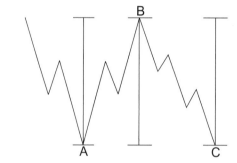

Figure 4-10

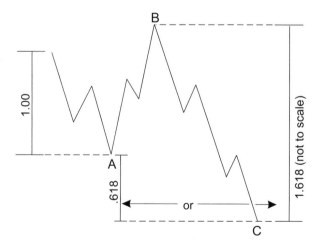

Figure 4-11

the length of wave A. Wave B in an expanded flat is sometimes 1.236 or 1.382 times the length of wave A.

In a triangle, we have found that at least two of the *alternate* waves are typically related to each other by .618. I.e., in a contracting or barrier triangle, wave e = .618c, wave c = .618a, or wave d = .618b, as illustrated in Figure 4-12. In an expanding triangle, the multiple is 1.618.

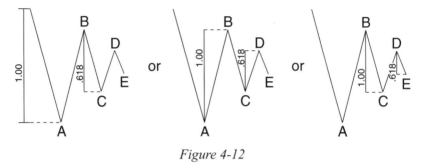

Figure 4-12

In double and triple corrections, the net travel of one simple pattern is sometimes related to another by equality or, particularly if one of the threes is a triangle, by .618.

Finally, wave 4 quite commonly spans a gross and/or net price range that has an equality or Fibonacci relationship to its corresponding wave 2. As with impulse waves, these relationships usually occur in percentage terms.

Applied Ratio Analysis

Elliott himself, a few years after Rhea's book, was the first to realize the applicability of ratio analysis. He noted that the number of DJIA points between 1921 and 1926, encompassing the first through third waves, was 61.8% of the number of points in the fifth wave from 1926 to 1928 (1928 is the orthodox top of the bull market according to Elliott). Exactly the same relationship occurred again in the five waves up from 1932 to 1937 (for reference, see Figures 2-11 and 2-12).

A. Hamilton Bolton, in the 1957 Elliott Wave Supplement to the *Bank Credit Analyst*, gave this price forecast based on expectations of typical wave behavior:

The powerhouse that will be building up if the market con-
solidates for another year or so along orthodox lines, it seems
to us, will offer the probability that Primary V could be quite
sensational, taking the DJIA to 1000 or more in the early 1960s
in a wave of great speculation.

Then, in *The Elliott Wave Principle — A Critical Appraisal*,
reflecting on examples cited by Elliott, Bolton stated,

Should the 1949 market to date adhere to this formula,
then the advance from 1949 to 1956 (361 points in the DJIA)
should be completed when 583 points (161.8% of 361 points)
have been added to the 1957 low of 416, or a total of 999 DJIA.
Alternatively, 361 over 416 would call for 777 in the DJIA.

Later, when Bolton wrote the 1964 Elliott Wave Supplement,
he concluded,

Since we are now well past the 777 level, it looks as if 1000
in the averages could be our next target.

The year 1966 proved those statements to be the most accurate prediction in stock market history, when the 3:00 p.m.
hourly reading on February 9th registered a high at 995.82 (the
"intraday" high was 1001.11). Six years prior to the event, then,
Bolton was right to within 3.18 DJIA points, less than one third
of one percent error.

Despite this remarkable portent, it was Bolton's view, as it
is ours, that wave form analysis must take precedence over the
implications of proportionate relationships. Indeed, when under-
taking a ratio analysis, it is *essential* that one understand and
apply the Elliott counting and labeling method to determine from
which points the measurements should be made in the first place.
Ratios between lengths based on orthodox pattern termination
levels are reliable; those based on nonorthodox price extremes
generally are not.

The authors themselves have used ratio analysis, often with
satisfying success. A.J. Frost became convinced of his ability to
recognize turning points by catching the "Cuban crisis" low in
October 1962 the hour it occurred and telegraphing his conclusion
to Hamilton Bolton in Greece. Then, in 1970, in a supplement to

The Bank Credit Analyst, he determined that the bear market low for the Cycle wave correction in progress would probably occur at a level .618 times the distance of the 1966 decline below the 1966 low, or 572. Four years later, the DJIA's hourly reading in December 1974 at the exact low was 572.20, from which the explosive rise into 1975-76 occurred.

Ratio analysis has value at smaller degrees as well. In the summer of 1976, in a published report for Merrill Lynch, Robert Prechter identified the fourth wave then in progress as a rare expanding triangle, and in October used the 1.618 ratio to determine that the maximum expected low for the eight-month pattern should be 922 on the Dow. The low occurred five weeks later at 920.63 at 11:00 on November 11, launching the year-end fifth-wave rally.

In October 1977, five months in advance, Mr. Prechter computed a probable level for the 1978 major bottom as "744 or slightly lower." On March 1, 1978, at 11:00, the Dow registered its low at exactly 740.30. A follow-up report published two weeks after the bottom reaffirmed the importance of the 740 level, noting that:

> ...the 740 area marks the point at which the 1977-78 correction, in terms of Dow points, is exactly .618 times the length of the entire bull market rise from 1974 to 1976. Mathematically we can state that $1022 - (1022-572).618 = 744$ (or using the orthodox high on December 31st, $1005 - (1005-572).618 = 737$). Second, the 740 area marks the point at which the 1977-78 correction is exactly 2.618 times the length of the preceding correction in 1975 from July to October, so that $1005 - (885-784)2.618 = 742$. Third, in relating the target to the internal components of the decline, we find that the length of wave C = 2.618 times the length of wave A if wave C bottoms at *746.* Even the wave factors as researched in the April 1977 report mark 740 as a likely level for a turn. At this juncture then, the wave count is compelling, the market appears to be stabilizing, and the last acceptable Fibonacci target level under the Cycle dimension bull market thesis has been reached at 740.30 on March 1st. It is at such times that the market, in Elliott terms, must "make it or break it."

The three charts from that report are reproduced here as Figures 4-13 (with a few extra markings to condense comments

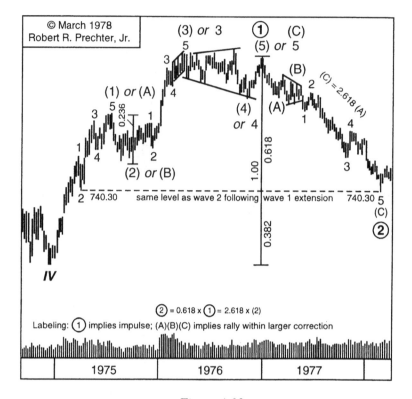

Figure 4-13

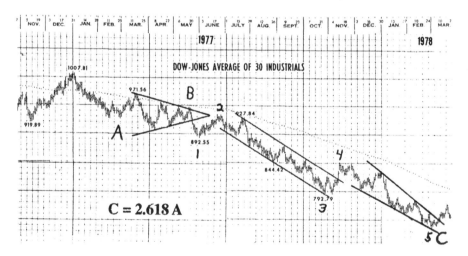

Figure 4-14

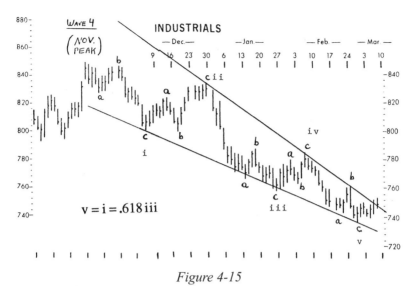

Figure 4-15

from the text), 4-14 and 4-15. They illustrate the wave structure into the recent low from Primary down to Minuette degree. Even at this early date, 740.30 seems to be firmly established as the low of Primary wave ② in Cycle wave V.

The 740 level has proved important other times in the past as well, quite possibly because while the 1974 low at 572.20 lies exactly 423.60 points under the 1966 peak at 995.82, 740.30 lies approximately 261.80 points under the 1004.65 level, the orthodox top in 1976. Both of these distances are expressions of Fibonacci ratios. Mr. Prechter further discussed the 740 level as follows:

> It is certainly not coincidence that the 740 level has proved of some importance in the past. In 1961, the intraday Dow peak at 741.30 accompanied the highest market P/E ratio in history; in 1966, the intraday low of 735.74 marked the end of the first slide to the measuring low in the Cycle wave IV bear market (the point which was 61.8% of the entire decline of Cycle wave IV); in 1963, 1970, 1974 and 1975, breaks through 740 in each direction accompanied extreme violence; in 1978, the 740 level corresponds with long term trendline support. Furthermore, the Wave Principle holds that the limit of any market correction is the bottom of the previous fourth wave of lesser degree. When the first wave in a five-wave sequence extends, however, the limit of the ensuing correction is often the bottom of the sec-

ond wave of that five-wave sequence. Given this guideline, the recent low on March first at 740.30 was a remarkable level at which to stop. A check with the hourly back figures as printed in the *Wall Street Journal* reveals that on March 25, 1975 the DJIA bottomed at 740.30 to complete the pullback of the second wave. [See note on Figure 4-13.]

In addition to the more traditional Elliott forecasting methods, Mr. Prechter has begun to research mathematical wave factors in terms of both time and price, of which motive waves have been found to be whole number multiples and corrective waves Fibonacci ratio multiples. The approach was discussed recently in several reports for Merrill Lynch.

Undoubtedly to some it will seem that we are patting ourselves on the back, which we most certainly are! Truthfully, though, we are hoping that an account of the successes which we have personally experienced with Elliott will inspire others to strive for similar achievements using this approach. To our knowledge, only the Wave Principle can be used to forecast with such accuracy. Of course, we have experienced failures as well, but nevertheless we feel that any drawbacks in the Elliott wave approach have been grossly overstated in the past, and that when expectations with regard to the market are not fulfilled, the Wave Principle warns the analyst in plenty of time to chart the next most likely course and to avoid losses by letting the market itself dictate his course of action.

We have found that predetermined price objectives are useful in that *if* a reversal occurs at that level and the wave count is acceptable, a doubly significant point has been reached. When the market ignores such a level or gaps through it, you are put on alert to expect the *next* calculated level to be achieved. As the next level is often a good distance away, this can be extremely valuable information. Moreover, targets are based upon the most satisfying wave count. Thus, if they are not met or are exceeded by a significant margin, in many instances you will be forced in a timely manner to reconsider your preferred count and investigate what may be rapidly developing as a more attractive inter- pretation. This approach helps keep you one step ahead of nasty surprises. It is a good idea to keep all reasonable wave interpretations in mind so you can use ratio analysis to obtain additional clues as to which one is operative.

Multiple Wave Relationships

Keep in mind that *all degrees of trend are always operating in the market at the same time*. Therefore, at any given moment, the market will be full of Fibonacci ratio relationships, all occurring with respect to the various wave degrees unfolding. It follows that future levels that will create *several* Fibonacci relationships have a greater likelihood of marking a turn than a level that will create only one.

For instance, if a .618 retracement of Primary wave ① by Primary wave ② gives a particular target, and within it, a 1.618 multiple of Intermediate wave (A) in an irregular correction gives the *same* target for Intermediate wave (C), and within that, a 1.00 multiple of Minor wave 1 gives the *same* target yet again for Minor wave 5, then you have a powerful argument for expecting a turn at that calculated price level. Figure 4-16 illustrates this example.

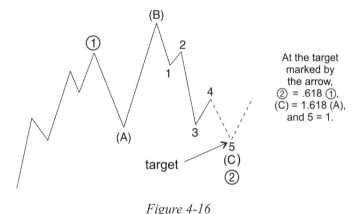

Figure 4-16

Figure 4-17 is an imaginary rendition of a reasonably ideal Elliott wave, complete with parallel trend channel. It has been created as an example of how ratios are often present throughout the market. In it, the following eight relationships hold:

$$
\begin{aligned}
② &= .618 \times ①; \\
④ &= .382 \times ③; \\
⑤ &= 1.618 \times ①; \\
⑤ &= .618 \times ⓪ \rightarrow ③;
\end{aligned}
$$

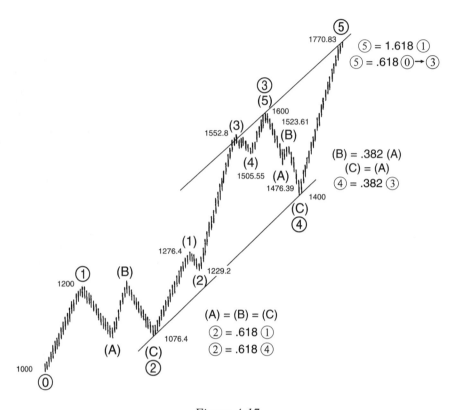

Figure 4-17

$$\text{②} \quad = .618 \times \text{④};$$
$$\text{in ②, (A) = (B) = (C);}$$
$$\text{in ④, (A) = (C);}$$
$$\text{in ④, (B) = .382 × (A).}$$

If a complete method of ratio analysis could be successfully resolved into basic tenets, forecasting with the Elliott Wave Principle would become more scientific. It will always remain an exercise to determine probability, however, not certainty. Nature's laws governing life and growth, though immutable, nevertheless allow for an immense diversity of specific outcome, and the market is no exception. All that can be said at this point is that comparing the price lengths of waves frequently confirms, often with pinpoint accuracy, that Fibonacci ratios are a key determinant of where waves will stop. It was awe-inspiring, but no surprise to us, for instance, that the advance from December 1974 to July 1975 traced just over 61.8% of the preceding 1973-74 bear slide, and that the 1976-78 market decline traced exactly 61.8% of the preceding rise from December 1974 to September 1976. Despite the continual evidence of the importance of the .618 ratio, however, our basic reliance must be on *form*, with ratio analysis as evidence to support or challenge what we see in the patterns of movement. Bolton's advice with respect to ratio analysis was, "Keep it simple." Research may still achieve further progress, as ratio analysis is still in its infancy. We are hopeful that those who labor with the problem of ratio analysis will add worthwhile material to the Elliott approach.

Fibonacci Time Sequences

There is no sure way of using the time factor by itself in forecasting. Elliott said that the time factor often "conforms to the pattern," for instance with regard to trend channels, and therein lies its primary significance. Frequently, however, durations and time relationships themselves reflect Fibonacci measurements. Exploring Fibonacci numbers of time units appears to go beyond an exercise in numerology, fitting wave spans with remarkable accuracy. They serve to give the analyst added perspective by indicating possible times for a turn, especially if they coincide with price targets and wave counts.

In *Nature's Law*, Elliott gave the following examples of Fibonacci time spans between important turning points in the market:

1921 to 1929	8 years
July 1921 to November 1928	89 months
September 1929 to July 1932	34 months
July 1932 to July 1933	13 months
July 1933 to July 1934	13 months
July 1934 to March 1937	34 months
July 1932 to March 1937	5 years (55 months)
March 1937 to March 1938	13 months
March 1937 to April 1942	5 years
1929 to 1942	13 years

In *Dow Theory Letters* on November 21, 1973, Richard Russell gave some additional examples of Fibonacci time periods:

1907 panic low to 1962 panic low	55 years
1949 major bottom to 1962 panic low	13 years
1921 recession low to 1942 recession low	21 years
January 1960 top to October 1962 bottom	34 months

Walter E. White, in his 1968 monograph on the Elliott Wave Principle, concluded that "the next important low point may be in 1970." As substantiation, he pointed out the following Fibonacci sequence: 1949 + 21 = 1970; 1957 + 13 = 1970; 1962 + 8 = 1970; 1965 + 5 = 1970. May 1970, of course, marked the low point of the most vicious slide in thirty years. Taken *in toto,* these distances appear to be a bit more than coincidence.

The progression of years from the 1928 (possible orthodox) and 1929 (nominal) high of the last Supercycle produces a remarkable Fibonacci sequence as well:

1929	+	3	=	1932 bear market bottom
1929	+	5	=	1934 correction bottom
1929	+	8	=	1937 bull market top
1929	+	13	=	1942 bear market bottom
1928	+	21	=	1949 bear market bottom
1928	+	34	=	1962 crash bottom
1928	+	55	=	1983 probable Supercycle peak

A similar series has begun at the 1965 (possible orthodox) and 1966 (nominal) highs of the third Cycle wave of the current Supercycle:

1965	+	1	=	1966 nominal high
1965	+	2	=	1967 reaction low
1965	+	3	=	1968 blowoff peak for secondaries
1965	+	5	=	1970 crash low
1966	+	8	=	1974 bear market bottom
1966	+	13	=	1979 low for 9.2 and 4.5 year cycles
1966	+	21	=	1987 probable Supercycle low

Thus, we foresee some interesting possibilities with respect to DJIA turning points in the near future. These possibilities are further explored in Chapter 8.

Besides their significant frequency, there is reason to believe that Fibonacci numbers and ratios of time units in the stock market are something other than numerology. For one thing, natural time units are related to the Fibonacci sequence. There are 365.24 days in a year, just shy of 377. There are 12.37 lunar cycles in a year, just shy of 13. The ratios between these actual numbers and Fibonacci numbers are .9688 and .9515. When the Earth's orbit and rotation were faster, these numbers would have been concurrently quite close to actual Fibonacci numbers. (Might the solar system have begun its periodicities at those frequencies?) Music of the spheres, indeed.

There are also 52.18 weeks in a year, just shy of 55. Weeks may not be natural time units, but the fact that there are four weeks in a month forces weeks into a near-Fibonacci relationship with months because Fibonacci numbers x 4.236 yield other Fibonacci numbers. Any duration of a Fibonacci number of months will be close to a Fibonacci number of weeks as well. For example, 13 months = 56 (55 + 1) weeks. There is no reason to believe that man-made time constructs such as minutes and centuries should follow Fibonacci time sequences, but we have not investigated such durations.

We have noted that the longer the duration of a wave sequence, the further it tends to deviate from a Fibonacci number of time units. The range of deviation itself appears to create a Fibonacci progression as the durations increase. Here are the typical time durations of wave sequences in natural units of time (days, weeks, months, years), along with their ranges of deviation:

$$
\begin{array}{rl}
5 & + \text{ or } - 0 \\
8 & + \text{ or } - 0 \\
13 & + \text{ or } - 0 \\
21 & + \text{ or } - 1 \\
34 & + \text{ or } - 1 \\
55 & + \text{ or } - 2 \\
89 & + \text{ or } - 2 \\
144 & + \text{ or } - 3 \\
233 & + \text{ or } - 3
\end{array}
$$

In applying Fibonacci time periods to the pattern of the market, Bolton noted that time "permutations tend to become infinite" and that time "periods will produce tops to bottoms, tops to tops, bottoms to bottoms or bottoms to tops." Despite this reservation, he successfully indicated within the same book, which was published in 1960, that 1962 or 1963, based on the Fibonacci sequence, could produce an important turning point. 1962, as we now know, saw a vicious bear market and the low of Primary wave ④, which preceded a virtually uninterrupted advance lasting nearly four years.

In addition to this type of time sequence analysis, the time relationship between bull and bear as discovered by Robert Rhea has proved useful in forecasting. Robert Prechter, in writing for Merrill Lynch, noted in March 1978 that "April 17 marks the day on which the A-B-C decline would consume 1931 market hours, or .618 times the 3124 market hours in the advance of waves (1), (2) and (3)." Friday, April 14 marked the upside breakout from the lethargic inverse head and shoulders pattern on the Dow, and Monday, April 17 was the explosive day of record volume, 63.5 million shares (see Figure 1-18). While this time projection did not coincide with the low, it did mark the exact day when the psychological pressure of the preceding bear was lifted from the market.

Benner's Theory

Samuel T. Benner was an ironworks manufacturer until the post Civil War panic of 1873 ruined him financially. He turned to wheat farming in Ohio and took up the statistical study of price movements as a hobby to find, if possible, the answer to the recurring ups and downs in business. In 1875, Benner wrote a book entitled *Business Prophecies of the Future Ups and Downs in Prices*. The forecasts contained in his book are based mainly on cycles in pig iron prices and the recurrence of financial panics. Benner's forecasts proved remarkably accurate for many years, and he established an enviable record for himself as a statistician and forecaster. Even today, Benner's charts are of interest to students of cycles and are occasionally seen in print, sometimes without due credit to the originator.

Benner noted that the highs of business tend to follow a repeating 8-9-10 yearly pattern. If we apply this pattern to high points in the Dow Jones Industrial Average over the past seventy-five years starting with 1902, we get the following results. These dates are not projections based on Benner's forecasts from earlier years, but are only an application of the 8-9-10 repeating pattern applied in retrospect.

Year	Interval	Market Highs
1902		April 24, 1902
1910	8	January 2, 1910
1919	9	November 3, 1919
1929	10	September 3, 1929
1937	8	March 10, 1937
1946	9	May 29, 1946
1956	10	April 6, 1956
1964	8	February 4, 1965
1973	9	January 11, 1973

With respect to economic low points, Benner noted two series of time sequences indicating that recessions (bad times) and depressions (panics) tend to alternate (not surprising, given Elliott's rule of alternation). In commenting on panics, Benner observed that 1819, 1837, 1857 and 1873 were panic years and showed them in his original "panic" chart to reflect a repeating 16-18-20 pattern, resulting in an irregular periodicity of these recurring events. Although he applied a 20-18-16 series to recessions, or "bad times," less serious stock market lows seem rather to follow the same 16-18-20 pattern as do major panic lows. By applying the 16-18-20 series to the alternating stock market lows, we get an accurate fit, as the Benner-Fibonacci Cycle Chart (Figure 4-18), first published in the 1967 supplement to the *Bank Credit Analyst*, graphically illustrates.

The Benner-Fibonacci Cycle Chart 1902-1987

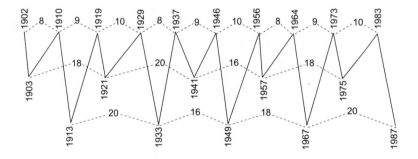

PEAKS:8-9-10, repeat. TROUGHS: 16-18-20, repeat. MAJOR TROUGHS: 16-18-20, repeat.

Figure 4-18

Note that the last time the cycle configuration was the same as the present was the period of the 1920s, paralleling both the Kondratieff picture, which we discuss in Chapter 7, and the last occurrence of a fifth Elliott wave of Cycle degree.

This formula, based upon Benner's idea of repeating time series for tops and bottoms, has fit most of this century's stock market turning points. Whether the pattern will always reflect future highs is another question. These are fixed cycles, after all, not Elliott. Nevertheless, in our search for the reason for its fit with reality, we find that Benner's theory conforms reasonably closely to the Fibonacci sequence in that the repeating series of 8-9-10 produces Fibonacci numbers up to the number 377, allowing for a marginal difference of one point, as shown below.

8-9-10 Series		Selected Subtotals	Fibonacci Numbers	Differences
8	=	8	8	0
+ 9				
+10				
+ 8	=	35	34	+1
+ 9				
+10	=	54	55	-1
...+ 8	=	89	89	0
...+ 8	=	143	144	-1
...+ 9	=	233	233	0
...+10	=	378	377	+1

Our conclusion is that Benner's theory, which is based on different rotating time periods for bottoms and tops rather than constant repetitive periodicities, falls within the framework of the Fibonacci sequence. Had we no experience with the approach, we might not have mentioned it, but it has proved useful in the past when applied in conjunction with a knowledge of Elliott wave progression. A.J. Frost applied Benner's concept in late 1964 to make the inconceivable (at the time) prediction that stock prices were doomed to move essentially sideways for the next ten years, reaching a high in 1973 at about 1000 DJIA and a low in the 500 to 600 zone in late 1974 or early 1975. A letter sent by Frost to Hamilton Bolton at the time is reproduced on the following page. Figure 4-19 is a reproduction of the accompanying chart, complete with notes. As the letter was dated December 10, 1964, it represents yet another long term Elliott prediction that turned out to be more fact than fancy.

December 10, 1964

Mr. A. H. Bolton
Bolton, Tremblay, & Co.
1245 Sherbrooke Street West
Montreal 25, Quebec

Dear Hammy:

Now that we are well along in the current period of economic expansion and gradually becoming vulnerable to changes in investment sentiment, it seems prudent to polish the crystal ball and do a little hard assessing. In appraising trends, I have every confidence in your bank credit approach except when the atmosphere becomes rarefied. I cannot forget 1962. My feeling is that all fundamental tools are for the most part low pressure instruments. Elliott, on the other hand, although difficult in its practical application, does have special merit in high areas. For this reason, I have kept my eye cocked on the Wave Principle and what I see now causes me some concern. As I read Elliott, the stock market is vulnerable and the end of the major cycle from 1942 is upon us.

...I shall present my case to the effect that we are on dangerous ground and that a prudent investment policy (if one can use a dignified word to express undignified action) would be to fly to the nearest broker's office and throw everything to the winds.

The third wave of the long rise from 1942, namely June 1949 to January 1960, represents an extension of primary cycles ...then the entire cycle from 1942 may have reached its orthodox culmination point and what lies ahead of us now is probably a double top and a long flat of Cycle dimension.

...applying Elliott's theory of alternation, the next three primary moves should form a flat of considerable duration. It will be interesting to see if this develops. In the meantime, I don't mind going out on the proverbial limb and making a 10-year projection as an Elliott theorist using only Elliott and Benner ideas. No self-respecting analyst other than an Elliott man would do such a thing, but then that is the sort of thing this unique theory inspires.

Best to you,

A. J. Frost

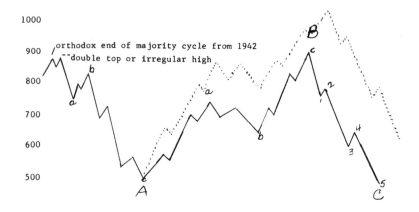

FLAT OF CYCLE DIMENSION

1965. '66. '67. '68. '69. '70. '71. '72. '73. '74. '75

DJIA

NOTES:

a) Elliott's theory of alternation calls for a FLAT of major or cycle dimension comprised of the next three primaries. The last major bear market 1929-42 appears to be on an upward zig-zag.

b) Massive monetary stimulation would likely give the above pattern an upward and forward tilt as indicated by dotted line

c) Wave 3 extension from June 1949 to January 1960 (post war bull market) of cycle wave from 1942 should not be violated to any great extent. The downward limit therefore should not be too far off 500.

d) Benner's rules of fixed periodicity have been applied to primary tops and bottoms - marked A, B & C.

Figure 4-19

Although we have been able to codify ratio analysis substantially as described in the first half of this chapter, there appear to be many ways that the Fibonacci ratio is manifest in the stock market. The approaches suggested here are merely carrots to whet the appetite of prospective analysts and set them on the right track. Parts of the following chapters further explore the use of ratio analysis and give perspective on its complexity, accuracy and applicability. Obviously, the key is there. All that remains is to discover how many doors it will unlock.

CHAPTER 5

LONG TERM WAVES AND AN UP-TO-DATE COMPOSITE

In September 1977, *Forbes* published an interesting article on the complexity theory of inflation entitled "The Great Hamburger Paradox," in which the writer, David Warsh, asks, "What really goes into the price of a hamburger? Why do prices explode for a century or more and then level off?" He quotes Professor E.H. Phelps Brown and Sheila V. Hopkins of Oxford University as saying,

> For a century or more, it seems, prices will obey one all-powerful law; it changes and a new law prevails. A war that would have cast the trend up to new heights in one dispensation is powerless to deflect it in another. Do we yet know what are the factors that set this stamp on an age, and why, after they have held on so long through such shakings, they give way quickly and completely to others?

Brown and Hopkins state that prices seem to "obey one all-powerful law," which is exactly what R. N. Elliott said. This all-powerful law is the harmonious relationship found in the Golden Ratio, which is basic to nature's laws and forms part of the fabric of man's physical, mental and emotional structure as well. As Mr. Warsh additionally observes quite accurately, human progress seems to move in sudden jerks and jolts, not as in the smooth clockwork operation of Newtonian physics. We agree with Mr. Warsh's conclusion but further posit that these shocks are not of only one noticeable degree of metamorphosis or age, but occur at *all* degrees along the logarithmic spiral of man's progress, from Minuette degree and smaller to Grand Supercycle degree and greater. To introduce another expansion on the idea, we suggest that *these shocks themselves are part of the clockwork*. A watch may appear to run smoothly, but its progress is controlled by the spasmodic jerks of a timing mechanism, whether mechanical or quartz crystal. Quite likely the logarithmic spiral of man's progress is propelled in a similar manner, though with the jolts tied not to time periodicity, but to repetitive form.

If you say "nuts" to this thesis, please consider that we are probably not talking about an exogenous force, but an endogenous one. Any rejection of the Wave Principle on the grounds that it is deterministic leaves unanswered the how and why of the social patterns we demonstrate in this book. All we want to propose is that there is a natural psychodynamic in men that generates form in social behavior, as revealed by market behavior. Most important, understand that the form we describe is primarily *social,* not individual. Individuals have free will and indeed can learn to recognize these typical patterns of social behavior, then use that knowledge to their advantage. It is not easy to act and think contrarily to the crowd and to your own natural tendencies, but with discipline and the aid of experience, you can certainly train yourself to do so once you establish that initial crucial insight into the true essence of market behavior. Needless to say, it is quite the opposite of what people have believed it to be, whether they have been influenced by the cavalier assumptions of event causality made by fundamentalists, the mechanical models posited by economists, the "random walk" offered by academics, or the vision of market manipulation by "Gnomes of Zurich" (sometimes identified only as "they") proposed by conspiracy theorists.

We suppose the average investor has little interest in what may happen to his investments when he is dead or what the investment environment of his great-great-great-great grandfather was. It is difficult enough to cope with current conditions in the daily battle for investment survival without concerning ourselves with the distant future or the long buried past. However, we should take the time to assess long term waves, first because the developments of the past serve greatly to determine the future, and secondly because it can be illustrated that the same law that applies to the long term applies to the short term and produces the same patterns of stock market behavior.

In other words, the stock market's patterns are the same at all degrees. The patterns of movement that show up in small waves, using hourly plots, show up in large waves, using yearly plots. For example, Figures 5-1 and 5-2 show two charts, one reflecting the hourly fluctuations in the Dow over a ten-day period

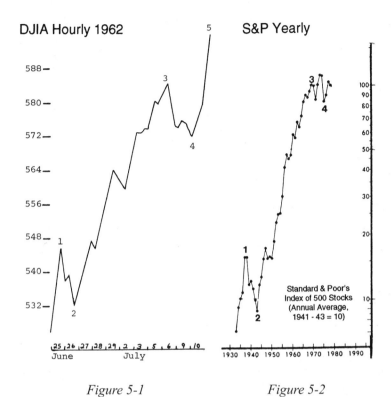

Figure 5-1   *Figure 5-2*

from June 25th to July 10th, 1962 and the other a yearly plot of the S&P 500 Index from 1932 to 1978 (courtesy of *The Media General Financial Weekly*). Both plots indicate similar patterns of movement despite a difference in the time span of over 1500 to 1. The long term formulation is still unfolding, as wave V from the 1974 low has not run its full course, but to date the pattern is along lines parallel to the hourly chart. At each degree, the form is constant.

In this chapter we shall outline the current position of the progression of "jerks and jolts" from what we call the Millennium degree to today's Cycle degree bull market. Moreover, as we shall see, because of the position of the current Millennium wave and the pyramiding of "fives" in our final composite wave picture, this decade could prove to be one of the most exciting times in world history to be writing about and studying the Elliott Wave Principle.

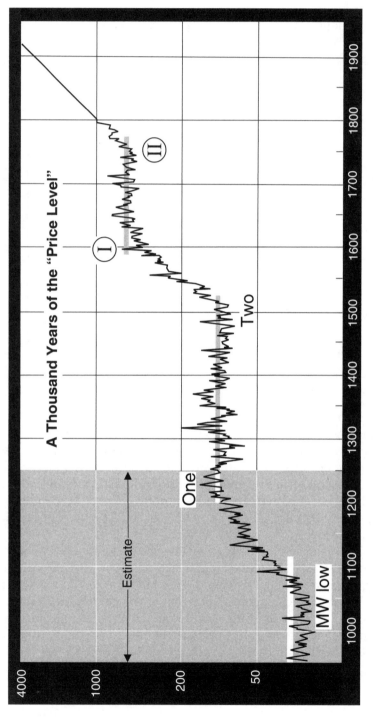

Figure 5-3

1. The Millennium Wave from the Dark Ages

Data for researching price trends over the last two hundred years is not especially difficult to attain, but we have to rely on less exact statistics for perspective on earlier trends and conditions. The long term price index compiled by Professor E. H. Phelps Brown and Sheila V. Hopkins and further enlarged by David Warsh is based on a simple "market basket of human needs" for the period from 950 A.D. to 1954.

By splicing the price curves of Brown and Hopkins onto industrial stock prices from 1789, we get a long-term picture of prices for the last one thousand years. Figure 5-3 shows approximate general price swings from the Dark Ages to 1789. For the fifth wave from 1789, we have overlaid a straight line to represent stock price swings in particular, which we will analyze further in the next section. Strangely enough, this diagram, while only a very rough indication of price trends, suggests a five-wave Elliott pattern.

Paralleling the broad price movements of history are the great periods of commercial and industrial expansion over the centuries. Rome, whose great culture at one time may have coincided with the peak of the previous Millennium wave, finally fell in 476 A.D. For five hundred years afterward, during the ensuing Millennium degree bear market, the search for knowledge became almost extinct. The Commercial Revolution (950-1350) eventually sparked the first new Grand Supercycle wave of expansion. The leveling of prices from 1350 to 1520 represents a "correction" of the progress during the Commercial Revolution.

The next period of rising prices, coincided with both the Capitalist Revolution (1520-1640) and with the greatest period in English history, the Elizabethan period. Elizabeth I (1533-1603) came to the throne of England just after an exhausting war with France. The country was poor and in despair, but before Elizabeth died, England had defied all the powers of Europe, expanded her empire, and become the most prosperous nation in the world. This was the age of Shake-speare, Martin Luther, Drake and Raleigh, truly a glorious epoch in world history. Business expanded and prices rose during this period of creative brilliance and luxury. By 1650, prices had reached a peak, leveling off to form a century-long Grand Supercycle correction.

The next Grand Supercycle advance within this Millennium wave appears to have begun for commodity prices around 1760 rather than our presumed time period for the stock market around 1770 to 1790, which we have labeled "1789" where the stock market data begins. However, as a study by Gertrude Shirk in the April/May 1977 issue of *Cycles* magazine points out, trends in commodity prices have tended to precede similar trends in stock prices generally by about a decade. Viewed in light of this knowledge, the two measurements actually fit together extremely well. This Grand Supercycle wave coincides with the burst in productivity generated by the Industrial Revolution and parallels the rise of the United States of America as a world power.

Elliott logic suggests that the Grand Supercycle from 1789 to date must both follow and precede other waves in the ongoing Elliott pattern, with typical relationships in time and amplitude. If this be true, then the 1000-year Millennium wave, unless it is extending, has almost run its full course and stands to be corrected by three Grand Supercycles (two down and one up), which could extend over the next five hundred years. It is difficult to think of a low-growth situation in world economies lasting for such a long period. This broad hint of long term trouble does not preclude that technology will mitigate the severity of what might be presumed to develop socially. The Elliott Wave Principle is a law of probability and degree, not a predictor of exact conditions. Nevertheless, the end of the current Supercycle (V) should lead to some form of economic or social shock ushering in another era of decline and despair. After all, if it was the Barbarians who finally toppled a rotting Rome, can it be said that the modern day barbarians do not have adequate means and a similar purpose?

2. The Grand Supercycle Wave from 1789 to Present

This long wave has the right look of three waves in the direction of the main trend and two against the trend for a total of five, complete with an extended third wave corresponding with the most dynamic and progressive period of U.S. history. In Figure 5-4, the Supercycle subdivisions have been marked (I), (II), (III) and (IV), with wave (V) currently in progress.

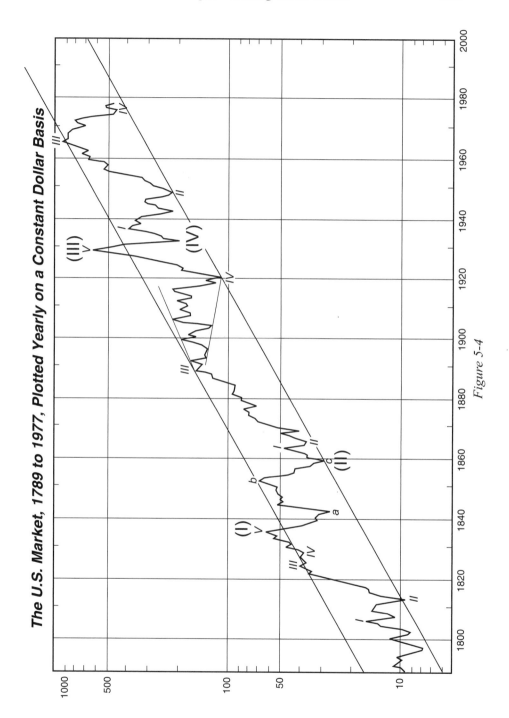

The U.S. Market, 1789 to 1977, Plotted Yearly on a Constant Dollar Basis

Figure 5-4

Considering that we are exploring market history back to the days of canal companies, horse-drawn barges and meager statistics, it is surprising that the record of "constant dollar" industrial share prices, which was developed by Gertrude Shirk for *Cycles* magazine, forms such a clear Elliott pattern. Especially striking is the trend channel, the baseline of which connects several important Cycle and Supercycle wave lows and the upper parallel of which connects the peaks of several advancing waves. A market high in 1983 would touch the upper parallel reasonably within our target area of 2500-3000, assuming no radical net change in the wholesale price index.

Wave (I) is a fairly clear "five," assuming 1789 to be the beginning of the Supercycle. Wave (II) is a flat, which neatly predicts a zigzag or triangle* for wave (IV), by rule of alternation. Wave (III) is extended and can easily be subdivided into the necessary five subwaves, including an expanding triangle characteristically in the fourth wave position. Wave (IV), from 1929 to 1932, terminates within the area of the fourth wave of lesser degree.

An inspection of wave (IV) in Figure 5-5 illustrates in greater detail the zigzag of Supercycle dimension that marked the most devastating market collapse in U.S. history. In wave a of the decline, daily charts show that the third subwave, in characteristic fashion, included the Wall Street crash of October 29, 1929. Wave a was then retraced approximately 50% by wave b, the "famous upward correction of 1930," as Richard Russell terms it, during which even Robert Rhea was led by the emotional nature of the rally to cover his short positions. Wave c finally bottomed at 41.22, a drop of 253 points or about 1.382 times the length of wave a. It completed an 89 (a Fibonacci number) percent drop in stock prices in 3 (another Fibonacci number) years.

It should be mentioned again that Elliott always interpreted 1928 as the orthodox top of wave (III), with the 1929 peak marking an irregular top. We find several faults with this contention, as does Charles Collins, who agrees with us that 1929 probably marked the orthodox high. First, the decline from 1929 to 1932

---

*Figure 5-4 shows wave (IV) as a zigzag. While it was a zigzag in actual prices, it was a triangle in inflation-adjusted prices, as recognized a year later (see Appendix).

is a fine specimen of a 5-3-5 zigzag decline. Next, for wave (III) to have topped in 1928, wave (IV) would have to assume a shape that is not consistent with the "right look" for a 3-3-5 expanded flat correction. Under that interpretation, wave c is way out of proportion to the smaller a and b waves and terminates an uncomfortably great distance below the low of wave a. Another problem is the power of the supposed b wave, which remains well within the uptrend channel and terminates through the upper trendline, as a fifth wave often does. Ratio analysis of wave (IV) supports both Elliott's contention of an irregular top and our thesis of an orthodox top, since wave c under Elliott's analysis is 2.618 times as long as the net decline of wave a from November 1928 to November 1929, and under our analysis wave c is 1.382 (.382 is the inverse of 2.618) times as long as wave a from September 1929 to November 1929.

Wave (V) of this Grand Supercycle is still in progress, but has so far conformed beautifully to the expectation that since wave (III) was an extension, wave (V) should be approximately equal to wave (I) in terms of time and percentage magnitude. Wave (I) took about fifty years to complete, as should wave (V) if it ends when we expect. Its height on the constant dollar chart is about equal to the height of wave (V), expressing equality in terms of percentage advance. Even their "looks" are not dissimilar. Wave (V) of the Grand Supercycle is further analyzed below.

3. The Supercycle Wave from 1932

Supercycle wave (V) has been in progress since 1932 and is still unfolding (see Figure 5-5). If there were such a thing as a perfect wave formation under the Wave Principle, this long term sequence of Elliott waves would be a prime candidate. The breakdown of Cycle waves is as follows:

Wave I: 1932 to 1937 — This wave is a clear cut five-wave sequence according to the rules established by Elliott. It retraces .618 of the market decline from the 1928 and 1930 highs and, within it, the extended fifth wave travels 1.618 times the distance of the first through third waves.

Wave II: 1937 to 1942 — Within wave II, subwave Ⓐ is a five, and wave Ⓒ is a five, so the entire formation is a zigzag. Most of the price damage occurs in wave Ⓐ. Thus, there is great strength in the structure of the entire corrective wave, much

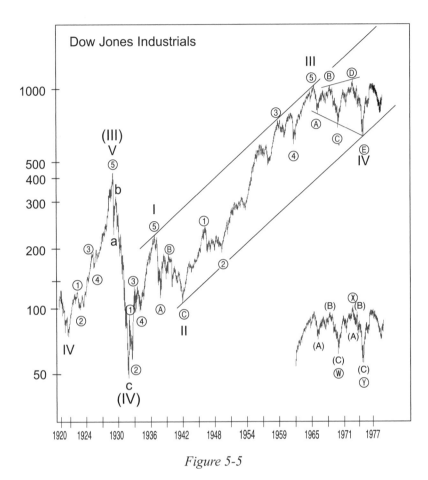

Figure 5-5

beyond what we would normally expect, as wave Ⓒ travels only slightly into new low ground for the correction. Most of the damage of wave Ⓒ was due to erosion, as continued deflation pushed price/earnings levels to below those even of 1932.

Wave III: 1942 to 1965(6) — This wave is an extension, by which the Dow rose nearly 1000% in twenty-four years. Its principal features are as follows:

1) Wave ④ is a flat, alternating with a zigzag, wave ②.

2) Wave ③ is the longest Primary wave and an extension.

3) Wave ④ corrects to near the top of the preceding fourth wave of one lesser degree and holds well above the peak of wave ①.

4) The length of subwaves ① and ⑤ are related by the Fibonacci ratio in terms of percentage advance (129% and 80% respectively, where 80 = 129 x .618), as is often the case between two non-extended waves.

Wave IV: 1965(6) to 1974 — In Figure 5-5, wave IV bottoms in the area of wave ④, as is normal, and holds well above the peak of wave I. We show two possible interpretations: a five-wave expanding triangle from February 1965 and a double three from January 1966. Both counts are admissible, although the triangle interpretation might suggest a lower objective, where wave V would trace an advance approximately as long as the widest part of the triangle. No other Elliott evidence, however, suggests that such a weak wave is in the making. Some Elliott theorists attempt to count the last decline from January 1973 to December 1974 as a five, thus labeling Cycle wave IV a large flat. Our technical objections to a five-wave count are that the supposed third subwave is too short, and the first wave is then overlapped by the fourth, thereby offending two of Elliott's basic rules. It is clearly an A-B-C decline.

Wave V: 1974 to ? — This wave of Cycle degree is still unfolding. It is likely that two Primary waves have been completed at this juncture and that the market is in the process of tracing out the third Primary, which should accompany a break-out to new all time highs. The last chapter will cover in somewhat more detail our analysis and expectations with respect to the current market.

Thus, as we read Elliott, the current bull market in stocks is the fifth wave from 1932 of the fifth wave from 1789 of possibly even the fifth wave from the Dark Ages. Figure 5-6 gives the composite picture and speaks for itself.*

The history of the West from the Dark Ages appears in retrospect to have been an almost uninterrupted period of human progress, which, as we have proposed, might be termed a wave of Millennium degree. The cultural rise of Europe and North

---

At the Crest of the Tidal Wave (1995) presents a variation of this picture involving a developing extension from the Dark Ages. It therefore moderates somewhat the vision presented here, concluding that the coming setback is more likely to be "only" of Grand Supercycle degree rather than of Millennium degree.

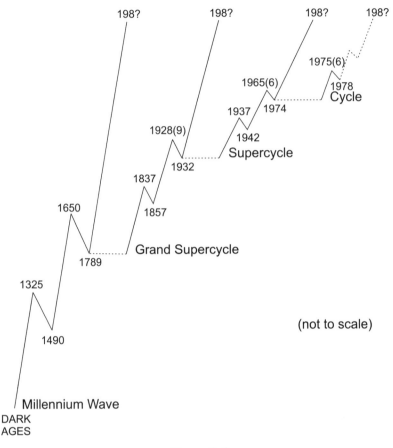

Figure 5-6

America, and before that the rise of the Greek city-states and the expansion of the Roman Empire, and before that the thousand-year wave of social progress in Egypt, might be termed waves of Cultural degree, each of which was separated by Cultural degree waves of stagnation and regress, each lasting centuries. One might argue that even these five waves, constituting the entirety of recorded history to date, may constitute a developing wave of Epochal degree, and that some period of social catastrophe centuries hence (involving nuclear or biological war, perhaps?) will ultimately ensure the occurrence of the largest human social regress in five thousand years.

Of course, the theory of the spiraling Wave Principle suggests that there exist waves of larger degree than Epochal. The ages in the development of the species *Homo sapiens* might be waves of even higher degree. Perhaps Homo sapiens himself is one stage in the development of hominids, which in turn are one stage in the development of even larger waves in the progress of life on Earth. After all, if the existence of the planet Earth is conceived to have lasted one year so far, life forms emerged from the oceans five weeks ago, while manlike creatures have walked the Earth for only the last six hours of the year, less than one one-hundredth of the total period during which forms of life have existed. On this basis, Rome dominated the Western world for a total of five seconds. Viewed from this perspective, a Grand Supercycle degree wave is not really of such large degree after all.

CHAPTER 6

STOCKS AND COMMODITIES

Individual Stocks

The art of managing investments is the art of acquiring and disposing of stocks and other securities so as to maximize gains. When to make a move in the investment field is more important than what issue to choose. Stock selection is not unimportant, but it is of secondary importance compared to timing. To be a winner in the stock market, either as a trader or as an investor, one must know the direction of the primary trend and proceed to invest with it, not against it. Fundamentals alone are seldom a proper justification for investing in stocks. U.S. Steel in 1929 was selling at $260 a share and was considered a sound investment for widows and orphans. The dividend was $8.00 a share. The Wall Street crash reduced the price to $22 a share, and the company did not pay a dividend for four years. The stock market is usually a bull or a bear, seldom a cow.

As a mass psychological phenomenon, the market averages unfold in Elliott wave patterns regardless of the price movements of individual stocks. As we shall illustrate, while the Wave Principle has some application to individual stocks, the count for many issues is often too fuzzy to be of great practical value. In other words, Elliott will tell you if the track is fast but not which horse is going to win. With regard to individual stocks, other types of analysis are probably more rewarding than trying to force the stock's price action into an Elliott count that may or may not exist.

There is reason to this. The Wave Principle broadly allows for individual attitudes and circumstances to affect price patterns of any single issue and, to a lesser degree, a narrow group of stocks, simply because what the Elliott Wave Principle reflects is only that part of each man's decision process which is shared by the mass of investors. In the larger reflection of wave form, then, the unique circumstances of individual investors and individual companies cancel each other out, leaving as residue a mirror of the mass mind alone. In other words, the form of the Wave Principle reflects the progress not necessarily of each man or company but certainly of mankind as a whole and his enterprise. Companies come and go. Trends, fads, cultures, needs and desires ebb and flow with the human condition. Therefore, the progress of *general* business activity is well reflected by the Wave Principle, while each *individual* area of activity has its own essence, its own life expectancy, and a set of forces that may relate to it alone. Thus, each company, like each man, appears on the scene as part of the whole, plays its part, and eventually returns to the dust from which it came.

If, through a microscope, we were to observe a tiny droplet of water, its individuality might be quite evident in terms of size, color, shape, density, salinity, bacteria count, etc., but when that droplet is part of a wave in the ocean, it becomes swept along with the force of the waves and the tides, despite its individuality. With over twenty million "droplets" owning stocks listed on the New York Stock Exchange, is it any wonder that the market averages are one of the greatest manifestations of mass psychology in the world?

Despite this important distinction, many stocks tend to move more or less in harmony with the general market. It has been shown that on average, seventy-five percent of all stocks move up with the market, and ninety percent of all stocks move down with the market, although price movements of individual stocks are usually more erratic than those of the averages. Closed-end stocks of investment companies and stocks of large cyclical corporations, for obvious reasons, tend to conform to the patterns of the averages more closely than most other stocks. Emerging growth stocks, however, tend to create the clearest individual Elliott wave patterns because of the strong investor emotion that accompanies their progress. The best approach seems to be to avoid trying to analyze each issue on an Elliott basis unless a clear, unmistakable wave pattern unfolds before your eyes and commands attention. Decisive action is best taken only then, but it should be taken, regardless of the wave count for the market as a whole. Ignoring such a pattern is always more dangerous than paying the insurance premium.

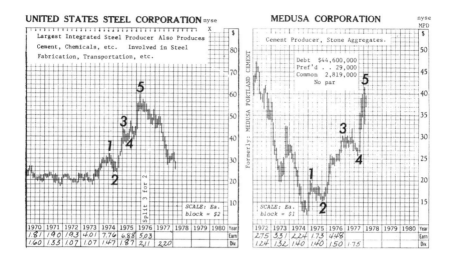

Figure 6-1

Figure 6-2

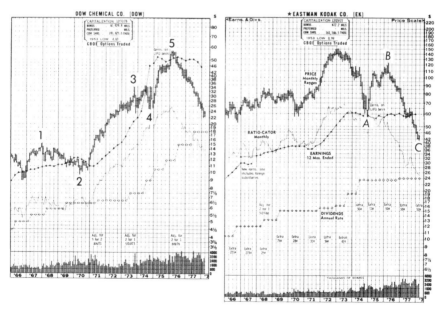

Figure 6-3

Figure 6-4

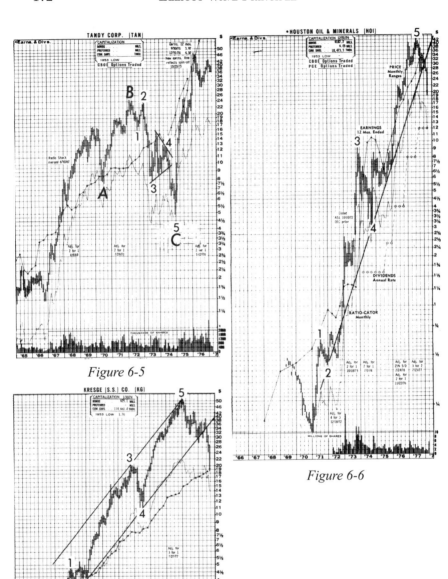

Figure 6-5

Figure 6-6

Figure 6-7

Despite the above detailed caveat, there are numerous examples of times when individual stocks reflect the Wave Principle. The seven individual stocks shown in Figures 6-1 through 6-7 show Elliott wave patterns representing three types of situations. The bull markets for U.S. Steel, Dow Chemical and Medusa show five-wave advances from their major bear market lows. Eastman Kodak and Tandy show A-B-C bear markets into 1978. The charts of Kmart (formerly Kresge) and Houston Oil and Minerals illustrate long term "growth" type advances that trace out Elliott patterns and break their long term supporting channel lines only after completing satisfactory wave counts.

Commodities

Commodities have as much individual character as stocks. One difference between the behavior of commodities and stock market averages is that in commodities, primary bull and bear markets at times overlap each other. Sometimes, for instance, a complete five-wave bull market will fail to take a commodity to a new all-time high, as the chart of soybean futures illustrates in Figure 6-9. Therefore, while beautiful charts of Supercycle degree waves do exist for a number of commodities, it seems that the peak observable degree in some cases is the Primary or Cycle degree. Beyond this degree, the Principle gets bent here and there.

Also in contrast to the stock market, commodities most commonly develop extensions in *fifth* waves within Primary or Cycle degree bull markets. This tendency is entirely consistent with the Wave Principle, which reflects the reality of human emotions. Fifth wave advances in the stock market are propelled by *hope*, while fifth wave advances in commodities are propelled by a comparatively dramatic emotion, *fear*: fear of inflation, fear of drought, fear of war. Hope and fear look different on a chart, which is one of the reasons that commodity market *tops* often look like stock market *bottoms*. Commodity bull market extensions, moreover, often appear following a *triangle* in the fourth wave position. Thus, while post-triangle thrusts in the stock market are often "swift and short," triangles in commodity bull markets of large degree often precede extended blowoffs. One example is shown in the chart of silver in Figure 1-44.

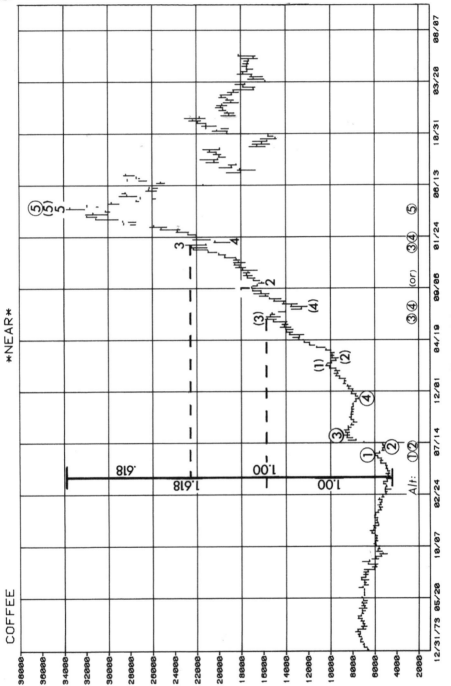

Figure 6-8

The best Elliott patterns are born from important long term breakouts from extended sideways base patterns, as occurred in coffee, soybeans, sugar, gold and silver at different times in the 1970s. Unfortunately, semilogarithmic chart scale, which may have indicated applicability of Elliott trend channels, was not available for this study.

Figure 6-8 shows the two-year price explosion in coffee from mid-1975 to mid-1977. The pattern is unmistakably "Elliott," even down to Minor degree. The ratio analyses employed beautifully project the peak price level. In these computations, the length of the rise to the peak of wave (3) and to the peak of wave 3 *each* divide the bull market into the Golden Section at equivalent distances. As you can see by the equally acceptable counts listed at the bottom of the chart, each of those peaks can also be labeled as the top of wave ③, fulfilling typical ratio analysis guidelines. After the pattern reached the peak of the fifth wave, a devastating bear market struck apparently from out of the blue.

Figure 6-9 displays five and a half years of price history for soybeans. The explosive rise in 1972-73 emerged from a long base, as did the explosion in coffee prices. The target area was met here as well, in that the length of the rise to the peak of wave 3, multiplied by 1.618, gives almost exactly the distance from the end of wave 3 to the peak of wave 5. In the ensuing A-B-C bear market, a perfect Elliott zigzag unfolded, bottoming in January 1976. Wave B of this correction is just shy of .618 times the length of wave A. A new bull market took place in 1976-77, although of subnormal extent since the peak of wave 5 falls just short of the minimum target of $10.90. In this case, the gain to the peak of wave 3 ($3.20) times 1.618 gives $5.20, which when added to the low within wave 4 at $5.70 gives the $10.90 target. In each of these bull markets, the initial measuring unit is the same, the length of the advance from its beginning to the peak of wave three. That distance is then .618 times the length of wave 5 measured from the peak of wave 3, the low of wave 4, or in between. In other words, in each case, some point within wave 4 divides the entire rise into the Golden Section, as described in Chapter 4.

Figure 6-10 is a weekly high-low chart of Chicago wheat futures. During the four years after the peak at $6.45, prices traced out an Elliott A-B-C bear market with excellent internal

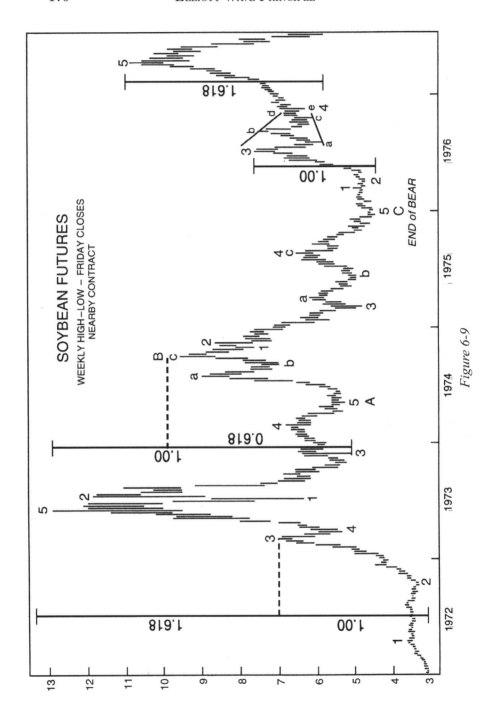

Figure 6-9

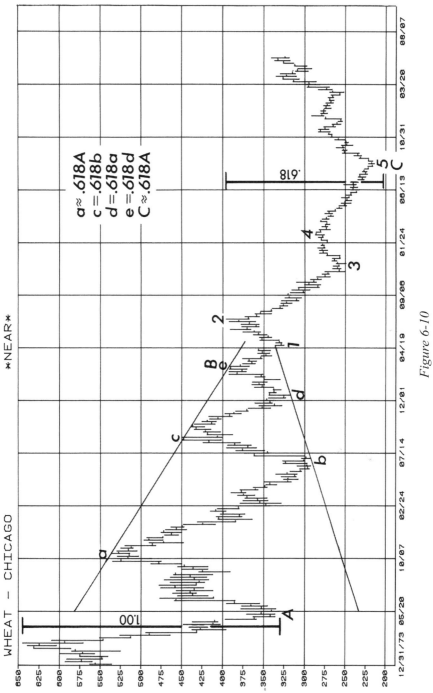

Figure 6-10

interrelationships. Wave B is a contracting triangle exactly like those discussed in Chapters 2 and 3. The five touch points conform perfectly to the boundaries of the trendlines. Though in an unusual manner, the triangle's subwaves develop as a reflection of the Golden Spiral, with each leg related to another by the Fibonacci ratio (c = .618b; d = .618a; e = .618d). A typical "false breakout" occurs near the end of the progression, although this time it is accomplished not by wave e, but by wave 2 of C. In addition, the wave A decline is approximately 1.618 times the length of wave a of B, and of wave C.

Thus, we can demonstrate that commodities have properties that reflect the universal order that Elliott discovered. It seems reasonable to expect, though, that the more individual the personality of a commodity, which is to say, the less it is a necessary part of human existence, the less it will reliably reflect an Elliott pattern. One commodity that is unalterably tied to the psyche of mass humanity is *gold*.

Gold

Gold in the recent past has often moved "contra-cyclically" to the stock market. A reversal in the price of gold to the upside after a downtrend often occurs concurrently with a turn for the worse in stocks, and vice versa. Therefore, an Elliott reading of the gold price has upon occasion provided confirming evidence for an expected turn in the Dow.

In April 1972, the U.S. government raised its long-standing fixed price for gold from $35 an ounce to $38 an ounce, and in February 1973 increased it again to $42.22. This "official" price used by central banks for currency convertibility purposes and the rising trend in the unofficial price in the early seventies led to what was called the "two-tier" system. In November 1973, the official price and the two-tier system were abolished by the inevitable workings of supply and demand in the free market.

The free-market price of gold rose from $35 per ounce in January 1970, reaching a closing "London fix" peak of $197 an ounce on December 30, 1974. The price then started to slide, and on August 31, 1976 reached a low of $103.50. The fundamental "reasons" given for this decline were U.S.S.R. gold sales, U.S. Treasury gold sales and I.M.F. auctions. Since then, the price of gold has recovered substantially and is trending upward again.

Despite the efforts of the U.S. Treasury to diminish gold's monetary role and the highly charged emotional factors affecting gold as a store of value and a medium of exchange, its price has traced out an inescapably clear Elliott pattern. Figure 6-11 is a graph of London gold, and on it we have indicated the correct wave labels. Note that the rise from the free-market liftoff to the peak at $179.50 an ounce on April 3rd, 1974 is a complete five-wave sequence. The officially maintained price of $35 an ounce before 1970 prevented wave formation prior to that time and thus helped create the necessary long-term base. The dynamic breakout from that base fits well the criterion for the clearest Elliott count for a commodity, and clear it is.

The rocketing five-wave advance forms a nearly perfect wave, with the fifth terminating well against the upper boundary of the trend channel (not shown). The Fibonacci target projection

Figure 6-11

method typical of commodities is fulfilled in that the $90 rise to the peak of wave ③ provides the basis for measuring the distance to the orthodox top. $90 x .618 = $55.62, which when added to the peak of wave III at $125, gives $180.62. The actual price at wave V's peak was $179.50, quite close indeed. Also noteworthy is that at $179.50, the price of gold had multiplied by just over five (a Fibonacci number) times its price at $35.

Then in December 1974, after the initial wave Ⓐ decline, the price of gold rose to an all-time high of nearly $200 an ounce. This wave was wave Ⓑ of an expanded flat correction, which crawled upward along the lower channel line, as corrective wave advances often do. As befits the personality of a "B" wave, the phoniness of the advance was unmistakable. First, the news background, as *everyone knew*, appeared to be bullish for gold, because legalization of American ownership was due on January 1, 1975. Wave Ⓑ, in a seemingly perverse but market-logical manner, peaked precisely on the last day of 1974. Second, gold mining stocks, both North American and South African, were noticeably underperforming on the advance, forewarning of trouble by refusing to confirm the assumed bullish picture.

Wave Ⓒ, a devastating collapse, accompanied a severe decline in the valuation of gold stocks, carrying some back to where they had begun their advances in 1970. In terms of the bullion price, the authors computed in early 1976 by the usual relationship that the low should occur at about $98, since the length of wave Ⓐ at $51, times 1.618, equals $82, which when subtracted from the orthodox high at $180, gives a target at $98. The low for the correction was well within the zone of the previous fourth wave of lesser degree and quite near the target, hitting a closing London price of $103.50 on August 25, 1976, the month just between the Dow Theory stock market peak in July and the slightly higher DJIA peak in September.

The ensuing advance so far has traced out four complete Elliott waves and entered a fifth, which should push the gold price to new all-time highs. Figure 6-12 gives a near term picture of the first three waves up from the August 1976 bottom, where each advancing wave divides clearly into a five-wave impulse. Each upward wave also conforms to an Elliott trend channel on semilog chart paper. The slope of the rise is not as steep as the initial bull market advance, which was a one-time explosion following years

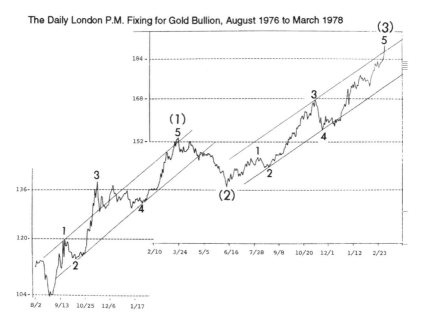

Figure 6-12

of price control. The current rise seems mostly to be reflecting the decline in the value of the dollar since in terms of other currencies, gold is not nearly as close to its all- time high.

Since the price of gold has held the previous fourth wave level on a normal pullback, the count could be a nearly completed five-wave sequence or a developing third wave extension, suggesting coming hyperinflationary conditions under which both the stock market and commodities climb together, although we offer no definite opinions on the subject. However, the Ⓐ-Ⓑ-Ⓒ expanded flat correction implies great thrust in the next wave into new high ground. It should be remembered, though, that commodities can form contained bull markets, ones that need not develop into waves of higher and higher degree. Therefore, one cannot necessarily assume that gold has entered a giant third wave from the low at $35. If the advance forms a distinct five-wave sequence from the low at $103.50 adhering to all Elliott rules, it should be regarded as at least an interim sell signal. Under all cases, the $98 level still should be the maximum extent of any important decline.

Gold, historically speaking, is one of the anchors of economic life, with a sound record of achievement. It has nothing more to offer the world than discipline. Perhaps that is the reason politicians work tirelessly to ignore it, denounce it, and attempt to demonetize it. Somehow, though, governments always seem to manage to have a supply on hand "just in case." Today, gold stands in the wings of international finance as a relic of the old days, but nevertheless also as a harbinger of the future. The disciplined life is the productive life, and that concept applies to all levels of endeavor, from dirt farming to international finance.

Gold is the time-honored store of value, and although the price of gold may flatten for a long period, it is always good insurance to own some until the world's monetary system is intelligently restructured, a development that seems inevitable, whether it happens by design or through natural economic forces. That paper is no substitute for gold as a store of value is probably another of nature's laws.

CHAPTER 7

OTHER APPROACHES TO THE STOCK MARKET & THEIR RELATIONSHIP TO THE WAVE PRINCIPLE

Dow Theory

According to Charles H. Dow, the primary trend of the market is the broad, all-engulfing "tide," which is interrupted by "waves," or secondary reactions and rallies. Movements of smaller size are the "ripples" on the waves. The latter are generally unimportant unless a line (defined as a sideways structure lasting at least three weeks and occurring within a price range of five percent) is formed. The main tools of the theory are the Transportation Average (formerly the Rail Average) and the Industrial Average. The leading exponents of Dow's theory, William Peter Hamilton, Robert Rhea, Richard Russell and E. George Schaefer, rounded out Dow's theory but never altered its basic tenets.

As Charles Dow once observed, stakes can be driven into the sands of the seashore as the waters ebb and flow to mark the direction of the tide in much the same way as charts are used to show how prices are moving. Out of experience came the fundamental Dow Theory tenet that since both averages are part of the same ocean, the tidal action of one average must move in unison with the other to be authentic. Thus, a movement to a new extreme in an established trend by one average alone is a new high or new low that is said to lack "confirmation" by the other average.

The Elliott Wave Principle has points in common with Dow Theory. During advancing impulse waves, the market should be a "healthy" one, with breadth and the other averages confirming the action. When corrective and ending waves are in progress, divergences, or non-confirmations, are likely. Dow's followers also recognized three psychological "phases" of a market advance. Naturally, since both methods describe reality, the Dow Theorists' brief descriptions of these phases conform to the personalities of Elliott's waves 1, 3 and 5 as we outlined them in Chapter 2.

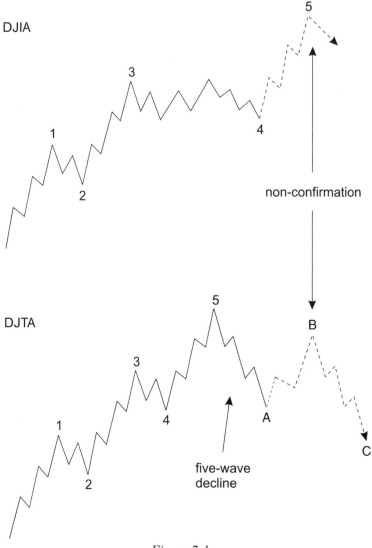

Figure 7-1

The Wave Principle validates much of Dow Theory, but of course Dow Theory does not validate the Wave Principle since Elliott's concept of wave action has a mathematical base, needs only one market average for interpretation, and unfolds according to a specific structure. Both approaches, however, are based on empirical observations and complement each other in theory and practice. Often, for instance, wave counts for the averages will forewarn the Dow Theorist of an upcoming non-confirmation. If, as Figure 7-1 shows, the Industrial Average has completed four waves of a primary swing and part of a fifth, while the Transportation Average is rallying in wave B of a zigzag correction, a non-confirmation is inevitable. In fact, this type of development has helped the authors more than once. As an example, in May 1977, when the Transportation Average was climbing to new highs, the preceding *five*-wave decline in the Industrials during January and February signaled loud and clear that any rally in that index would be doomed to create a non-confirmation.

On the other side of the coin, a Dow Theory non-confirmation can often alert the Elliott analyst to examine his count to see whether or not a reversal should be the expected event. Thus, knowledge of one approach can assist in the application of the other. Since Dow Theory is the grandfather of the Wave Principle, it deserves respect for its historical significance as well as its consistent record of performance over the years.

The "Kondratieff Wave" Economic Cycle

The fifty- to sixty- (averaging fifty-four) year cycle of catastrophe and renewal had been known and observed by the Mayas of Central America and independently by the ancient Israelites. The modern expression of this cycle is the "long wave" of economic and social trends observed in the 1920s by Nikolai Kondratieff, a Russian economist. Kondratieff documented, with the limited data available, that economic cycles of modern capitalist countries tend to repeat a cycle of expansion and contraction lasting a bit over half a century. These cycles correspond in size to Supercycle degree (and occasionally Cycle degree when an extension is involved) waves under the Wave Principle.

Figure 7-2, courtesy of *The Media General Financial Weekly*, shows the idealized concept of Kondratieff cycles from the 1780s to the year 2000 and their relationship to wholesale prices. Notice that within the Grand Supercycle wave shown in Figure 5-4, the beginning of wave (I) to the deep low of wave a of (II) in 1842 roughly tracks one Kondratieff cycle, the extended wave (III) and wave (IV) track most of two Kondratieffs, and our current Supercycle wave (V) will last throughout most of one Kondratieff.

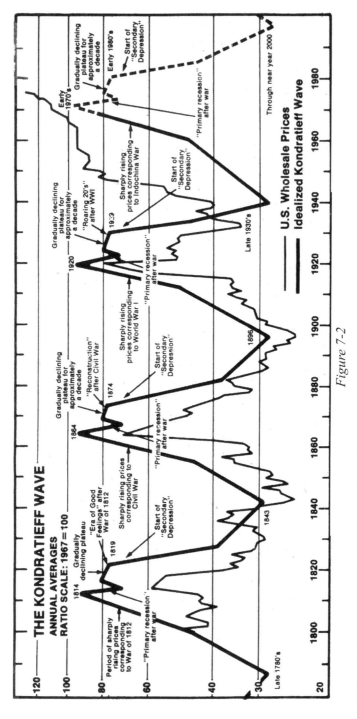

Figure 7-2

* The April 6, 1983 Special Report (see Figure A-8 in the Appendix) recognized that the last contraction ended later than depicted in this standard illustration, in 1949, pushing all forecast dates forward accordingly. See Appendix B of *At The Crest of the Tidal Wave* for an update of this graph.

Kondratieff noted that "trough" wars, i.e., wars near the bottom of the cycle, usually occur at a time when the economy stands to benefit from the price stimulation generated by a war economy, resulting in economic recovery and an advance in prices. "Peak" wars, on the other hand, usually occur when recovery is well advanced and, as the government pays for the war by the usual means of inflating the money supply, prices rise sharply. After the economic peak, a primary recession occurs, which is then followed by a disinflationary "plateau" of about ten years' duration in which relatively stable and prosperous times return. The end of this period is followed by several years of deflation and a severe depression.

The first Kondratieff cycle for the U.S. began at the trough that accompanied the Revolutionary War, peaked with the War of 1812, and was followed by a plateau period called the "Era of Good Feeling," which preceded the depression of the 1830s and '40s. As James Shuman and David Rosenau describe in their book, *The Kondratieff Wave*, the second and third cycles unfolded economically and sociologically in a surprisingly similar manner, with the second plateau accompanying the "Reconstruction" period after the Civil War and the third aptly referred to as the "Roaring Twenties," which followed World War I. The plateau periods generally supported good stock markets, especially the plateau period of the 1920s. The roaring stock market of that time was followed ultimately by collapse, the Great Depression and general deflation until about 1942.

As we interpret the Kondratieff cycle, we have now reached another plateau, having had a trough war (World War II), a peak war (Vietnam) and a primary recession (1974-75). This plateau should again be accompanied by relatively prosperous times and a strong bull market in stocks. According to a reading of this cycle, the economy should collapse in the mid-1980s* and be followed by three or four years of severe depression and a long period of deflation through to the trough year 2000 A.D. This scenario fits ours like a glove and would correspond to our fifth Cycle wave advance and the next Supercycle decline, as we discussed in Chapter 5 and further outline in the last chapter.

Cycles

The "cycle" approach to the stock market has become quite fashionable in recent years as investors search for tools to help them deal with a volatile, net-sideways trend. This approach has a great deal of validity, and in the hands of an artful analyst can be an excellent approach to market analysis. However, in our opinion, while it can make money in the stock market as can many other technical tools, the "cycle" approach does not reflect the true essence of the law behind the progression of markets.

Unfortunately, just as the Elliott Wave Principle in conjunction with Dow Theory and one or two related methods spawned a large public following for the "all bull markets have three legs" thesis, cycle theories have recently spawned a rigid adherence to the "four-year cycle" idea by many analysts and investors. Some comments seem appropriate. First, the existence of any cycle does not mean that moves to new highs within the second half of the cycle are impossible. The measurement is always low to low, regardless of intervening market action. Second, while the four-year cycle has been visible for the postwar period (about thirty years), evidence of its existence prior to that time is spotty and irregular, revealing a history that will allow for its contraction, expansion, shift or disappearance at any time.

For those who have found success using a cyclic approach, we feel that the Wave Principle can be a useful tool in predicting changes in the lengths of cycles, which seem to fade in and out of existence at times, usually with little or no warning. Note, for instance, that the four-year cycle has been quite visible in most of the current Supercycle's subwaves II, III and IV but was muddled and distorted in wave I, the 1932-1937 bull market, and prior to that time. If we remember that the two shorter waves in a five-wave bull move tend to be quite similar, we can deduce that the current Cycle wave V should more closely resemble wave I (1932-37) than any other wave in this sequence, since wave III from 1942 to 1966 was the extended wave and will be dissimilar to the two other motive waves. The current wave V, then, should be a simpler structure with shorter cycle lengths and could provide for the sudden contraction of the popular four-year cycle to more like three and a half years. In other words, *within* waves, cycles may tend toward time constancy. When the next wave begins, however, the analyst should be on the alert for changes in periodicity. Since we believe that the debacle currently predicted for 1978 and 1979 by the cycle theorists on the basis of the four- and nine-year cycles will not occur, we would like to present the following quotation from "Elliott's Wave Principle — A Reappraisal" by Charles J. Collins, published in 1954 by Bolton, Tremblay & Co.:

> Elliott alone among the cycle theorists (despite the fact he died in 1947, while others lived) provided a basic background of cycle theory compatible with what actually happened in the postwar period (at least to date).
>
> According to orthodox cycle approaches, the years 1951-1953 were to produce somewhat of a holocaust in the securities and commodity markets, with depression centering in this period. That the pattern did not work out as anticipated is probably a good thing, as it is quite doubtful if the free world could have survived a decline which was scheduled to be almost as devastating as 1929-32.

In our opinion, the analyst could go on indefinitely in his attempt to verify fixed cycle periodicities, with negligible results. The Wave Principle reveals that the market reflects more the properties of a spiral than a circle, more the properties of nature than of a machine.

The Decennial Pattern

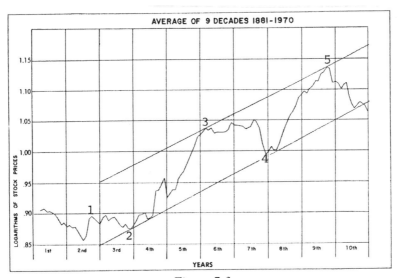

Figure 7-3

Figure 7-3 is a chart, courtesy of Edson Gould and Anametrics, Inc., of the "decennial pattern," as averaged out over the past seven decades in the stock market. In other words, this chart is a reproduction of the DJIA action, since its inception, for the composite decade, years one through ten. The tendency toward similar market action in each year of the decade is well documented and is referred to as the "decennial pattern." Our approach, however, gives this observation a new and startling meaning. Look for yourself: a perfect Elliott wave.

News

While most financial news writers explain market action by current events, there is seldom any worthwhile connection. Most days contain a plethora of both good and bad news, which is usually selectively scrutinized to come up with a plausible explanation for the movement of the market. In *Nature's Law,* Elliott commented on the value of news as follows:

> At best, news is the tardy recognition of forces that have already been at work for some time and is startling only to those unaware of the trend. The futility in relying on anyone's ability to interpret the value of any single news item in terms of the stock market has long been recognized by experienced and successful traders. No single news item or series of developments can be regarded as the underlying cause of any sustained trend. In fact, over a long period of time the same events have had widely different effects because trend conditions were dissimilar. This statement can be verified by casual study of the 45 year record of the Dow Jones Industrial Average.
>
> During that period, kings have been assassinated, there have been wars, rumors of wars, booms, panics, bankruptcies, New Era, New Deal, "trust busting," and all sorts of historic and emotional developments. Yet all bull markets acted in the same way, and likewise all bear markets evinced similar characteristics that controlled and measured the response of the market to any type of news as well as the extent and proportions of the component segments of the trend as a whole. These characteristics can be appraised and used to forecast future action of the market, regardless of news.
>
> There are times when something totally unexpected happens, such as earthquakes. Nevertheless, regardless of the

degree of surprise, it seems safe to conclude that any such development is discounted very quickly and *without reversing the
indicated trend under way before the event*. Those who regard
news as the cause of market trends would probably have better
luck gambling at race tracks than in relying on their ability
to guess correctly the significance of outstanding news items.
Therefore the only way to "see the forest clearly" is to take a
position above the surrounding trees.

Elliott recognized that not news, but something else forms
the patterns evident in the market. Generally speaking, the
important analytical question is not the news *per se*, but the importance the market places or appears to place on the news. In
periods of increasing optimism, the market's apparent reaction
to an item of news is often different from what it would have
been if the market were in a downtrend. It is easy to label the
progression of Elliott waves on a historical price chart, but it is
impossible to pick out, say, the occurrences of war, the most dramatic of human activities, on the basis of recorded stock market
action. The psychology of the market in relation to the news, then,
is sometimes useful, especially when the market acts contrarily
to what one would "normally" expect.

Our studies suggest not simply that news tends to lag the
market but that it nevertheless *follows exactly the same progression*. During waves 1 and 2 of a bull market, the front page
of the newspaper reports news that engenders fear and gloom.
The fundamental situation generally seems its worst as wave
2 of the market's new advance bottoms out. Favorable fundamentals return in wave 3 and peak temporarily in the early
part of wave 4. They return partway through wave 5, and like
the technical aspects of wave 5, are less impressive than those
present during wave 3 (see "Wave Personality" in Chapter 3). At
the market's peak, the fundamental background remains rosy,
or even improves, yet the market turns down despite it. Negative fundamentals then begin to wax again after the correction
is well under way. The news, or "fundamentals," then, are offset
from the market temporally by a wave or two. This parallel progression of events is a sign of unity in human affairs and tends
to confirm the Wave Principle as an integral part of the human
experience.

Technicians argue, in an understandable attempt to account for the time lag, that the market "discounts the future," i.e., actually guesses correctly in advance changes in the social condition. This theory is initially enticing because in preceding economic developments and even socio-political events, the market appears to sense changes before they occur. However, the idea that investors are clairvoyant is somewhat fanciful. It is almost certain that in fact people's emotional states and trends, as reflected by market prices, *cause* them to behave in ways that ultimately affect economic statistics and politics, i.e., produce "news." To sum up our view, then, the market, for forecasting purposes, *is* the news.

Random Walk Theory

Random Walk theory has been developed by statisticians in the academic world. The theory holds that stock prices move randomly and not in accord with predictable patterns of behavior. On this basis, stock market analysis is pointless as nothing can be gained from studying trends, patterns, or the inherent strength or weakness of individual securities.

Amateurs, no matter how successful they are in other fields, usually find it difficult to understand the strange, "unreasonable," sometimes drastic, seemingly random ways of the market. Academics are intelligent people, and to explain their own inability to predict market behavior, some of them simply assert that prediction is impossible. Many facts contradict this conclusion, and not all of them are at the abstract level. For instance, the mere existence of very successful professional traders who make hundreds, or even thousands, of trading decisions a year flatly disproves the Random Walk idea, as does the existence of portfolio managers and analysts who manage to pilot brilliant careers over a professional lifetime. Statistically speaking, these performances prove that the forces animating the market's progression are not random or due solely to chance. The market has a *nature*, and some people perceive enough about that nature to attain success. A very short-term trader who makes tens of decisions a week and makes money each week has accomplished something far less probable (in a random world) than tossing a coin fifty times in a row with the coin falling "heads" each time. David Bergamini, in *Mathematics,* stated,

Tossing a coin is an exercise in probability theory which everyone has tried. Calling either heads or tails is a fair bet because the chance of either result is one half. No one expects a coin to fall heads once in every two tosses, but in a large number of tosses, the results tend to even out. For a coin to fall heads fifty consecutive times would take a million men tossing coins ten times a minute for forty hours a week, and then it would only happen once every nine centuries.

An indication of how far the Random Walk theory is removed from reality is the chart of the first 89 days of trading on the New York Stock Exchange after the 740 low on March 1, 1978, as shown in Figure 2-16 and discussed therewith. As demonstrated there and in the chart of the Supercycle in Figure 5-5, action on the NYSE does not create a formless jumble wandering without rhyme or reason. Hour after hour, day after day and year after year, the DJIA's price changes create a succession of waves dividing and subdividing into patterns that perfectly fit Elliott's basic tenets as he laid them out forty years ago. Thus, as the reader of this book may witness, the Elliott Wave Principle challenges the Random Walk theory at every turn.

Technical Analysis

The Elliott Wave Principle not only supports the validity of chart analysis, but it can help the technician decide which formations are most likely of real significance. As does the Wave Principle, technical analysis (as described by Robert D. Edwards and John Magee in their book, *Technical Analysis of Stock Trends)* recognizes the "triangle" formation as generally an intra-trend phenomenon. The concept of a "wedge" is the same as that for Elliott's diagonal and has the same implications. Flags and pennants are zigzags and triangles. "Rectangles" are usually double or triple threes. "Double tops" are generally caused by flats, "double bottoms" by truncated fifths.

The famous "head and shoulders" pattern can be discerned in a normal Elliott top (see Figure 7-4), while a head and shoulders pattern that "doesn't work out" might involve an expanded flat correction under Elliott (see Figure 7-5). Note that in both patterns, the decreasing volume that usually accompanies a head and shoulders formation is a characteristic fully compatible with

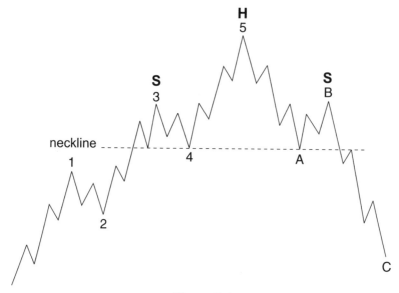

Figure 7-4

the Wave Principle. In Figure 7-4, wave 3 will have the heaviest volume, wave 5 somewhat lighter, and wave B usually lighter still when the wave is of Intermediate degree or lower. In Figure 7-5, the impulse wave will have the highest volume, wave B usually somewhat less, and wave four of C the least.

Trendlines and trend channels are used similarly in both approaches. Support and resistance phenomena are evident in

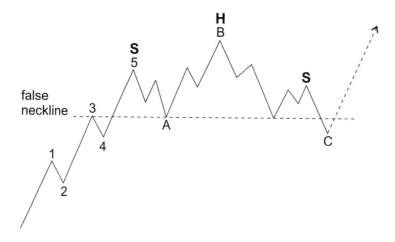

Figure 7-5

normal wave progression and in the limits of bear markets (the congestion of wave four is support for a subsequent decline). High volume and volatility (gaps) are recognized characteristics of "breakouts," which generally accompany third waves, whose personality, as discussed in Chapter 2, fills the bill.

Despite this compatibility, after years of working with the Wave Principle we find that applying classical technical analysis to stock market averages gives us the feeling that we are restricting ourselves to the use of stone tools in an age of modern technology.

The technical analytic tools known as "indicators" are often extremely useful in judging and confirming the momentum status of the market or the psychological background that usually accompanies waves of each type. Indicators of investor psychology, such as those that track short selling, option transactions and market opinion polls, reach extreme levels at the end of C waves, second waves and fifth waves. Momentum indicators reveal an ebbing of the market's power (i.e., speed of price change, breadth and in lower degrees, volume) in fifth waves and in B waves in expanded flats, creating "momentum divergences." Since the utility of an individual indicator can change or evaporate over time due to changes in market mechanics, we strongly suggest their use as tools to aid in correctly counting Elliott waves but would not rely on them so strongly as to ignore wave counts of obvious portent. Indeed, the associated guidelines within the Wave Principle at times have suggested a market environment that made the temporary alteration or impotence of some market indicators predictable.

The "Economic Analysis" Approach

Currently extremely popular with institutional fund managers and advisors is the method of trying to predict the stock market by forecasting changes in the economy using interest rate trends, typical postwar business cycle behavior, rates of inflation and other measures. In our opinion, attempts to forecast the market without listening to the market itself are doomed to fail. If anything, the market is a far more reliable predictor of the economy than vice versa. Moreover, taking a historical perspective, we feel strongly that while various economic conditions may be related to the stock market in certain ways during one period of time, those relationships are subject to change seem-

ingly without notice. For example, sometimes a recession begins
near the start of a bear market, and sometimes one does not occur
until the end. Another changing relationship is the occurrence of
inflation or deflation, each of which has appeared bullish for the
stock market in some cases and bearish for the stock market in
others. Similarly, tight money fears have kept many fund managers out of the 1978 market to date, just as the lack of such fears
kept them invested during the 1962 collapse. Falling interest
rates often accompany bull markets but also accompany the very
worst market declines, such as that of 1929-1932.

While Elliott claimed that the Wave Principle was manifest
in all areas of human endeavor, even in the frequency of patent
applications, for instance, the late Hamilton Bolton specifically
asserted that the Wave Principle was useful in telegraphing
changes in monetary trends as far back as 1919. Walter E. White,
in his work, "Elliott Waves in the Stock Market," also finds wave
analysis useful in interpreting the trends of monetary figures,
as this excerpt indicates:

> The rate of inflation has been a very important influence on
> stock market prices during recent years. If percentage changes
> (from one year earlier) in the consumer price index are plotted,
> the rate of inflation from 1965 to late 1974 appears as an Elliott
> 1-2-3-4-5 wave. A different cycle of inflation than in previous
> postwar business cycles has developed since 1970 and the fu-
> ture cyclical development is unknown. The waves are useful,
> however, in suggesting turning points, as in late 1974.

Elliott wave concepts are useful in the determination of turning points in many different series of economic data. For instance,
net free banking reserves, which White said "tend to precede
turning points in the stock market," were essentially negative
for about eight years from 1966 to 1974. The termination of a
five-wave decline in late 1974 suggested a major buying point.

As testimony to the utility of wave analysis in the money
markets, we present in Figure 7-6 a wave count for the price of
a long term U.S. Treasury bond, the 8 and 3/8 of the year 2000.
Even in this brief nine-month price pattern, we see a reflection
of the Elliott process. On this chart, we have three examples of
alternation, as each second wave alternates with each fourth,

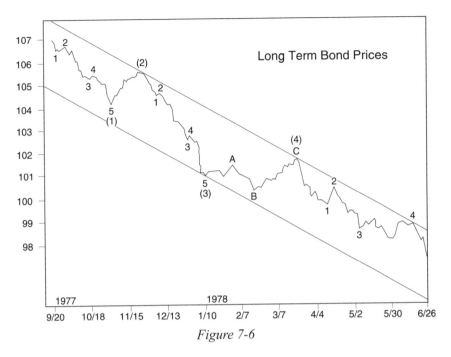

Figure 7-6

one being a zigzag, the other a flat. The upper trendline contains all rallies. The fifth wave constitutes an extension, which itself is contained within a trend channel. At the current stage of interpretation, the best bond market rally in almost a year is due quite soon.

Thus, while monetary phenomena may relate to stock prices in a complex way, our experience is that price movements always create an Elliott pattern. Apparently, what influences investors in managing their portfolios is likely influencing bankers, businessmen and politicians as well. It is difficult to separate cause from effect when the interactions of forces at all levels of activity are so numerous and intertwined. Elliott waves, as a reflection of the mass psyche, extend their influence over all categories of human behavior.

Exogenous Forces

We do not reject the idea that exogenous forces may be triggering cycles and patterns that man has yet to comprehend. For instance, for years, some analysts have suspected a connection between sunspot frequency and stock market prices on the basis that changes in magnetic radiation have an effect on the mass psychology of people, including investors. In 1965, Charles J. Collins published a paper entitled "An Inquiry into the Effect of Sunspot Activity on the Stock Market." Collins noted that since 1871, severe bear markets generally followed years when sunspot activity had risen above a certain level. More recently, Dr. R. Burr, in *Blueprint for Survival*, reported that he had discovered a striking correlation between geophysical cycles and the varying level of electrical potential in plants. Several studies have indicated an effect on human behavior from changes in atmospheric bombardment by ions and cosmic rays, which may in turn be regulated by lunar and planetary cycles. Indeed, some analysts successfully use planetary alignments, which apparently affect sunspot activity, to predict the stock market. In October 1970, *The Fibonacci Quarterly* (issued by The Fibonacci Association, Santa Clara University, Santa Clara, CA) published a paper by B.A. Read, a captain with the U.S. Army Satellite Communications Agency. The article is entitled "Fibonacci Series in the Solar System" and establishes that planetary distances and periods conform to Fibonacci relationships. The tie-in with the Fibonacci sequence suggests that there may be more than a random connection between stock market behavior and the extraterrestrial forces affecting life on Earth. Nevertheless, we are content for the time being to assume that Elliott wave patterns of social behavior result from the mental and emotional makeup of men and their resulting behavioral tendencies in social situations. If these tendencies are triggered or tied to exogenous forces, someone else will have to prove the connection.

CHAPTER 8

ELLIOTT SPEAKS

The Next Ten Years

While it may be quite dangerous to attempt the "impossible," a long term prediction for the stock market, we have decided to run the risk, if only to demonstrate the methods we use to analyze the position of the market in terms of the Wave Principle. The risk lies in the problem that if our thinking changes course during the next few years along with the stock market, this book will remain unaltered in its presentation of our analysis, which is based on our knowledge as of early July, 1978. We can only hope that our readers will not reject outright the theory of the Wave Principle because one rather daring prediction happens not to work out. With our reservations stated at the outset, we proceed directly to our analysis.

In Elliott terms, the Supercycle bull move that began in 1932 has nearly run its course. Currently, the market is within a bull phase of Cycle degree, which in turn will be composed of five waves of Primary degree, two of which have likely been completed. Several conclusions can already be drawn from the long term picture. First, stock prices should not develop a bear market downswing similar to 1969-70 or 1973-74 for several years to come, most likely not until the early or middle eighties, at least. Next, "secondary" stocks should be leaders during the entire Cycle wave V, [but to a lesser degree than they were in Cycle wave III]. Finally, and perhaps most important, this Cycle wave should not develop into a steady, prolonged 1942-66 type of bull market since within a wave structure of any degree, generally only one wave develops an extension. Therefore, since 1942 to 1966 was the extended wave, the current Cycle bull market should resemble a more simple structure and a shorter time period such as the 1932-37 and 1921-29 markets.

With the DJIA in a persistent downtrend until just recently, pervasive pessimism has worked to produce several distorted

"Elliott" interpretations that call for a calamitous decline to emerge from what is only a Primary second wave correction. Targets below 200 DJIA have been forecast for the near future by taking Elliott's principles and twisting them into pretzels. To such analyses, we can only quote Hamilton Bolton from page 12 of the 1958 Elliott Wave Supplement to the *Bank Credit Analyst*, in which he states:

> Whenever the market gets into a bear phase, we find correspondents who think that "Elliott" can be interpreted to justify much lower prices. While "Elliott" can be interpreted with considerable latitude, it still cannot be twisted entirely out of context. In other words, as in amateur vs. professional hockey, you can change some of the rules, but basically you must stick to the ground rules, or else you are in danger of creating a new game.

The most bearish allowable interpretation, as we see it, is that Cycle wave IV is not yet over, and that the final wave down is still in progress. Even given this case, the maximum expected low is 520 DJIA, the low of wave ④ in 1962. Based on the trend channel we have constructed in Figure 5-5 however, we have assigned this scenario a very low probability.

Basically, two plausible interpretations present themselves at the current time. Some evidence suggests the formation of a large diagonal (see Figure 8-1) that could be constructed entirely by stampede-type swings and persistent intervening declines. Since the October 1975 low at 784.16 was broken in January 1978, leaving behind what could be a three-wave Primary advance, the diagonal seems quite a plausible Cycle bull market scenario, since in a diagonal each of the actionary waves is composed of three waves rather than five. Only because this Cycle wave beginning in December 1974 is a fifth in the Supercycle is it possible that a large diagonal is being formed. Since a diagonal is essentially a weak structure, our ultimate upside target may have to be reduced to the 1700 area if this case indeed develops. To date, the drastic underperformance of the DJIA relative to the rest of the market seems to support this thesis.

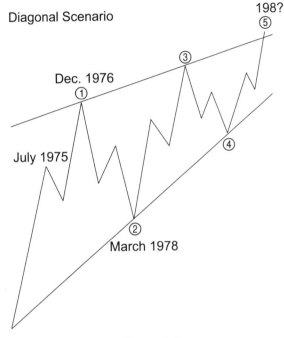

Figure 8-1

The most convincing alternative to the diagonal scenario is that all of the action from July 1975 to March 1978 is a large A-B-C expanded flat correction similar to the 1959-62 market pattern. This interpretation is illustrated in Figure 8-2 and suggests a very strong upward thrust to follow. Our target should be easily met if this interpretation turns out to be correct.

Our price projection for the Dow comes from the tenet that two of the impulse waves in a five-wave sequence, especially when the third is the extended wave, tend toward equality in length. For the current Cycle wave, semilogarithmic (percentage) equality to wave I from 1932 to 1937 puts the orthodox high of the market close to 2860 [2724 using an exactly equivalent 371.6% gain], which is quite a reasonable target, since trendline projections suggest highs in the 2500 to 3000 area. For those who think these numbers are ridiculously high, a check of history will verify that such percentage moves in the market are not uncommon.

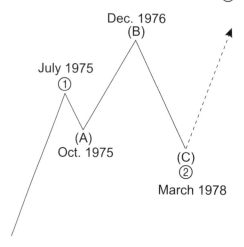

Figure 8-2

It is a fascinating comparison that like the nine years of "work" under the 100 level prior to the bull market of the 1920s, the last fifth Cycle wave, the Dow has currently concluded thirteen years of work under the 1000 level. And, as the Dow's orthodox peak in 1928 occurred at 296 according to Elliott's interpretation, the next peak is estimated at about the same relative level, although an expanded flat correction could carry the averages into even higher ground temporarily. We expect the terminal point to be close to the upper Supercycle channel line. If there is a throw-over, the ensuing reaction could be breathtakingly fast.

If the interpretation of the current market status presented in Figure 8-2 is correct, a reasonable picture of the 1974-87 market progression could be constructed by attaching a reverse inverted image of the 1929-37 period onto the recent March 1978 low at 740, as we have done in Figure 8-3. This picture is only a suggestion of the profile, but it does provide five Primary waves with the fifth extending. The rule of alternation is satisfied, as wave ② is a flat and wave ④ is a zigzag. Remarkably, the rally that would be scheduled for 1986 would halt exactly on the dotted line at 740, a level whose importance already has been established (see Chapter 4). Since the 1932-37 Cycle bull market lasted five years, its addition to the current level after three years of bull

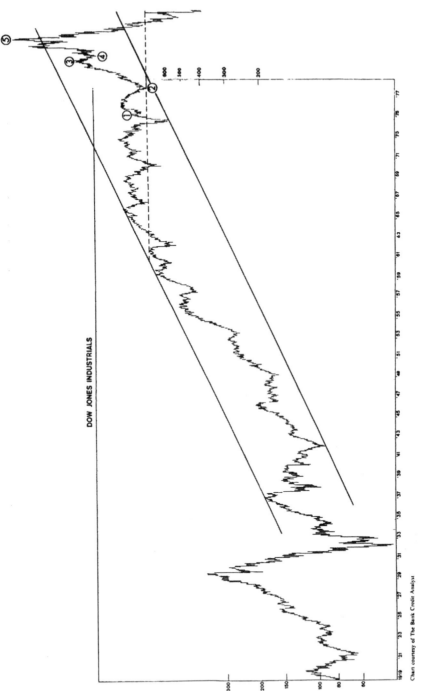

DOW JONES INDUSTRIALS

Chart courtesy of The Bank Credit Analyst

Figure 8-3

market gives a length of eight years (1.618 times the length of wave I) for the current Cycle wave.

To bolster our conclusions with regard to the time element, let us first examine Fibonacci time sequences from some of the major turning points in the market, starting with 1928-29.

Fibonacci Timetable

Turning Points	Time Period	High ?	Low ?
1928-29	55	1983-84	
1932	55		1987
1949	34	1983	
1953	34		1987
1962	21	1983	
1966	21		1987
1970	13	1983	
1974	13		1987
1974	8	1982	
1979?	8		1987

The reverse Fibonacci timetable in Chapter 4 points to the same years as turning point years.

The above formulas relate only to time and considered alone pose the question of whether 1982-84 will be a top or a bottom and whether 1987 will be a top or a bottom. From the context of the previous market structure, however, one would expect the 1982-84 period to be a major top area and 1987 a major low. Since the third wave constituted an extension, the first and fifth waves will be the shortest in this Supercycle. Since wave I was five years long, a Fibonacci number, wave V could well be eight years long, the next Fibonacci number, and last through the end of 1982. A certain symmetry, often evident in wave structures, will be created if waves IV and V are each eight years long, since waves I and II were each five years long. Furthermore, the total time length of waves I, II, IV and V will then be approximately equal to the entire period of the extended wave III.

Another ground for concluding that the 1982-84 zone is the probable terminal area of the current Supercycle V is purely arithmetical. An advance within the trend channel containing the price action of the current Supercycle should reach the upper parallel line at our price objective near 2860 in about 1983.

Some additional perspective may be gained from the Benner-Fibonacci Cycle chart shown in Figure 4-17 which, as we demonstrated, was used quite successfully in forecasting broad stock market movements from 1964 to 1974. At least for the time being, Benner's theory seems to substantiate our conclusions about the future, since at this time it clearly calls for a high in 1983 and a deep low in 1987. However, while we expect the projections to hold for the next decade, like all other cycle formulas, it could very well fade in the next down Supercycle.

Even the fifty-four year economic cycle discovered by Nikolai Kondratieff, which we discussed in Chapter 7, suggests that 1987, being fifty-four years from the depression depths of 1933, would be well within a reasonable time period for some kind of stock market bottom, especially if the current plateau period generates enough optimism to allow for a strong stock market prior to that time. One of our objections to the "killer wave" occurring now or in 1979, as most cycle theorists suggest, is that the psychological state of the average investor does not seem poised for a shock of disappointment. Most important stock market collapses have come out of optimistic, high-valuation periods. Such conditions definitely do not prevail at this time, as eight years of a raging bear market have taught today's investor to be cautious, conservative and cynical. Defensiveness is not in evidence at tops.

O.K., what next? Are we in for another 1929 to 1932 period of chaos?

In 1929, as bids were withdrawn, "air pockets" developed in the market structure, and prices tumbled precipitously. The best efforts of the leaders of the financial community could not stem the panic once the tides of emotion took control. Situations of this nature that have happened over the last two hundred years usually have been followed by three or four years of chaotic conditions in the economy and the markets. We have not seen a 1929 situation in fifty years and, while it is to be hoped that it never recurs, history suggests otherwise.

In fact, four fundamental changes in market conditions may be part of the basis for a real panic some time in the future. First is the increasing institutional dominance of the market, greatly magnifying the impact of one man's emotions on the behavior of the market, since millions or even billions of dollars may be under the control of one man or a small committee. Second is the birth of the options market, where many "little guys" will have their stake as the market approaches its peak. In that situation, billions of dollars worth of paper assets could disappear in a day's trading on the NYSE. Third, the change in the holding period from six months to one year for declaration of long term gains could exacerbate the "can't sell" syndrome of those who insist upon logging only long-term gains for tax purposes. Finally, the SEC-mandated abolition of the specialists' role on the NYSE, which will force the securities industry to operate a dealer's market, could necessitate some brokerage firms to assume very high equity positions in order to maintain a liquid market, thus leaving them quite vulnerable in a precipitous decline.

A panic is an emotional problem, not an Elliott problem. The Wave Principle simply warns the investor of impending changes in the trend of the market for better or for worse. Deciding what to look for in the next ten years is more important than trying to predict what definitely to expect. No matter how we struggle with long term future probabilities, our interpretations must remain tentative until the fifth Minor wave of the fifth Intermediate of the fifth Primary is under way from the 1974 low. As the "fifth of the fifth" nears its terminal point, the Elliott wave analyst should be able to recognize the end of the Cycle bull market in stocks. In analyzing market movements under the tenets of the Wave Principle, remember that it is always the count that is most significant. Our advice is to count correctly and never, never proceed blindly on the assumptions of a preconceived scenario. Despite the evidence presented here, *we will be the first to discard our predictions if the waves tell us we must.*

If our scenario proves correct, however, a new Grand Supercycle will get under way once the current Supercycle V has terminated. The first phase could end about 1987 and bring the market down from its peak to about the 1000 level again. Eventually, the Grand Supercycle bear should carry to its expected target within the range of the previous Supercycle fourth wave, between 41 and 381 on the Dow. However, we certainly do not make any definite forecast, despite our suspicions, with respect to a panic occurring directly after the peak. The market often does move impulsively during A waves, but precipitous action more assuredly develops in C waves of A-B-C formations. Charles J. Collins, however, fears the worst when he states,

My thought is that the end of Supercycle V will probably also witness a crisis in all the world's monetary high-jinks and Keynesian tomfoolery of the past four and one-half decades and, since wave V ends a Grand Supercycle, we then had better take to the hurricane shelters until the storm blows over.

Nature's Law

Why does man continuously have to shelter himself from hurricanes of his own making? Andrew Dickinson White's book, *Fiat Money Inflation in France,* examines in great detail a time in the past when "experience yielded to theory, plain business sense to financial metaphysics." In consternation, Henry Hazlitt, in the introduction to the book, ponders man's repeated experiments with inflation:

> Perhaps the study of other great inflations — of John Law's experiments with credit in France between 1716 and 1720; of the history of our own Continental currency between 1775 and 1780; of the Greenbacks of our Civil War; of the great German inflation which culminated in 1923 — would help to underscore and impress that lesson. Must we, from this appalling and repeated record, draw once more the despairing conclusion that the only thing man learns from history is that man learns nothing from history? Or have we still time enough, and sense enough, and courage enough, to be guided by these dreadful lessons of the past?

We have given this question due thought and come up with the conclusion that apparently it is one of nature's laws that man at times will refuse to accept the rest of its laws. If this assumption were untrue, the Elliott Wave Principle may never have been discovered because it may never have existed. The Wave Principle exists partly because man refuses to learn from history, because he can always be counted upon to be led to believe that two and two can and do make five. He can be led to believe that the laws of nature do not exist (or more commonly, "do not apply in this case"), that what is to be consumed need not be first produced, that what is lent need never be paid back, that promises are equal to substance, that paper is gold, that benefits have no costs, that the fears which reason supports will evaporate if they are ignored or derided.

Panics are sudden emotional mass realizations of reality, as are the initial upswings from the bottoms of those panics. At these points, reason suddenly impresses itself upon the mass psyche, saying, "Things have gone too far. The current levels are not justified by reality." To the extent that reason is disregarded, then, will be the extent of the extremes of mass emotional swings and their mirror, the market.

Of the many laws of nature, the one most blindly ignored in the current Elliott Supercycle is that, except in cases of family or charity, each living thing in the natural setting either provides for its own existence or is granted no existence. The very beauty of nature is its functional diversity, as each living element intertwines with the others, often providing for many others merely by providing for itself. No living thing other than man ever demands that its neighbors support it because that is its right, as there is no such right. Each tree, each flower, each bird, each rabbit, each wolf, takes from nature that which it provides and expects nothing from the efforts of its living neighbors; to do so would reduce the flourishing beauty of those neighbors and thus of the whole of nature in the process. One of the noblest experiments in the history of mankind was the American structure of human liberty and its necessary environment of free enterprise capitalism. That concept freed men from being bonded by others, whether they be feudal lords, squires, kings, bishops, bureaucrats or mobs demanding free bread and circuses. The diversity, richness and beauty of the experiment have stood out in the annals of history, a monument to one of the greatest laws of nature, the final burst of achievement in the Millennium wave.

The Founding Fathers of the Republic did not choose the pyramid capped by an all-seeing eye as the seal of the United States on a whim. They used the Egyptian symbol of cosmic truth to proclaim the organization of the perfect society, a society based on the knowledge of human nature and the workings of natural law. Over the past one hundred years, for political reasons, the meanings of the Founders' words have been distorted and their intentions perverted, eventually producing a social framework quite different from that established. It is ironic that the decline in the value of the dollar bill, which bears the seal of the United States, mirrors the decline in values within its social and political framework. As of this writing, in fact, the dollar's value relative to that in 1913 when the Federal Reserve Board was created is twelve cents. Depreciating currencies have virtually always been accompanied by declining standards of civilization.

Our friend Richard Russell describes the problem this way:

> I firmly believe the world's troubles would be solved (and the earth would resemble heaven) if everyone would take total RESPONSIBILITY for himself. In talking to hundreds of people, I don't find that 1 in 50 holds himself up, takes responsibility for his own life, does his own thing, accepts his own pain (instead of inflicting it on others). This same refusal to take responsibility spills over into the financial sphere. Today, people insist on their right to everything — as long as you and I pay for it. There's the right to work, the right to go to college, the right to happiness, the right to three meals a day. Who promised everyone all those rights? I believe in freedom of all kinds, except where freedom becomes license and inflicts damage. But Americans confuse freedom with rights.

Lord Thomas Babington Macaulay, British historian and statesman, whom we quote in part, correctly ascertained the root of the problem over a hundred years ago in a letter to H. S. Randall of New York dated May 23rd, 1857:

> I heartily wish you a good deliverance. But my reason and my wishes are at war, and I cannot help foreboding the worst. It is quite plain that your government will never be able to restrain a distressed and discontented majority. For with you the majority is the government, and has the rich, who are always a minority, absolutely at its mercy. The day will come when, in the State of New York, a multitude of people, none of whom had more than half a breakfast, or expects to have more than half a dinner, will choose the legislature. Is it possible to doubt what sort of legislature will be chosen? On one side is a statesman preaching patience, respect for vested rights, strict observance of public faith. On the other is a demagogue ranting about the tyranny of capitalists and usurers, and asking why anybody should be permitted to drink champagne, and to ride in a carriage while thousands of honest folk are in want of necessaries?
>
> I seriously apprehend that you will, in some such season of adversity as I have described, do things which will prevent prosperity from returning; that you will act like people who should

in a year of scarcity devour all the seedcorn, and thus make the next a year, not of scarcity, but of absolute famine. Either some Caesar or Napoleon will seize the reins of government with a strong hand, or your Republic will be as fearfully plundered and laid waste by barbarians in the twentieth century as the Roman Empire was in the fifth; with this difference, that the Huns and Vandals who ravaged the Roman Empire came from without, and that your Huns and Vandals will have been engendered within your country by your own institutions.

The function of capital (seedcorn) is to produce more capital as well as income, assuring the well being of future generations. Once squandered through socialist spending policies, capital is gone; man can make jam out of berries, but he can never reconstitute the berries.

As this century progresses, it becomes clearer that in order to satisfy the demands of some individuals and groups for the output of others, man, through the agency of the state, has begun to leech off that which he has created. He has not only mortgaged his present output, but he has mortgaged the output of future generations by eating the capital that took generations to accumulate.

In the name of a right that does not exist within the laws of nature, man has forced acceptance of paper that represents nothing but costs everything, he has bought, spent and promised at an exponential rate, creating in the process the greatest debt pyramid in the history of the world, refusing to acknowledge that these debts must ultimately be paid in one form or another. Minimum wages that deny employment to the unskilled, socialization of schools that smothers diversity and discourages innovation, rent control that consumes housing, extortion through transfer payments, and stifling regulation of markets are all man's political attempts to repeal the natural laws of economics and sociology, and thus of nature. The familiar results are crumbling buildings and rotting railroads, bored and uneducated students, reduced capital investment, reduced production, inflation, stagnation, unemployment and ultimately widespread resentment and unrest. Institutionalized policies such as these create increasing instability and have the power to turn a nation of conscientious producers into a private sector full of impatient gamblers and a public sector full of unprincipled plunderers.

When the fifth wave of the fifth wave tops out, we need not ask why it has done so. Reality, again, will be forced upon us. When the producers who are leeched upon disappear or are consumed, the leeches who remain will have lost their life support system, and the laws of nature will have to be patiently relearned.

The trend of man's progress, as the Wave Principle points out, is ever upward. However, the path of that progress is not a straight line and never will be unless human nature, which is one of the laws of nature, is repealed. Ask any archaeologist. He knows.

APPENDIX

LONG TERM FORECAST UPDATE, 1982-1983

Elliott Wave Principle concluded that the wave IV bear market in the Dow Jones Industrial Average ended in December 1974 at 572. The authors labeled the March 1978 low at 740 as the end of Primary wave ② within the new bull market. Neither level was ever broken on a daily or hourly closing basis. That wave labeling still stands, except that the low of wave ② is better placed in March 1980.

The analysis that follows, from Robert Prechter's *Elliott Wave Theorist*, details his real-time conclusion that the 1982 low may also be labeled as the end of the wave IV bear market, particularly when taking the "constant-dollar" Dow into account. This text includes *The Elliott Wave Theorist*'s dramatic market analysis of September 1982. Published one month after the low of a 16½-year downtrend in the inflation-adjusted Dow, it identified the start of the great "liftoff" for Cycle wave V.

This Appendix, which first appeared in the April 1983 edition, has been expanded to include all long-term commentary through the first year of the bull market.

All text that follows is quoted as published in
Robert Prechter's *The Elliott Wave Theorist*
on the dates cited below.

January 1982

BLUEPRINT FOR THE '80s

Sometimes obtaining perspective on a current situation necessitates taking a good hard look at what has happened in the
past. This report will take a look at the long-term picture to get
a sense of what the decade of the 1980s has in store. One of the
most revealing presentations of data is the chart of U.S. stock
prices going back over two hundred years, the longest period for
which such data is available. The accompanying chart [Figure
A-1] was first presented in 1978 in A.J. Frost's and my book *Elliott Wave Principle* [see Figure 5-4], although the wave count
near the end has been amended to reflect current knowledge.

The wave structure from the late 1700s to 1965 on the accompanying chart now unmistakably shows a *completed pattern*
of five waves. The third wave is characteristically long, the fourth
wave does not overlap the first, and the guideline of alternation
is satisfied in that wave (II) is a flat, while wave (IV) is a triangle. Furthermore, the first and fifth waves are related by the
Fibonacci ratio .618, in that the percentage advance of wave (V)
is roughly .618 times that of wave (I).

Some analysts have tried to argue that the wave count on
the "current dollar" chart [the actual Dow, Figure 5-5] shows a
full five waves into 1966. As I have been arguing for years, such a
count is highly suspect, if not impossible. In order to accept such a
count, one has to accept Elliott's argument of a triangle formation
ending in 1942 (detailed in *R.N. Elliott's Masterworks*), a count
that was quite correctly shown to be in error by the late A. Hamilton Bolton in his 1960 monograph, "The Elliott Wave Principle
— A Critical Appraisal" [see *The Complete Elliott Wave Writings
of A. Hamilton Bolton*]. Bolton's alternative proposal, a triangle
that ends in 1949 as the accompanying inflation-adjusted chart
shows, contained problems at the time he proposed it (namely
accepting 1932-1937 as a "three") and subsequent evidence has
confirmed that interpretation as impossible.

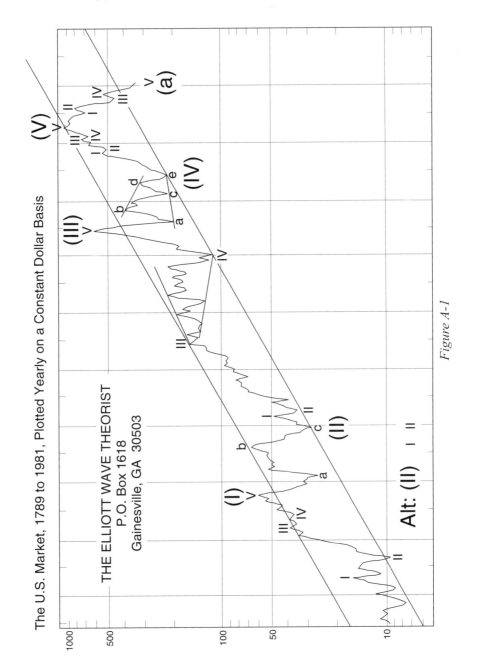

Figure A-1

The Dow, from the perspective of the [sideways trend], has been in a "bear market" the entire time [since 1965], although all other indexes have been in bull markets since 1974. Elliott was about the only analyst ever to recognize that sideways trends are bear markets. For evidence of this contention, all one need do is look at the chart of the inflation-adjusted Dow from 1966 [and compare it to the same period in Figure 5-5]. Raging inflation plus bear market equals sideways formation.*

More important is that a clear five-wave downward Elliott pattern from the 1965 peak appears to be in its final stage. As a shorter-term consideration, we can see from the chart that stocks are now deeply oversold and [, having fallen below the long term support line,] historically cheap in terms of value relative to the wholesale price index. Thus, *the next few years could witness a countertrend three-wave (a-b-c) rally in **real** terms that should translate into a dramatic 'breakout' in the Dow Industrial Average to new all-time highs in **current dollar** terms.* Such an advance would satisfy the Dow's wave count from 1932 in nominal dollars by letting it complete its final fifth Cycle wave from 1974. So we still need one more dramatic new high on the Dow Jones Industrial Average, giving us a fifth wave in actual prices and a B wave in inflation-adjusted prices.**

September 13, 1982

THE LONG TERM WAVE PATTERN — NEARING A RESOLUTION

This is a thrilling juncture for a wave analyst. For the first time since 1974, some incredibly large wave patterns may have been completed, patterns which have important implications for the next five to eight years. The next fifteen weeks should clear up all the long term questions that have persisted since the market turned sloppy in 1977.

---

* These last three sentences are from the immediately preceding December 1979 issue of EWT.
** The ensuing portion of this report, which presented an outlook for the bear market ultimately to follow, is reprinted in Chapter 3 of *At the Crest of the Tidal Wave.*

Elliott wave analysts sometimes are scolded for forecasts that reference very high or very low numbers for the averages. But the task of wave analysis often requires stepping back and taking a look at the big picture and using the evidence of the historical patterns to judge the onset of a major change in trend. Cycle and Supercycle waves move in wide price bands and truly are the most important structures to take into account. Those content to focus on 100-point swings will do extremely well as long as the Cycle degree trend of the market is neutral, but if a truly *persistent* trend gets under way, they'll be left behind at some point while those in touch with the big picture stay with it.

In 1978, A.J. Frost and I forecast a target for the Dow of 2860 for the final target in the current Supercycle from 1932. That target is still just as valid, but since the Dow is still where it was four years ago, the time target is obviously further in the future than we originally thought.

A tremendous number of long term wave counts have crossed my desk in the past five years, each attempting to explain the jumbled nature of the Dow's pattern from 1977. Most of these have proposed failed fifth waves, truncated third waves, substandard diagonals, and scenarios for immediate explosion (usually submitted near market peaks) or immediate collapse (usually submitted near market troughs). Very few of these wave counts showed any respect for the rules of the Wave Principle, so I discounted them. But the *real* answer remained a mystery. Corrective waves are notoriously difficult to interpret, and I, for one, have alternately labeled as "most likely" one or the other of two interpretations, given changes in market characteristics and pattern. At this point, the two alternates I have been working with are still valid, but I have been uncomfortable with each one for reasons that have been explained. There is a third one, however, that fits the guidelines of the Wave Principle as well as its rules, and has only now become a clear alternative.

Double Three Correction Still in Progress

This wave count argues that the giant Cycle wave correction from 1966 is still in progress. The final low [before the great bull market begins] would occur between Dow 563 and 554. Only a break of 766 would have made it certain, however, and no such break has yet occurred.

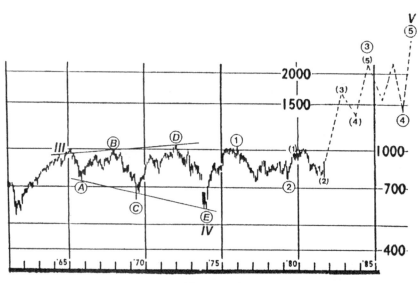

Figure A-2

Series of 1s and 2s in Progress

This count [see Figure A-2] has been my ongoing hypothesis for most of the time since 1974, although the uncertainty in the 1974-1976 wave count and the severity of the second wave corrections have caused me a good deal of grief in dealing with the market under this interpretation.

This wave count argues that the Cycle degree correction from 1966 ended in 1974 and that Cycle wave V began with the huge breadth surge in 1975-1976. The technical name for wave IV is an expanding triangle. The complicated subdivision so far in wave V suggests a *very long bull market*, perhaps lasting another ten years, with long corrective phases, waves (4) and ④, interrupting its progress. Wave V will contain a clearly defined extension within wave ③, subdividing (1)-(2)-(3)-(4)-(5), of which waves (1) and (2) have been completed. The peak would ideally occur at 2860, the original target calculated in 1978. [The main] disadvantage of this count is that it suggests too long a period for the entire wave V, as per the guideline of equality.

Advantages

1) Satisfies all rules under the Wave Principle.

2) Allows to stand A.J. Frost's 1970 forecast for an ultimate low for wave IV at 572.
3) Accounts for the tremendous breadth surge in 1975-1976.
4) Accounts for the breadth surge in August 1982.
5) Keeps nearly intact the long-term trendline from 1942.
6) Fits the idea of a four-year cycle bottom.
7) Fits the idea that the fundamental background looks bleakest at the bottom of second waves, not at the actual market low.
8) Fits the idea that the Kondratieff Wave plateau is partly over. Parallel with 1923.

Disadvantages

1) 1974-1976 is probably best counted as a "three," not a "five."
2) Wave (2) takes six times as much time to complete as does wave (1), putting the two waves substantially out of proportion.
3) The breadth of the 1980 rally was substandard for the first wave in what should be a powerful Intermediate third.
4) Suggests too long a period for the entire wave V, which should be a short and simple wave resembling wave I from 1932 to 1937 rather than a complex wave resembling the extended wave III from 1942 to 1966 (see *Elliott Wave Principle*, Figure 5-5).

Double Three Correction Ending in August 1982

The technical name for wave IV by this count is a "double three," with the second "three" an ascending [barrier] triangle. [See Figure A-3.] This wave count argues that the Cycle wave correction from 1966 ended last month (August 1982). The lower boundary of the trend channel from 1942 was broken briefly at the termination of this pattern, similar to the action in 1949 as that sideways market broke a major trendline briefly before launching a long bull market. A brief break of the long term trendline, I should note, was recognized as an occasional trait of fourth waves, as shown in [*R.N. Elliott's Masterworks*]. [The main] disadvantage of this count is that a double three with this construction, while perfectly acceptable, is so rare that no example in any degree exists in recent history.

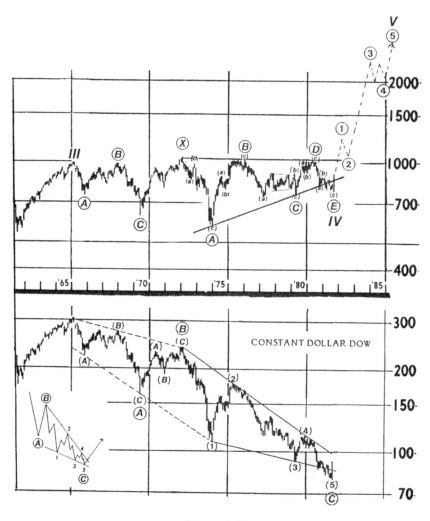

Figure A-3

A surprising element of time symmetry is also present. The 1932-1937 bull market lasted 5 years and was corrected by a 5-year bear market from 1937 to 1942. The 3½-year bull market from 1942 to 1946 was corrected by a 3½-year bear market from 1946 to 1949. The 16½-year bull market from 1949 to 1966 has now been corrected by a 16½-year bear market from 1966 to 1982!

The Constant Dollar (Inflation-Adjusted) Dow

If the market has made a Cycle wave low, it coincides with a satisfactory count on the "constant dollar Dow," which is a plot of the Dow divided by the consumer price index to compensate for the loss in purchasing power of the dollar. The count is a downward sloping Ⓐ-Ⓑ-Ⓒ, with wave Ⓒ a diagonal [see Figure A-3]. As usual in a diagonal, its final wave, wave (5), terminates below the lower boundary line.

I have added the expanding boundary lines to the upper portion of the chart just to illustrate the symmetrical diamond-shaped pattern constructed by the market. Note that each long half of the diamond covers 9 years 7½ months (5/65 to 12/74 and 1/73 to 8/82), while each short half cover 7 years 7½ months (5/65 to 1/73 and 12/74 to 8/82). The center of the pattern (June-July 1973) cuts the price element in half at 190 and the time element into two halves of 8+ years each. Finally, the decline from January 1966 is 16 years, 7 months, exactly the same length as the preceding rise from June 1949 to January 1966.

Advantages

1) Satisfies all rules and guidelines under the Wave Principle.
2) Keeps nearly intact the long-term trendline from 1942.
3) A break of triangle boundaries on wave E is a normal occurrence.
4) Allows for a simple bull market structure as originally expected.
5) Coincides with an interpretation for the constant dollar (deflated) Dow and with the corresponding break of its lower trendline.
6) Takes into account the sudden and dramatic rally beginning in August 1982, since triangles produce "thrust."
7) Final bottom occurs during a depressionary economy.
8) Fits the idea of a four-year cycle bottom.
9) Fits the idea that the Kondratieff Wave plateau has just begun, a period of economic stability and soaring stock prices. Parallel with late 1921.
10) Celebrates the end of the inflationary era or accompanies a "stable reflation."

Disadvantages

1) A double three with this construction, while perfectly acceptable, is so rare that no example in any degree exists in recent
   history.
2) A major bottom would be occurring with broad recognition
   by the popular press.

Outlook

Triangles portend "thrust," or swift moves in the opposite
direction traveling approximately the distance of the widest part
of the triangle. This guideline would indicate a minimum move of
495 points (1067-572) from Dow 777, or **1272**. Since the triangle
boundary extended below January 1973 would add about 70
more points to the "width of the triangle," a thrust could carry
as far as 1350. *Even this target would only be a first stop*, since
the extent of the fifth wave would be determined not merely by
the triangle, but by the entire wave IV pattern, of which the
triangle is only part. Therefore, one must conclude that a bull
market beginning in August 1982 would ultimately carry out
its full potential of five times its starting point, making it the
percentage equivalent of the 1932-1937 market, thus target-
ing **3873-3885**. The target should be reached either in 1987 or
1990, since the fifth wave would be of simple construction. An
interesting observation regarding this target is that it parallels
the 1920s, when after 17 years of sideways action under the 100
level (similar to the recent experience under the 1000 level), the
market soared almost nonstop to an intraday peak at 383.00.
As with this fifth wave, such a move would finish off not only a
Cycle, but a Supercycle advance.

[Near Term Wave Structure]

In the [August 17] Interim Report, I mentioned the possibility of a diagonal having been completed at the [Friday,] August
[12th] low. The two daily charts below illustrate this count. A
diagonal from last December would be wave [v of] c of a large a-b-c
from the August 1980 peak [see Figure A-4] or wave c of a large
a-b-c from the June 1981 peak [see Figure A-5]. The strength of
the explosion off the August low supports this interpretation.

Figure A-4 (pertains to Figure A-2)

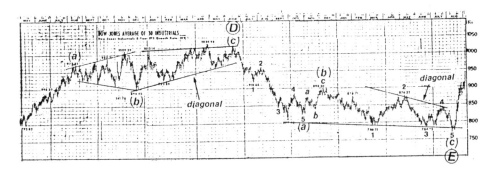

Figure A-5 (pertains to Figure A-3)

October 6, 1982

This bull market should be the first "buy-and-hold" market since the 1960s. The experience of the last 16 years has turned us all into traders, and it's a habit that will have to be abandoned. The market may have 200 points behind it, but it's got over 2000 left to go! The Dow should hit an ultimate target of **3880**, with interim stops at **1300*** (an estimate for the peak of wave ①, based on post-triangle thrust) and **2860*** (an estimate for the peak of wave ③, based on the target measuring from the 1974 low).

---

* Wave ① topped at 1286.64 (about 1300 intraday) in 1983-1984. EWT later reduced the rough estimate of 2860 for wave ③, as precise figures came out to 2724 (see bracket on page 201). Wave ③ topped at 2722.42 in 1987. Wave ⑤ reached and well surpassed Prechter's "pie-in-the-sky" target of 3880.

The confirmed status of the long-term trend of the stock market has tremendous implications. It means: (1) no new lows in the averages on the next reactions, (2) no crash or depression in 1983 (although a "mini-crisis" could develop soon), and (3) for those who fear one, *no international war for at least ten years.*

November 8, 1982

From the perspective of Elliott wave analysis, the stock market is in sharp focus. Surveying all the market's action over the past 200 years, it is comforting to know exactly where you are in the wave count. [Figure A-6] is Securities Research Company's yearly range chart. Note that waves II and IV in the DJIA accurately reflect the guideline of alternation, since wave II is a short sharp zigzag, while wave IV is a long sideways combination. As unusual as the Dow's structure was from 1966 to 1982,

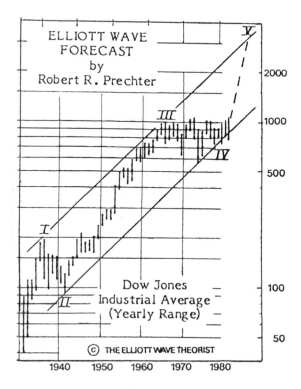

Figure A-6

it was perfect Elliott, showing that no matter how difficult the pattern is to read sometimes, it always resolves satisfactorily into a classic pattern.

Make no mistake about it. The next few years will be profitable beyond your wildest imagination. *Make sure you make it while the making is good.* Tune your mind to 1924. Plan during these five years to make your fortune. Then be prepared to lock it up safely for the bad years that are sure to follow.

November 29, 1982

A PICTURE IS WORTH A THOUSAND WORDS

The arrow on the chart below [see Figure A-7] illustrates my interpretation of the position of the Dow within the current bull market. Now if an Elliotter tells you that the Dow is in wave (2)

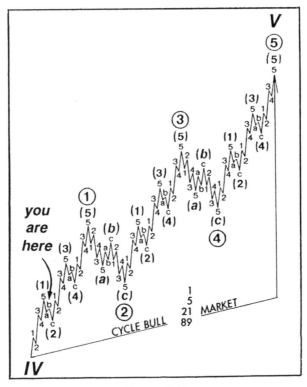

Figure A-7

of ① of V, you know exactly what he means. Whether he's right, of course, only time will tell.

The easiest thing to forecast is that the bull market *will* happen; the second easiest is a price estimate; the last is time. I'm currently looking for 1987 to mark a top, but it could carry into 1990. The important thing is *wave form*. In other words, it will be a lot easier to *recognize* when we're there than to forecast it in advance. We'll just have to be patient.

Breadth measures almost always begin to show weakness during a fifth-wave advance when compared to the first through third waves. For this reason, I would expect a very broad market through wave ③, then increasing selectivity until the peak of wave ⑤, by which time the leaders in the Dow may be almost the only things going. For now, play any stocks you like. Later on, we may have to pick and choose more carefully.

April 6, 1983

A RISING TIDE:
THE CASE FOR WAVE V
IN THE DOW JONES INDUSTRIAL AVERAGE

In 1978, A.J. Frost and I wrote a book called *Elliott Wave Principle*, which was published in November of that year. In the forecast chapter of that book, we made the following assessments:

1) That wave V, a tremendous bull market advance, was required in order to complete the wave structure that began in 1932 for the Dow Industrial Average.
2) That there would be no "crash of '79" and in fact no '69-'70 or '73-'74 type decline until wave V had been completed.
3) That the 740 low in March 1978 marked the end of Primary wave ② and would not be broken.
4) That the bull market in progress would take a simple form, unlike the extended advance from 1942 to 1966.
5) That the Dow Industrial Average would rise to the upper channel line and hit a target based on a 5x multiple of the wave IV low at 572, then calculated to be 2860.
6) That, if our conclusion that 1974 marked the end of wave IV was correct, the fifth-wave peak would occur in the 1982-1984 time period, with 1983 being the most likely year for the actual top [and 1987 the next most likely].

7) That "secondary" stocks would provide a leadership role throughout the advance.

8) That after wave V was completed, the ensuing crash would be the worst in U.S. history.

One thing that continuously surprised us since we made those arguments was how long it took the Dow Jones Industrial Average finally to lift off. The broad market averages continued to rise persistently from 1978, but the Dow, which appeared to mirror more accurately the fears of inflation, depression and international banking collapse, didn't end its corrective pattern, dating from 1966, until 1982. (For a detailed breakdown of that wave, see *The Elliott Wave Theorist*, September 1982 issue.) Despite this long wait, it fell only briefly beneath its long term trendline, and the explosive liftoff finally began when that downside break failed to precipitate any significant further selling.

If our overall assessment is correct, the forecasts Frost and I made based on the Wave Principle back in 1978 will still occur, with one major exception: the *time target*. As we explained in our book, R.N. Elliott said very little about time, and in fact our estimate for the time top was not something that the Wave Principle required, but simply an educated guess based on the conclusion that wave IV in the Dow ended in 1974. When it finally became clear that the long sideways wave IV correction hadn't ended until 1982, the time element had to be shifted ahead to compensate for that change in assessment. At no time was there a doubt that wave V would occur; it was only a matter of when, and after what.

I would like to take this space to answer these important questions:

1) Has the sideways correction in the Dow that began in 1966 actually ended?

2) If so, how big a bull market can we expect?

3) What will be its characteristics?

4) What will happen afterward?

1) *In 1982, the DJIA finished a correction of very large degree.* The evidence for this conclusion is overwhelming.

First, as those who take the Wave Principle seriously have argued all along, the pattern from 1932 [see Figure A-8] is still incomplete and requires one final rise to finish a five-wave Elliott pattern. Since a Supercycle crash was not in the cards, what

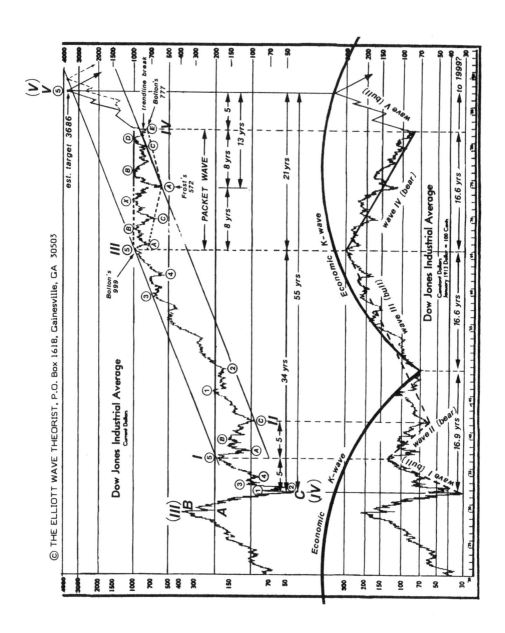

Figure A-8

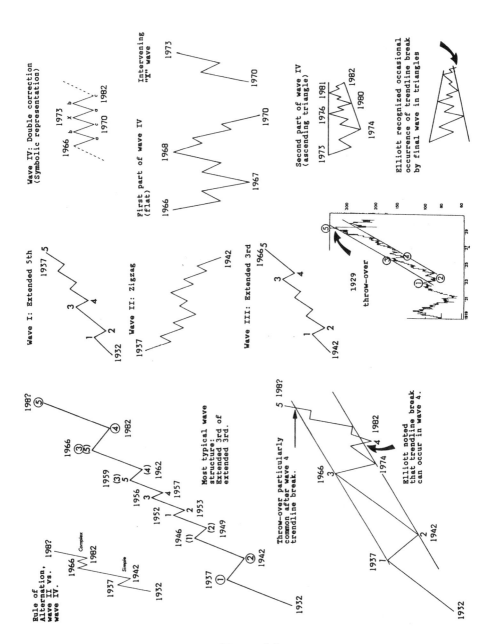

Figure A-9

has occurred since 1966 is more than adequate for a correction of Cycle degree (the same degree as the 1932-1937, 1937-1942 and 1942-1966 waves).

Second, the sideways pattern from 1966 (or arguably 1964 or 1965, if you enjoy talking theory) pushed to the absolute limit the long-term parallel trend channel from 1932. As you can see in the illustration from Elliott's own *Nature's Law* [see Figure A-9], it is an occasional trait of fourth waves that they will break beneath the lower boundary of the uptrend channel just prior to the onset of wave five. The price action in 1982 simply leaves no more room for the correction to continue.

Third, the pattern between the mid-'60s and 1982 is another wonderful real-life example of standard corrective formations outlined by Elliott over forty years ago. The official name for this structure is a "double three" correction, which is two basic corrective patterns back-to-back. In this case, the market traced out a "flat" (or by another count, a[n unorthodox] triangle [from 1965]) in the first position and an "ascending [barrier] triangle" in the second, with an intervening simple three-wave advance, labeled "X," which serves to separate the two component patterns. Elliott also recognized and illustrated the occasional propensity for the final wave of a triangle to fall out of the lower boundary line, as occurred in 1982. The doubling of a correction is moderately rare, and since the 1974 low had already touched the long term uptrend line, Frost and I weren't expecting it. Moreover, a "double three" with a *triangle* in the second position is so rare that in my own experience it is unprecedented.

Fourth, the pattern has some interesting properties if treated as a single formation, that is, one correction. For instance, the *first* wave of the formation (996 to 740) covers almost exactly the same distance as the *last* wave (1024 to 777). The advancing portion, moreover, takes the same time as the declining portion, 8 years. The symmetry of the pattern prompted Frost and me to come up with the label "Packet Wave" in 1979, to describe a single pattern starting at "rest," going through wider, then narrower swings, and returning to the point from which it began. (This concept is detailed in the December 1982 issue of *The Elliott Wave Theorist*.) Using the alternate count of two triangles, it happens that the middle wave (wave C) of each triangle covers the same territory, from the 1000 level to 740. Numerous Fibonacci relationships occur within the pattern, many of which were detailed in a Special

Report of *The Elliott Wave Theorist* dated July 1982. Far more important, however, is the Fibonacci relationship of its *starting* and *ending* points to part of the *preceding bull market*. Hamilton Bolton made this famous observation in 1960:

> Elliott pointed out a number of other coincidences. For instance, the number of points from 1921 to 1926 were 61.8% of the points of the last wave from 1926 to 1928 (the orthodox top). Likewise in the five waves up from 1932 to 1937. Again the wave from the top in 1930 (297 DJIA) to the bottom in 1932 (40 DJIA) is 1.618 times the wave from 40 to 195 (1932 to 1937). Also, the decline from 1937 to 1938 was 61.8% of the advance from 1932 to 1937. *Should the 1949 market to date adhere to this formula, then the advance from 1949 to 1956 (361 points DJIA) should be complete when 583 points (161.8% of the 361 points) have been added to the 1957 low of 416, or a total of 999 DJIA.*

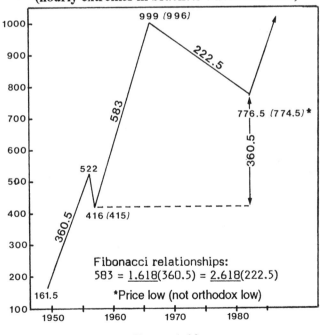

BOLTON'S FIBONACCI CALCULATIONS, 1960
(hourly extremes in brackets where different)

Figure A-10

So in projecting a Fibonacci relationship, Bolton forecast a peak that turned out to be just three points from the exact hourly reading at the top in 1966. But what was largely forgotten (in the wake of A.J. Frost's successful forecast for the wave IV low at 572, which was borne out in 1974 at the hourly low of 572.20) was Bolton's very next sentence:

> Alternately, 361 points over 416 would call for 777 in the DJIA.

Needless to say, 777 was nowhere to be found. That is, until August 1982. The exact orthodox low on the hourly readings was *776.92* on August 12. In other words, Bolton's calculations [see Figure A-10] defined the exact beginning and end of wave IV in advance, *based on their relationships to the previous price structure*. In price points, 1966-1982 is .618 of 1957-1982 *and* of 1949-1956, each of which, being equal, is .618 of 1957-1966, all within 1% error! When weekly and monthly patterns work out time after time to Fibonacci multiples, the typical response from Wall Street observers is, "Another coincidence." When patterns of this size continue to do it, it becomes a matter of faith to continue to believe that Fibonacci multiples are *not* characteristic of the stock market. As far as I know, Bolton is the only dead man whose forecasts continue to fit the reality of Wall Street.

From these observations, I hope to have established that Cycle wave IV in the DJIA, which the "constant dollar Dow" clearly supports as a single bear phase, ended in August 1982.

2) *The advance following this correction will be a much bigger bull market than anything seen in the last two decades.* **Numerous guidelines dealing with normal wave behavior support this contention.**

First, as Frost and I have steadfastly maintained, the Elliott wave structure from 1932 is unfinished and requires a fifth wave advance to complete the pattern. At the time we wrote our book, there was simply no responsible wave interpretation that would allow for the rise beginning in 1932 already to have ended. The fifth wave will be of the same degree and should be in relative proportion to the wave patterns of 1932-1937, 1937-1942, 1942-1966, and 1966-1982.

Second, a normal fifth wave will carry, based on Elliott's channeling methods, to the *upper channel line*, which in this case cuts through the price action in the **3500-4000** range in the latter half of the 1980s. Elliott noted that when a fourth wave breaks the trend channel, the fifth will often have a throw-over, or a brief penetration through the same trend channel on the other side.

Third, an important guideline within the Wave Principle is that when the third wave is extended, as was the wave from 1942 to 1966, the first and fifth waves tend toward equality in time and magnitude. This is a tendency, not a necessity, but it does indicate that the advance from 1982 should resemble the first wave up, which took place from 1932 to 1937. Thus, this fifth wave should travel approximately the same percentage distance as wave I, which moved in nearly a 5x multiple from an estimated (the exact figures are not available) hourly low of 41 to an hourly peak of 194.50. Since the orthodox beginning of wave V was 777 in 1982, an equivalent multiple of 4.744 projects a target of **3686**. If the exact hourly low for 1932 were known, one could project a precise number, Bolton style, with some confidence. As it stands, the "3686" number should be taken as probably falling within 100 points of the ideal projection (whether it comes true is another question).

Fourth, as far as *time* goes, the 1932-1937 bull market lasted five years. Therefore, one point to be watching for a possible market peak is 5 years from 1982, or *1987*. Coincidentally, as we pointed out in our book, 1987 happens to be a Fibonacci *13* years from the correction's low point in 1974, *21* years from the peak of wave III in 1966, and *55* years from the start of wave I in 1932. To complete the picture, 1987 is a perfect date for the Dow to hit its 3686 target since, to reach it, the Dow would have to burst briefly through its upper channel line in a "throw-over," which is typical of exhaustion moves (such as the 1929 peak). Based on a 1.618 time multiple of the time of wave I and on equality to the 1920s fifth Cycle wave, an 8-year wave V would point to 1990 as the next most likely year for a peak. It would be particularly likely if the Dow is still substantially below the price target by 1987. Keep in mind that in wave forecasting, *time is a consideration that is entirely secondary to both wave form, which is of primary importance, and price level.*

Fifth, while the Dow Industrial Average is only in its *first* Primary wave advance within Cycle wave V, *the broader indexes began wave V in 1974* and are already well into their *third* Primary wave [see Figure A-12]. These indexes, such as the Value Line Average, the Indicator Digest Average and the Fosback Total Return Index, are tracing out a traditional extended third, or middle wave, and have just entered the most powerful portion. Estimating conservatively, 60% of five-wave sequences have extended third waves, so this interpretation is along the lines of a textbook pattern, whereas attempts to interpret the broader indexes as being in their fifth and final wave are not. With a third wave extension under way in the broad indexes, a good deal of time will be necessary to complete the third wave, and then trace out the fourth and fifth waves. With all that ahead of us, the size of the current bull market will have to be substantial.

3) Now that the likelihood of wave V *occurring* has been established and its size and shape estimated, it might be helpful to assess its probable *characteristics*.

First, the advance should be very selective, and rotation from one group to another should be pronounced. *Breadth* during wave V should be unexceptional, if not outright poor relative to the spectacular breadth performance in the monolithic markets of the 1940s and '50s, during wave III. Since it's an impulse wave, however, it will certainly be broader than anything we saw within wave IV from 1966 to 1982.

*A moment's thought explains the reason why the wave V advance will be thin in relationship to waves I and III. In a fifth wave, the prolonged "bull" move is coming to its conclusion, and relative to the corrections within that bull phase, major damage is due to follow. In long term waves, fundamental background conditions have by then deteriorated to the point that fewer and fewer companies will increase their prosperity in the environment of the upswing. (It seems clear to me that these conditions exist today on a Supercycle basis.) Thus the bull market, while providing huge opportunities for profit, becomes observably more

---

* The next two paragraphs are from the April 11, 1983 issue of *The Elliott Wave Theorist*, published five days later. The sentences before and after the asterisk include wording from the December 1982 issue.

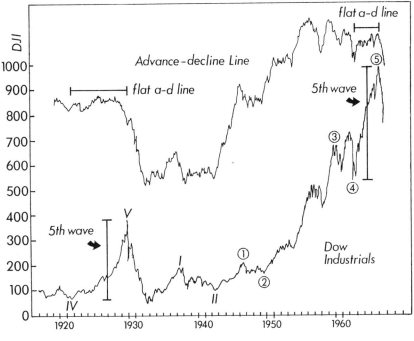

Figure A-11

selective, as reflected by an underperforming advance-decline line and fewer days of abundant "new highs" in stocks. Have you noticed how, since the 1974 low, stocks have rarely gone up all at once, but prefer to advance selectively, a few groups at a time?

All degrees of non-extended (and even most extended) fifth waves act this way, which is exactly what causes standard "sell signals" based on divergence. The problem is that most analysts apply this concept only to the *near or intermediate term swings*. However, *it is just as true of Supercycle swings as the smaller ones*. In effect, the flat a-d line of the 1920s [see Figure A-11] was a "sell signal" for the entire advance from 1857. Similarly, the flat a-d line in the mid-'60s was a "sell signal" for the 1942-1966 bull market. A relatively poorly performing a-d line from 1982 to (I expect) 1987 will be a "sell signal" for the entire Supercycle from 1932. The lesson for now is, *don't use that underperformance as a reason to sell too early* and miss out on what promises to be one of the most profitable uplegs in the history of the stock market.

COUNT BASED ON 1978 INTERPRETATION
(Still probable for broad indexes)

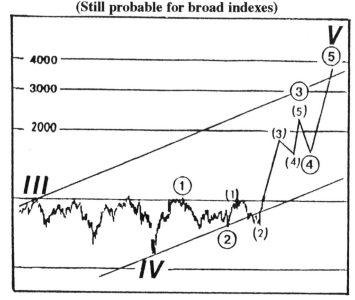

Figure A-12

Second, this bull market should be a simple structure, more akin to 1932-1937 than to 1942-1966. In other words, *expect a swift and persistent advance, with short corrections,* as opposed to long rolling advances with evenly spaced corrective phases. *Large institutions will probably do best by avoiding a market timing strategy and concentrating on stock selection, remaining heavily invested until a full five Primary waves can be counted.*

Third, the wave structure of the Dow and that of the broader indexes should fit together. If the count based on our 1978 interpretation [see Figure A-12] is still the correct one, then it is the same as that for the broad indexes, and their waves will coincide. If the preferred count is the correct one, then I would expect the third wave in the broad indexes to end when the Dow finishes its *first* wave, and the fifth wave in the broad indexes to end when the Dow finishes its *third* wave. That would mean that during the Dow's fifth wave, it would be virtually alone in making new highs, as market breadth begins to thin out more obviously. At the ultimate top, then, I would not be surprised to see the Dow Industrials in new high ground, unconfirmed by both the broad indexes and the advance-decline line, creating a classic technical divergence.

Finally, given the technical situation, what might we conclude about the psychological aspects of wave V? The 1920s bull market was a fifth wave of a *third* Supercycle wave, while Cycle wave V is the fifth wave of a *fifth* Supercycle wave. Thus, as the last hurrah, it should be characterized, at its end, by an almost unbelievable institutional mania for stocks and a public mania for stock index futures, stock options, and options on futures. In my opinion, the long term sentiment gauges will give off major trend sell signals two or three years before the final top, and the market will just keep on going. In order for the Dow to reach the heights expected by the year 1987 or 1990, *and* in order to set up the U.S. stock market to experience the greatest crash in its history, which, according to the Wave Principle, is due to follow wave V, investor mass psychology should reach manic proportions, with elements of 1929, 1968 and 1973 all operating together and, at the end, to an even greater extreme.

4) If all goes according to expectations, the last remaining question is, "what happens after wave V tops out?"

The Wave Principle would recognize the 3686 top as the end of wave V of (V), the peak of a Grand Supercycle. A Grand Supercycle bear market would then "correct" all the progress dating from the late 1700s. The downside target zone would be the price area (ideally near the low*) of the previous fourth wave of lesser degree, wave (IV), which fell from 381 to 41 on the Dow. Worldwide banking failures, government bankruptcy, and eventual destruction of the paper money system might be plausible explanations** for a bear phase of this magnitude. Since armed conflicts often occur after severe financial crises, one would have to consider the possibility that the collapse in value of financial assets of this magnitude would presage war between the superpowers. Regarding time, either wave (A) or wave (C) of the Grand Supercycle correction should bottom in 1999, + or - 1 year, based on several observations. From a 1987 top, a decline matching the 13 years up from 1974 would point to the year 2000. From a 1990 top, a decline matching the 8 years up from 1982 would point to 1998. It also happens that the very regular recurrence of turning points at 16.6-16.9-year intervals

---

* More likely near the high; see *At the Crest of the Tidal Wave.*
(The daily closing high was 381.17; the intraday high was 383.00.)
** Results, actually.

[see Figure A-8, bottom] projects 1999 for the next turning point. Finally, with the Kondratieff economic cycle due to bottom in 2003 (+ or - 5 years), a stock market low a few years prior to that time would fit the historical pattern.

August 18, 1983

THE SUPERBULL MARKET OF THE '80s —
Has the Last Wild Ride Really Begun?

When A.J. Frost and I wrote *Elliott Wave Principle* in 1978, the prevailing attitude was that the Kondratieff cycle was rolling over and would create the "Awful '80s." Books such as *How To Survive the Coming Depression* and *The Crash of '79* were on the bestseller lists. Gold and inflation were skyrocketing, and Jimmy Carter was battling the memory of Herbert Hoover for a place in history as the country's worst president.

In writing a book about how to apply Elliott's Wave Principle, it was virtually impossible to avoid making a forecast, since a wave interpretation of the past almost always implies something about the future. At that time, the evidence was overwhelming that the stock market was at the dawn of a tremendous bull market. Even at the stage, the Wave Principle revealed some of the details of what the bull might look like: a classic five-wave form in the price pattern, a 400% increase in the Dow Industrials in a short span of five to eight years, and a Dow target close to 3000. While that figure was met with some derision at the time and a good deal of skepticism even today, Elliott wave-based forecasts (even competent ones) can often appear extreme. The reason is that the Wave Principle is one of the few tools which can help an analyst anticipate *changes* in trends, including trends that are so long term that they have become accepted as the normal state of affairs. I have no doubt that by the time this bull market is ending, our call for a huge crash and depression will be laughed off the street. In fact, that's exactly what we should expect if there is to be any chance that we're right.

If our ongoing analysis is correct, the current environment is providing a once-in-a-generation money making opportunity. This opportunity takes on greater importance, however, because it may well precede not merely a Kondratieff cycle downswing, but the biggest financial catastrophe since the founding of the Republic. In other words, we had better make our fortunes now just in case "Elliott" is right about the aftermath. But for this article, let's forget the "crash" part of our forecast and concentrate on the "bull market" part. There are still plenty of questions to be answered about the expected bull market years. After all, no forecast is proven correct until it's fulfilled, and the Dow is still a long way from our recently refined target of 3600-3700 in 1987. Do we have any evidence that stocks have started what we call "Wave V" in the long advance from the Depression depths of 1932? The answer, in a word, is an emphatic "yes." Let's examine several powerfully confirming signs.

The Wave Principle

The wave structure coming off the August 1982 bottom has been strikingly clear in contrast to the corrective wave ramble which preceded it. Advancing waves are all "fives," while declines all take the form of one of Elliott's corrective patterns. The move channels well, contains no "overlaps," and follows all the rules and guidelines that R.N. Elliott spelled out over 40 years ago. Volume and internal momentum figures confirm the preferred wave count at every point along the way. Wave counting adjustments have been minimal in contrast to the frequent uncertainties during corrective periods. All of these elements strongly support the case that a bull market is in progress. Detailed evidence is continually presented in ongoing issues of *The Elliott Wave Theorist*, so there is no reason to recount it all here. What is particularly interesting at this stage is the corroboration provided by standard technical analysis, the social enviroment and the recently constructed machinery for financial speculation, all which have signaled a major change in the status of the market.

Momentum

Indicators of stock market momentum almost always "announce" the beginning of a huge bull market. They do so by creating a tremendously overbought condition in the initial stage of advance. While this tendency is noticeable at all degrees of trend, the Annual Rate of Change for the S&P 500 is particularly useful in judging the strength of "kickoff" momentum in large waves of Cycle and Supercycle degree. This indicator is created by plotting the percentage difference between the average daily close for the S&P 500 in the current month and its reading for the same month a year earlier. The peak momentum reading is

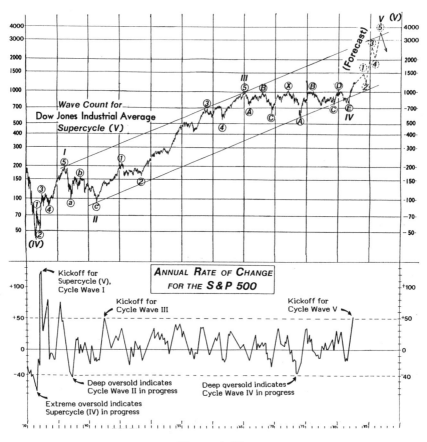

Figure A-13

typically registered about one year after the start of the move, due to the construction of the indicator. What's important is the *level* the indicator reaches. As you can see [in Figure A-13], *the level of "overbought" at the end of July 1983, approximately one year after the start of the current bull market, is the highest since May 1943, approximately one year after the start of Cycle wave III.* The fact that they each hit the 50% level is a strong confirmation that they mark the beginning of waves of equivalent degrees. In other words, August 1982 marked the start of something more than what has come to be regarded as the norm, a 2-year bull market followed by a 2-year bear. On the other hand, it has *not* indicated the start of a glorious "new era" either. If a wave of *Supercycle* degree were beginning, we would expect to see the kind of overbought reading generated in 1933, when the indicator hit 124% one year after the start of wave (V) from 1932. There is now no chance that such a level can even be approached. Thus, the highest overbought condition in forty years signals to me that our Elliott wave forecast for the launching of wave V is right on target.

Sentiment

Foreknowledge of how indicators might be expected to act is another example of just useful an Elliott wave perspective can be. As I have argued since the early days of the current advance, the sentiment indicators should reach much more extreme levels than they ever saw in the 1970s. This assessment has been proved by now, with the Dow over 300 points higher than when the sentiment figures first gave sell signals based on the old parameters. Sentiment figures are a function of the vitality and extent of the market in progress. The fact that the indicators' 10-year parameters *have* been exceeded is more good evidence that Cycle wave V has begun.

The Social Scene

By the top, the nostalgic conservatism of the current social scene should give way to a wild abandon characteristic of the *late 1920s* and *late 1960s*. [For the rest of this text, see page 41 of *Pioneering Studies in Socionomics* — Ed.]

Falling Into Place

With sentiment, momentum, wave characteristics and social phenomena all supporting our original forecast, can we say that the environment on Wall Street is conducive to developing a full-blown speculative mania? In 1978, an Elliott analyst had no way of knowing just what the mechanisms for a wild speculation would be. "Where's the 10% margin which made the 1920s possible?" was a common rebuttal. Well, to be honest, we didn't know. But now look! The entire structure is being built as if it were planned.

Options on hundreds of stocks (and now stock indexes) allow the speculator to deal in thousands of shares of stock for a fraction of their values. Futures contracts on stock indexes, which promise to deliver nothing, have been created for the most part as speculative vehicles with huge leverage. Options *on* futures carry the possibilities one step further. And it's not stopping there. Major financial newspapers are calling for the end of any margin requirements on stocks whatsoever. "Lookback" options are making a debut. S&L's are leaping into the stock brokerage business, sending flyers to little old ladies. And New York City banks are already constructing kiosks for quote machines so that depositors can stop off at lunch and punch out their favorite stocks. Options exchanges are creating new and speculative instruments — guess the C.P.I. and win a bundle! In other words, the financial arena is becoming the *place to be*. And, as if by magic, the media are geometrically increasing coverage of financial news. New financial newsletters and magazines are being created every few months. Financial News Network is now broadcasting 12 hours a day, bringing up-to-the-minute quotations on stocks and commodities via satellite and cable into millions of homes.

Remember, this is just the *set-up* phase. The average guy probably won't be joining the party until the Dow clears 2000. The market's atmosphere by then will undoubtedly become out-and-out euphoric. *Then* you can start watching the public's activity as if it were one huge sentiment indicator. When the stock market makes the news reports every single day (as gold did starting about two months before the top, remember?), when your neighbors find out you're "in the Business" and start telling you about *their* latest speculations, when stories of stock market riches hit the pages of the general newspapers, when the best seller list includes "How to Make Millions in Stocks," when Walden's and Dalton start stocking *Elliott Wave Principle*, when almost no one is willing to discuss financial calamity or nuclear war, when mini-skirts return and men dress with flash and flair, and when your friends stay home from work to monitor Quotron machines (since it's more lucrative than working), then you know we'll be close. At the peak of the fifth wave, the spectacle could rival Tulipomania and the South Sea Bubble.

Part of the character of a *fifth* wave of any degree is the occurrence of psychological denial on a mass scale. In other words, the fundamental problems are obvious and threatening to anyone who coldly analyzes the situation, but the average person chooses to explain them away, ignore them, or even deny their existence. This fifth wave should be no exception, and will be built more on unfounded *hopes* than on soundly improving fundamentals such as the U.S. experienced in the 1950s and early '60s. And since this fifth wave, wave V, is a fifth *within a larger fifth*, wave (V) from 1789, the phenomenon should be magnified by the time the peak is reached. By that time, we should be hearing that the global debt pyramid is "no longer a problem," that the market and the economy have "learned to live with high interest rates" and that computers have ushered in a "new era of unparalleled prosperity." Don't lose your perspective when the time comes. It will take great courage to make money during this bull market, because in the early stages it will be easy to be too cautious. However, it will take even *greater* courage to get out near the top, because that's when the world will call you a damn fool for selling.

Perspective

One way to avoid the premature selling that is so typical during bull markets is to obtain a *long term* perspective on the present which most investors lack. One of the reasons that the Wave Principle is so valuable is that it usually forces the analyst to look at the big picture in order to make all relevant conclusions about the market's current position. Put/call ratios and 10-day averages are valuable as far as they go, but they are best interpreted within the context of the broad sweep of the market events.

Take another look at the long term Dow chart and ask yourself a few questions about some points that are considered common knowledge.

— Is the market really "more volatile" today than it has ever been in the past? No. A look at 1921-1946 throws that idea right out the window.

— Is the 1000 level a "high" level? For that matter, is 1200 a "high" level? Not any more! The long period spent going sideways since 1966 has put the Dow back at the lower end of its fifty-year uptrend channel in "current dollar" terms (and down to a point of very low valuation in "constant dollar" terms).

— Is the current bull market an "old" bull market which began in 1974 and is therefore "running out of time"? Hardly. Both in "constant dollar" terms and with reference to the 40-year uptrend, the Dow was more undervalued in 1982 than at the crash low in 1974.

— Is my Elliott-based expectation of a 400% gain in 5-8 years a wild one? It appears to be, when compared to recent history. But not when compared to 1921-1929, a 500% gain in 8 years, or 1932-1937, a 400% gain in 5 years.

— Can you always extrapolate current trends into the future? Definitely not. The one rule of the market is change.

— Is any cycle ever "just like the last one"? Not too often! In fact, Elliott formulated a rule about it, called the Rule of Alternation. Broadly interpreted, it instructs the investor to look for a different style of patterns as each new phase begins.

— Is recent market action "too strong," "overextended," "unprecedented," or even a "new era"? No, variations on today's theme all happened before.

— Is the market a random walk, or an erratic wild ride, whipping back and forth without form, trend or pattern? If so, it's "wandered" into long-lasting periods of clear trend, rhythmic cyclical repetition and impeccable Elliott wave patterns.

At the very least, [Figure A-13] helps you picture the market's action within the broad sweep of history, thus making next week's money supply report appear as irrelevant as it really is. Furthermore, it helps you visualize why a bull market which is larger than the 30%-80% gains of the upward swings of the last sixteen years is probable, while illustrating the *potential* for a bull market bigger than any in the *fifty* years.

Although it is probably the best forecasting tool in existence, the Wave Principle is not *primarily* a forecasting tool; it is a detailed description of how markets behave. So far, the market is behaving in such a way as to reinforce our original Wave V forecast. As long as the market fulfills expectations, we can assume we're still on track. But ultimately, the market is the message, and a change in behavior can dictate a change in outlook. One reason that forecasts are useful is that they provide a good backdrop against which to measure current market action. But no matter what your convictions, it pays never to take your eye off what's happening in the wave structure in real time.

GLOSSARY OF TERMS

Alternation (guideline of): If wave two is a sharp correction, wave four will usually be a sideways correction, and vice versa.

Apex: Intersection of the two boundary lines of a contracting or barrier triangle.

Corrective Wave: A three-wave pattern, or combination of three-wave patterns, that moves in the opposite direction of the trend of one larger degree.

Diagonal: A wedge-shaped pattern containing overlap that usually occurs as a fifth or C wave and occasionally occurs as a first or A wave. Subdivides 3-3-3-3-3.

Double Three: Combination of two simple sideways corrective patterns, labeled W and Y, separated by a corrective wave labeled X.

Double Zigzag: Combination of two zigzags, labeled W and Y, separated by a corrective wave labeled X.

Equality (guideline of): In a five-wave sequence, when wave three is the longest, waves five and one tend to be equal in price length.

Expanded Flat: Flat correction in which wave B enters new price territory relative to the preceding impulse wave.

Failure: See Truncated Fifth.

Flat: Sideways correction labeled A-B-C. Subdivides 3-3-5.

Impulse: A five-wave pattern that subdivides 5-3-5-3-5 and contains no overlap.

Irregular Flat: See Expanded Flat.

Motive Wave: A five-wave pattern that moves in the same direction as the trend of one larger degree, i.e., any impulse or diagonal.

One-two, one-two: The initial development in a five-wave pattern, just prior to acceleration at the center of wave three.

Overlap: The entrance by wave four into the price territory of wave one. Not permitted in impulse waves.

Previous Fourth Wave: The fourth wave within the preceding impulse wave of the same degree. Corrective patterns typically terminate in this area.

Running: Refers to a flat or triangle in which wave B goes beyond the start of wave A, and wave C does not go below the end of wave A.

Sharp Correction: Any corrective pattern that does not contain a price extreme meeting or exceeding that of the ending level of the prior impulse wave; alternates with sideways correction.

Sideways Correction: Any corrective pattern that contains a price extreme meeting or exceeding that of the prior impulse wave; alternates with sharp correction.

Third of a Third: Powerful middle section within an impulse wave.

Thrust: Impulsive wave following completion of a triangle.

Triangle (barrier): Same as contracting triangle but the B-D trendline is horizontal. May be termed "ascending" or "descending" depending on direction.

Triangle (contracting): Corrective pattern, subdividing 3-3-3-3-3 and labeled A-B-C-D-E. Occurs as a fourth, B or Y wave. Trendlines converge as pattern progresses.

Triangle (expanding): Same as contracting triangle but trendlines diverge as pattern progresses.

Triple Three: Combination of three simple sideways corrective patterns labeled W, Y and Z, each separated by a corrective wave labeled X.

Triple Zigzag: Combination of three zigzags, labeled W, Y and Z, each separated by a corrective wave labeled X.

Truncated Fifth: The fifth wave in an impulsive pattern that fails to exceed the price extreme of the third wave.

Zigzag: Sharp correction, labeled A-B-C. Subdivides 5-3-5.

PUBLISHER'S POSTSCRIPT

As you have just read, the authors' powerful stock market analysis brought readers to the liftoff of a great bull market. It was a vantage point that afforded a remarkably clear perspective on both history and the future.

If some reader chances across this book today, he may not be able to judge adequately the background during which the prediction for a great bull market was made. The late 1970s were a period of widespread worry. The "doom and gloom" contingent held the attention of investors. Hard-money oriented investment survival seminars were held often and attracted attendees numbering in the hundreds and often the thousands. Inflation could not be controlled, and interest rates, widely perceived as the kiss of death for stocks, continued their relentless advance to new all-time highs. *The Crash of '79, Crisis Investing* and *New Profits from the Monetary Crisis* were flying out of the bookstores. Kondratieff cycle enthusiasts called for a depression. Portfolio strategists were awaiting the final smash of the secular bear market that began in 1966. The President at the time was widely considered to be the most inept in modern history. As evidenced by the results of a Roper poll, the U.S. public was more negative on "the future" than at any time since the poll began in the 1940s. In early 1978, the Dow had moved as low as 740, less than 170 points from its 1974 low. Though it was in the midst of an "October massacre" back to 790 as the book was being sent to the printer, the authors were quite willing to let stand their description of "the current bull market in stocks...which should accompany a breakout to new all time highs."

Over the next few years, skepticism remained entrenched. In 1980, inflation was in runaway mode, unemployment was high, the economy was in recession, Iran was holding U.S. citizens hostage, John Lennon was shot dead, and the Russians invaded Afghanistan. A prominent administration official publicly warned of a depression. Many fretted that Ronald "Ray-Gun" would blow up the world. Violent gyrations in interest rates and the near-bankruptcy of the Hunt business empire sent shock waves through the financial community. *How to Prosper During the Coming Bad Years* was lodged at the top of *The New York Times'* best-seller list, while the authors' forecast of a coming great wave of optimism, an "institutional and public mania," as Prechter put it in 1983, was mostly ignored.

Despite this veil of gloom, the stock market knew that better days lay ahead and said so by its pattern. The low of Cycle wave IV had already occurred at Dow 570, and the broad secondary market continued to hold up through 1979, 1980 and 1981, giving a clear signal that the underlying forces were bullish. Negative fundamental conditions, in typical fashion, "tested" the low in 1982, as recession and high interest rates returned. Then, just when the Dow Industrials appeared unable ever to rise again, Prechter raised the ante by another thousand Dow points to as high as 3885. "Dow 3800? You're crazy!" It was then that Cycle wave V began its upward march.

While these events proved the Wave Principle a remarkably useful tool for stock market forecasting, the authors had to change their opinion in two major areas: the time element, as Cycle wave V has taken far longer than originally, or even subsequently, expected, and finally as a result of the substantial extra time, the upside price potential as well. These developments certainly reveal why Elliott's observations about wave "equality" discussed in Chapter 2 constitute a *guideline*, in this case one that did not apply. The wave V that the authors forecasted lasted not 5 or 8 years, but 18 years from 1982 and 26 years from 1974! In doing so, it surpassed the 1974-1989 percentage gain in the Japanese Nikkei to achieve the status of the most extended stock mania *ever* in terms of both price and time.

It is some consolation that the only three years that Frost and Prechter projected as likely years for a peak (1983, 1987 and 1990) marked the three most important interim market tops within Cycle wave V. Taking imperfections fully into account, the only other examples of successfully published analysis such as that by Prechter as detailed in this book's Appendix are R.N. Elliott's superbullish long term outlook in October 1942, Hamilton Bolton's 1960 forecast for a top at Dow 999, Collins' bear market call at the 1966 high, and Frost's forecast for a wave IV low at 572. Reviewing that history, one is struck by the fact that the thematic progression in the Elliott wave outlook over the many decades since R.N. Elliott first sent a forecast to Charles J. Collins has been *consistent*. In contrast, most economists, analysts and forecasters change their views every six months, six weeks or six days. Each late-breaking news item has to be "factored in" to their analysis. Market patterns, on the other hand, often hint at what the next news item will be. While wave structures can at times be difficult to interpret, while scenarios may have to be abandoned if future price behavior forces a change in the ordering of probabilities for various outcomes, overall the Wave Principle provides a stable perspective from which sensible advance planning is possible.

Many books on the stock market, the economy or the future in general have taken a bullish stance or a bearish stance. Most are wrong, as they are written in a mental fever supported by the current social psychology when in fact the opposite stance should be taken. Even those that are correct on one general direction of trend must be questioned as to the extent of the "luck" factor. However, any sequence of forecasts this specific and encompassing a complete up-and-down cycle has never before been attempted, much less proved successful. One of the most important tests of the validity of a scientific theory is in its record of success in predicting events. In that regard, the Elliott Wave Principle has been delivering the goods to such an extent that no other theory of market behavior has ever come close. Real time forecasting such as that chronicled in Chapter 8 and the Appendix is an immense intellectual challenge. Mid-pattern decision making is particularly difficult. There are times, however, as in December 1974 and August 1982, when major patterns reach completion and a textbook picture stands right before your eyes. At such times, one's level of conviction rises to over 90%. Today, only the bear market half of the forecast remains to be fulfilled. If the authors' expectations are borne out, *Elliott Wave Principle* will further stand as the only book in stock market history to forecast correctly not only a great bull market but the ensuing great bear market, the details of which Robert Prechter has outlined in his recent book, *Conquer the Crash*.

So at this time, half of our great journey is over. The upward half has been intellectually rewarding in fulfilling the authors' conservative (in retrospect) expectations, which were simultaneously beyond most market observers' wildest dreams of potential market performance. The next phase, which will be downward, may not be as rewarding, but it will probably be far more important to anticipate, as its onset will mark the end of a sociological era. Being prepared the *first* time meant fortune and perhaps a bit of fame for its forecasters. *This* time, it will mean survival, both financial and (based upon Prechter's work correlating social and cultural trends with financial trends) ultimately physical for many people as well. Although it is generally believed (and tirelessly reiterated) that "the market can do anything," our money is once again on the Wave Principle to provide a proper perspective on humanity's great journey through the patterns of life and time.

Index